12/6

What's Wrong with
the United Nations
and How to Fix It

What's Wrong with the United Nations and How to Fix It

Thomas G. Weiss

polity

First published in 2008 by Polity Press

Reprinted in 2009 (thrice), 2010

Polity Press
65 Bridge Street
Cambridge CB2 1UR, UK

Polity Press
350 Main Street
Malden, MA 02148, USA

ISBN-13: 978-0-7456-4297-0
ISBN-13: 978-0-7456-4298-7(pb)

A catalogue record for this book is available from the British Library.

Typeset in 10.25 on 13 pt FF Scala
by Servis Filmsetting Ltd, Stockport, Cheshire
Printed and bound in United States by Odyssey Press, Inc., Gonic, New Hampshire

The publisher has used its best endeavors to ensure that the URLs for external
websites referred to in this book are correct and active at the time of going to
press. However, the publisher has no responsibility for the websites and can
make no guarantee that a site will remain live or that the content is or will
remain appropriate.

For further information on Polity, visit our website: www.politybooks.com

God, give us grace to accept with serenity the things that cannot be changed, courage to change the things that should be changed, and the wisdom to distinguish the one from the other.
  —Reinhold Niebuhr, "Serenity Prayer," 1943

Contents

About the Author

Thomas G. Weiss is Presidential Professor of Political Science at The Graduate Center of The City University of New York and Director of the Ralph Bunche Institute for International Studies, where he is also Co-director of the United Nations Intellectual History Project. He is President of the International Studies Association (2009–10) and Chair of the Academic Council on the UN System (2006–9). He was awarded the Grand Prix Humanitaire de France 2006 and the Médaille d'honneur de la ville de Marseille 2008 in recognition of his analytical contributions to global governance and UN studies. The former Editor of *Global Governance* and Research Director of the International Commission on Intervention and State Sovereignty, he has written extensively about international organization (especially the United Nations), peace and security, humanitarian action, and development. His recent authored books that bear on this one include *Ahead of the Curve? UN Ideas and Global Challenges* (2001); *The Responsibility To Protect: Research, Bibliography, and Background* (2001); *Military–Civilian Interactions: Humanitarian Crises and the Responsibility to Protect* (2nd edn. 2005); *UN Voices: The Struggle for Development and Social Justice* (2005); *Sword & Salve: Confronting New Wars and Humanitarian Crises* (2006); *Internal Displacement: Conceptualization and its Consequences* (2006); *Humanitarian Intervention: Ideas in Action* (2007); and *The United Nations and Changing World Politics* (5th edn. 2007). His recent edited volumes are *Terrorism and the UN: Before and After*

September 11 (2004); *Wars on Terrorism and Iraq: Human Rights, Unilateralism, and US Foreign Policy* (2004); *The Oxford Handbook on the United Nations* (2007); and *Humanitarianism in Question: Power, Politics, and Ethics* (2008). He is currently writing *The UN and Global Governance: An Unfinished Journey* and *UN Ideas Changing History*, and he is editing *The United Nations and Nuclear Orders*.

Foreword

Almost from the outset in 1945, the reform of the world organization has been a constant item on its agenda. UN reform has been the subject of hundreds of books, speeches, UN documents, and articles in the media. Governments have spent thousands of hours discussing the subject. Except for the reorganization of the Security Council, however, on which there is no agreement, reform has usually been taken to mean only the reform of the secretariat's bureaucracy and authority. Governments evidently prefer it that way. But the UN is a political organization, and the need to develop and strengthen its political basis and nature is an essential part of any serious effort to make it work better.

Thomas G. Weiss has had the courage—the temerity perhaps—to put the political aspect of UN reform front and center of his book, *What's Wrong with the United Nations and How to Fix It*. His main argument is simple and direct. National sovereignty, as defined in the Treaty of Westphalia in 1648, is the fundamental organizing principle of the United Nations. Since World War II, revolutionary change and the new demands of a global world have steadily reduced the relevance and importance of national sovereignty in most areas of human activity. At the United Nations, however, national sovereignty is as strong, or stronger, than ever. For proof of this, one need look no further than the obstacles that now confront the UN in dealing with the Darfur calamity.

The history of the UN has been, among other things, a continuous and often unsuccessful effort to find a working balance between national sovereignty on the one hand, and international responsibility and effective action on the other. This effort has become especially important because the present generation of "global problems" can truly be dealt with only by international management of an entirely new order. If global warming, terrorism, and nuclear proliferation are serious threats—as they surely are—we simply cannot limp along indefinitely with the current, severely limited generation of international organizations.

To devise and to rally support for serious reform, it is important that the current workings of the United Nations should be far better understood than is now the case. Weiss provides a clear and highly readable account of the main activities of the organization, as well as a brilliant analysis of its contemporary operations and problems. These include the UN's vital relationship with the remaining superpower, the United States, with its global reach and power. He examines the relationship between the secretariat and intergovernmental bodies, both in the UN itself and in the UN system of specialized agencies and special programs. He also considers the increasingly important part played by nongovernmental organizations on the world stage.

In a bold and original conclusion, Weiss proceeds to outline the need to go further than the present stage of international "governance," which has manifestly too many anomalies to provide an adequate response to the kind of problems the human race now faces. Weiss points out that earlier generations of scholars and citizens did not shy away, in the 1930s and 1940s, from the notion of world government, although it is now considered a heretical and impractical fantasy by a surprising number of people. Weiss suggests that world government is the necessary conceptual basis for adequate future management of the major problems of our planet. This is a bracing departure from the timidity and circumlocution on such subjects often induced by the jeremiads of our contemporary breed of neo-super-nationalists.

Weiss notes that there is an extraordinary lack of public interest in discussing the political nature of future institutions of international cooperation and management. We can, of course, wait passively for a new terrible disaster to prove the urgent need for such institutions, and our patience will no doubt be rewarded in time by new and unimaginable calamities. Instead, I hope that Weiss's book may give rise to the kind of productive and far-sighted discussions that the original governments of the United Nations, led by the United States, found time to engage in during a world war over 65 years ago.

Brian Urquhart
New York City
April 2008

Acknowledgements

General Charles de Gaulle famously nicknamed the United Nations *le machin* (the thing), in an attempt to dismiss multilateral cooperation as frivolous in comparison with the real meat of international affairs. He somehow forgot—as many historians have since—that the formal birth of "the thing" was not the signing of the UN Charter on June 26, 1945, but rather the adoption of the "Declaration by the United Nations" in Washington, DC, on January 1, 1942. The same 26 countries that constituted the wartime coalition that saved France from Nazi tyranny also looked forward to the formal establishment of the UN as an extension of the priorities set by the allies at war.[1] The world body and its system of agencies were seen as a vital necessity to international order, human rights, and economic stability and prosperity.

What happened to de Gaulle and others? What happened to the world organization and its Charter, which were the political culmination of the unified war effort? The question of the continued relevance of the world body is now a matter of serious political debate. In its starkest form, we can cite an ambassador in the US Mission to the United Nations in New York, who spoke publicly of "waving . . . a fond farewell as [the UN] sailed into the sunset."[2] The spirit of this folkloric declaration by a disgruntled official from the Ronald Reagan administration extends far beyond Washington.

In short, "What's Wrong with the UN?" is an intriguing puzzle for this new Polity Press series about the current state of global institutions.

Having already condensed what I thought was an enormous topic, humanitarian intervention,[3] into a concise and I hope authoritative volume for Polity, I was an easy target when Louise Knight contacted me and urged me to attempt a tougher synthesis. Having spent my analytical career steeped in the intricacies of the institutional behavior and misbehavior of the UN system—including my co-authored textbook that is going into a sixth edition and a co-edited massive handbook[4]— I decided to respond to her challenge and write a briefer book that might be read by non-specialists as well as UN junkies.

I wish clearly to acknowledge some precious research and editorial help from two very special graduate students in international relations at The CUNY Graduate Center. Janet Reilly helped me pull together various illustrations and citations as soon as the outline was accepted by the reviewers at Polity. With her keen judgment for what is and is not important, and with a very developed sense of what makes for nonsense, her helping hands were essential to assembling the early drafts. Danielle Zach Kalbacher, who has now helped shepherd numerous publications of mine in the last five years, once again applied her remarkable editorial skills. This book simply would not have been as readable or as sharp without her careful attention to content, logic, and presentation. Both Janet and Danielle have improved immeasurably the final text, and I am deeply grateful to them both. Two anonymous reviewers also helped ameliorate the final presentation and eliminate errors.

Finally, I also am extremely appreciative that Brian Urquhart agreed to grace these pages with his foreword. I have known Brian for two decades, though of course have been aware of his reputation since I was in graduate school. No one is more associated with the ideal of integrity by an international civil servant than he and his two mentors, Dag Hammarskjöld and Ralph Bunche. I have learned a great deal from his own books,[5] his continuing insights in the *New York Review of Books*, and from our congenial conversations over lunch. As the reader will see, one of the main solutions to what ails the United Nations would be to employ more Sir Brian's. I count myself lucky to be among his younger colleagues.

Notwithstanding the help of many individuals, I alone am responsible for remaining errors of fact or interpretation.

T.G.W.
New York City
April 2008

List of Figures and Tables

We are grateful to the following for permission to reproduce copyright material:

Cambridge University Press for table 5.1 "Features of the Human Rights Council Compared with Those of the Commission on Human Rights" by Nico Schrijver, "The UN Human Rights Council: 'Society of the Committed' or Just Old Wine in New Bottles?," published in *Leiden Journal of International Law* Vol 20(04), pp809-823 (2007); UN Human Rights Council for table 1.1 "Member States of the

List of Abbreviations

AMIS	African Union Mission in Sudan
AU	African Union
CERF	Central Emergency Response Fund
CHR	Commission on Human Rights
CPA	Comprehensive Peace Agreement
CSD	Commission on Sustainable Development
CSW	Commission on the Status of Women
DAW	Division for the Advancement of Women
DHA	Department of Humanitarian Affairs
DPA	Department of Political Affairs
DPKO	Department of Peacekeeping Operations
ECOSOC	Economic and Social Council
ECOWAS	Economic Community of West African States
ERC	Emergency Relief Coordinator
ERRF	European Rapid Reaction Force
EUFOR	European Union Force
FAO	Food and Agriculture Organization
FNI	Four Nations Initiative
G-8	Group of 8
G-77	Group of 77
GEF	Global Environment Facility
HLP	High-level Panel on Threats, Challenges and Change
HRC	Human Rights Council
IASC	Inter-Agency Standing Committee
ICBL	International Campaign to Ban Landmines

ICC	International Criminal Court
ICISS	International Commission on Intervention and State Sovereignty
ICRC	International Committee of the Red Cross
IDP	internally displaced person
IFI	international financial institution
IGO	intergovernmental organization
IMF	International Monetary Fund
INGO	international nongovernmental organization
INSTRAW	UN International Research and Training Institute for the Advancement of Women
IOM	International Organization for Migration
MCA	Millennium Challenge Account
MDG	Millennium Development Goal
NAM	Non-Aligned Movement
NATO	North Atlantic Treaty Organization
NGO	nongovernmental organization
NIEO	New International Economic Order
OCHA	Office for the Coordination of Humanitarian Affairs
ODA	official development assistance
OECD	Organisation for Economic Co-operation and Development
OFFP	Oil-for-Food Programme
OHCHR	Office of the High Commissioner for Human Rights
OPEC	Organization of the Petroleum Exporting Countries
OSAGI	Office of the Special Advisor to the Secretary-General on Gender Issues and the Advancement of Women
P-5	permanent five (members of the Security Council)
PBC	Peace-Building Commission

PBF	Peace-Building Fund
PBSO	Peace-Building Support Office
PID	Project on Internal Displacement
R2P	responsibility to protect
SFOR	NATO Stabilisation Force
SRSG	Special representative of the UN secretary-general
UNAMID	UN Assistance Mission in Darfur
UNEP	UN Environment Programme
UNCED	UN Conference on the Environment and Development
UNCHE	UN Conference on the Human Environment
UNCHS	UN Center for Human Settlements (Habitat)
UNCTAD	UN Conference on Trade and Development
UNDP	UN Development Programme
UNESCO	UN Educational, Scientific and Cultural Organization
UNFCCC	UN Framework Convention on Climate Change
UNFPA	UN Population Fund
UNHCR	UN High Commissioner for Refugees
UNICEF	UN Children's Fund
UNIFEM	UN Development Fund for Women
UNMIS	UN Mission in Sudan
UPR	universal periodic review
WFP	World Food Programme
WHO	World Health Organization
WMO	World Meteorological Organization

Introduction

Almost a decade into the twenty-first century, the United Nations seems remarkably ill-adapted to the times. What was ahead of the curve in 1945 is hardly apt for today, let alone tomorrow. While both World War I and World War II gave rise to ground-breaking efforts at international organization, neither the end of the Cold War nor September 11 has led to the creation of a "third generation" of multilateral institutions.

What exactly is wrong with the UN, and how can we fix it? Is it possible to retrofit the world body? I leave it to readers to determine whether the current generation of organizations is fixable, or whether we, sadly, require a cataclysm—a dirty nuclear bomb, a worldwide economic depression, catastrophic global warming—to generate new institutions capable of handling the challenges of our increasingly interconnected world. What, in short, would stimulate governments and "We the Peoples of the United Nations," the stirring words that head the UN Charter, to formulate and pursue more creative visions and substantially different kinds of intergovernmental organizations (IGOs)?

Looking Back: UN Shortcomings

Over six decades after its establishment, the United Nations and its "system" of related agencies and programs seemingly are perpetually in crisis. The somber departure in December 2006, after 10 years, of the controversial but telegenic and

Nobel Prize-winning seventh secretary-general, Kofi Annan, and his replacement in January 2007 by a rather faceless South Korean bureaucrat, Ban Ki-moon, is merely the latest of the about-faces so characteristic of UN history. It was not that long ago that the Cold War's end had supposedly signaled the "renaissance" of multilateralism. The heralded arrival and subsequent departure of the neo-con firebrand, US Ambassador John Bolton—who wreaked havoc during the so-called celebration of the UN's 60th anniversary in fall 2005 and its immediate follow-up—captured in a microcosm the long-standing US love-hate relationship with the United Nations. Ironically, of course, the UN system itself reflects American values and design—a history of ups-and-downs that Edward Luck calls "mixed messages."[1]

Annan's call to arms for the anniversary included appeals to an "historic turning point," a "fork in the road," and even a "San Francisco moment." In spite of the mantra of reform, the state-centric world organization continues to limp along as it has since the outset. The United Nations is not a monolith—even if it is often spoken of as if it were—but was set up after World War II in a very particular set of historical circumstances. In spite of decolonization processes and a massive membership expansion, along with fundamental geo-political and other changes, the world organization's basic structure and institutional make-up has remained fundamentally the same. Unlike earlier cataclysms, today's set of narrow escapes has not yet led to a transformation in the mechanics of international cooperation. The various moving parts of the UN organization itself, and the myriad institutions of the broader system, have evolved but undergone no major shake up, which the planet desperately requires.

Indeed, shortly after leaving his post as deputy-secretary-general and prior to becoming the UK's minister for Africa, Asia, and the United Nations, Mark Malloch Brown commented that neither governments nor Secretary-General Ban Ki-moon understood "the scale of change required." Member states "would have to rise above their own current sense of entrenched rights and privileges and find a grand bargain to allow a new more realistic governance model for the UN"; but, he continued, "that may take a crisis."[2]

On the one hand, the framers of the UN Charter would today have trouble recognizing the world organization because of extensive institutional adaptations and changes since 1945, when many contemporary topics (such as global warming, HIV/AIDS, and gender inequality) were not even on the international agenda. On the other hand, the founders would certainly find a familiar state-centric and decentralized institutional approach to problem-solving that is incapable of addressing the kinds of life-threatening global challenges increasingly and routinely confronting humanity. As the saying goes, "The more things change, the more they stay the same."

"Change," of course, can be a problematic concept. But an analysis of the nature and evolution of the world organization over the past six decades is crucial to understanding and determining the adaptability of the current system. Looking to identify momentous change through a crisis-by-crisis approach is misleading to the story I am trying to tell. In fact, the tale is about uneven change within the UN system despite substantial alterations in the nature of world politics. Thus, on the scorecard of change, we should evaluate quantitative data to appreciate when an indicator—budgets or staff numbers, for example—ratchets up or surges. However, we should also be concerned with what cannot be quantified.

In *Taming the Sovereigns*, Kal Holsti probes the concept of change and ways of measuring it. He points out that change is quite different for someone playing the stock market in comparison to those trying to understand international relations, where recent events are of no interest unless they have a demonstrable effect on how diplomatic, military, or humanitarian work is done. As Holsti notes, "This is the Hegelian and Marxist problem: at what point does quantitative change lead to qualitative consequences?"[3] In other words, we can also characterize as "new" a tipping point where quantitative change is so substantial that it constitutes something qualitatively new.

In the end, I do not expect to settle grand debates about change versus continuity in international affairs. The underlying proposition of this book is that there is continuity in the relationship between the UN system and world politics. At the same time, change has occurred in both the nature of the world organization as well as the material and normative dimensions of world politics.

Looking Forward: Why the UN is More Necessary than Ever

UN Secretary-General (1997–2006) Kofi Annan often employed the image of "problems without passports" to characterize challenges that require cooperation across borders but instead encounter decision makers who can speak only for the space inside national boundaries. The United Nations is, in the final analysis, what the French would call a "pis-aller"—a makeshift expedient that is the best organizational structure that we seem to have been able to create to deal with a set of problems that cannot be dealt with by a traditional state system. Unfortunately, these problems will persist—and likely multiply and intensify—because they are connected with the modern economy and the forces of globalization.

Given the skewed distribution of power in the international system, however, it is apparent that alongside the UN, which is global in membership, there is another "world organization"—the United States, which is global in reach and power. There is no precedent for its military, economic, and cultural predominance—what former French Foreign Minister Hubert Védrine dubbed the *hyper-puissance* (hyper-power). Much of contemporary UN debate can be compared with the Roman Senate's effort to control the emperor.

Pundits too often overlook how the UN system serves American interests and gives Washington cause to proceed with international acquiescence, if not jubilant support. In this context, Ted Sorensen, a former speechwriter for President John F. Kennedy, asks: "What is more unrealistic than to believe that this country can unilaterally decide the fate of others, without a decent respect for the opinions of mankind, or for the judgment of world institutions and our traditional allies?"[4] For his part, Princeton University's John Ikenberry points to a striking irony in Washington's approach since the election of George W. Bush: "The worst unilateral impulses coming out of the Bush administration are so harshly criticized around the world because so many countries have accepted the multilateral vision of international order that the United States has articulated over most of the twentieth century."[5]

Nonetheless, American unilateralism has been such a part of world politics since 2001 that it circumscribes the analysis on virtually every page of this book. Before the war in Iraq, the "hyper-power" was already spending more on its military than the next 15–25 countries (depending on who was counting); Washington now spends more (approximately $750 billion) than the rest of the world's militaries combined.[6] And, with regards to softer power—economic might and cultural influence—the United States remains without challenge a major player on the world stage for the foreseeable future.

UN-led or UN-approved operations with substantial military requirements take place only when Washington approves or at least acquiesces. Moving ahead on other issues without the United States is problematic, although experiments are underway with the implementation of the 1997 Convention on the Prohibition of the Use, Stockpiling, Production and Transfer of Anti-Personnel Mines and Their Destruction, and the International Criminal Court, created in 1998. While many observers emphasize the peculiarity of the George W. Bush administration, unilateralism is not new. Whether or not, as Joseph Nye claims, "the world's only superpower can't go it alone,"[7] for the foreseeable future Washington's sheer might and willingness to resort to unilateralism will dominate every level of UN affairs—normative, legal, and operational.[8] Indeed, Charles Krauthammer's "unipolar moment" seems to have lasted quite some time.[9]

Given the importance of the United States to multilateralism, Washington's policy toward the United Nations figures prominently in this discussion of "what's wrong." Readers without US passports will have to indulge me. This does not reflect parochialism but rather the fact that the role of the United States in world politics and in UN affairs is a global concern.

Far more obstacles to cooperation arise. The emphasis is on the United Nations Organization proper; but many of the illustrations can be strengthened by reference to the wider UN system in which similar structural, philosophical, bureaucratic, and operational problems are not only apparent but are also exacerbated by additional institutional layers and other players.

The trick is to convey complexity without overwhelming the reader with bureaucratic details. To do this, some familiarity with the basic UN system's organizational chart in figure I.1 is important. The UN proper includes not only the six principal organs—Security Council, General Assembly, Trusteeship Council, the Economic and Social Council (ECOSOC), Secretariat, and International Court of Justice (ICJ). It also includes a host of important creations and some large and semi-autonomous agencies—e.g., the UN High Commissioner

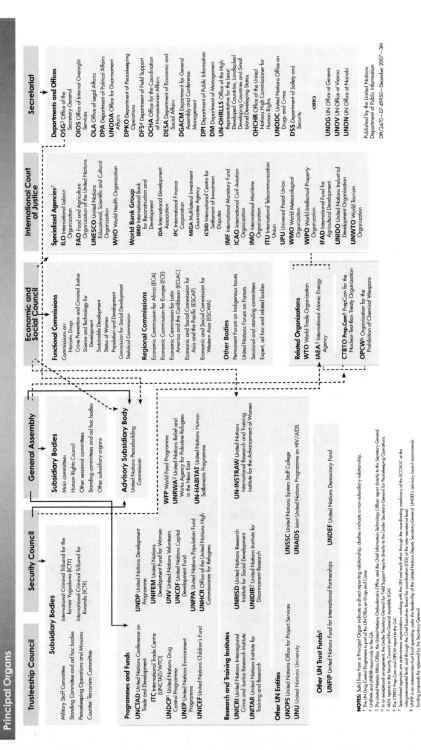

Source: United Nations website, http://www.un.org/aboutun/chart_en.pdf

Figure 1.1: Organizational Chart of the UN System

for Refugees (UNHCR), the UN Development Programme (UNDP), the UN Children's Fund (UNICEF), the World Food Programme (WFP), and the UN Conference on Trade and Development (UNCTAD)—as well as peacekeeping operations for which current expenditures are three times the UN's own regular budget. Meanwhile, the "system" has other more autonomous specialized agencies—e.g., the Food and Agriculture Organization (FAO), the World Health Organization (WHO), and the Educational, Scientific and Cultural Organization (UNESCO)—along with the *de facto* independent international financial institutions—the World Bank group and the International Monetary Fund (IMF).

One major thread in the chapters to follow is the extent to which member states paralyze decisions or actions. Another key theme is the distinction between the "first United Nations" (the stage or arena for state decision making) and the "second United Nations" (the secretariats who work for member states but who have a certain margin for maneuver). "There's a fundamental confusion between the UN as a stage and the UN as an actor," Assistant Secretary-General Robert Orr summarizes. "As an actor, there's so little we can do, and often the people accusing us are the same ones who prevent us from being able to act."[10]

No one should be surprised about the reality of the first UN and the second UN. After all, member states—51 in June 1945 and 192 today—establish priorities and pay the bills, more or less, thus determining what the world body does. That arena for debate and decision making is captured by Paul Kennedy's "Parliament of Man."[11] International civil servants would not exist without member states; but, equally, an institution of member states would not be much of a presence without the administrative support of a secretariat.

In addition, a "third United Nations" crops up in these pages. It consists of nongovernmental organizations (NGOs), independent experts, consultants, and committed citizens whose roles include pressing for action, research, policy analysis, and idea-mongering. They often combine forces to put forward new information and ideas, push for new policies, and mobilize public opinion around UN deliberations and operations. They include informed scholars, practitioners, and activists who maintain their independence but provide essential inputs into UN discussions, activities, advocacy, implementation, and monitoring. These actors are an integral part of today's United Nations. What once seemed marginal for *international* relations now is central to the analysis of multilateralism.[12] Numerous individuals and institutions that are neither states nor the creations of states (that is, intergovernmental bureaucracies) contribute to and circumscribe virtually every deliberation and decision by either of the other two United Nations.

The rebalancing of public and private, of states and markets, suggests the need to move beyond Inis Claude's 1956 two-part, textbook distinction between the world organization as an arena for state decision making and as a secretariat.[13] Why do I constantly remind readers to parse these actors? Because individuals matter—in governments, in the international civil service, and in global civil society. Success or failure in changing and implementing policy is, of course, not independent of states with their resources and vital interests. Yet there is more room for maneuver and autonomy on the part of international secretariats than is often supposed—particularly in the intellectual and advocacy realms and when pushed or inspired by the third UN.

In trying to hold accountable diplomats and politicians who are ultimately responsible for formulating international policies and their execution, of what value are these distinctions between the three United Nations? An old adage comes to mind—success has numerous parents, but failure is an orphan. States are rarely willing to blame themselves for breakdowns in international order and society; and international secretariats often indiscriminately blame governments for their lack of political will. The first UN has a convenient scapegoat in the second UN, and vice versa. As long as it is not directed at them, individual governments pay little heed to whether blame should be put on the collective first or the second UN. Sometimes the third UN adds to this confusion, blaming the world organization in general without distinction.

Indeed, a word is in order about one of my pet peeves, the shorthand label "international community," which usually introduces confusion into analyses of the United Nations and multilateralism. While international lawyers refer narrowly to the "peace-loving states"—that is, euphemistically the first UN—other observers frequently employ the term "international community" more expansively. Some observers include not merely states but also their creations in the form of intergovernmental bodies—that is, the second UN. Still other commentators use "international community" to embrace not only states and international secretariats but also nonstate actors operating internationally—that is, the third UN.

A special section of the journal *Foreign Policy* in fall 2002 was entitled "What is the International Community?"[14] As the lead-in to the essays summarized the problem: "Invoking the international community is a lot easier than defining it." Outside of public international law circles, it no longer makes sense to use the term restrictively because the cast of nonstate characters playing essential roles on the UN's stage is crucial to addressing virtually every global challenge to survival and dignity.

Thus, it is important to parse the components and interactions of the three United Nations, the contemporary international "community." Rather than use this term, however, it is preferable to identify precisely which actors are being discussed. In meeting the need to fill the glaring gaps in global governance,[15] "the UN"—in all its aspects—should continue to pool energies and make maximum use of comparative advantages to improve an international system that, as James Rosenau and Ernst Czempiel put it, has "governance without government."[16]

I acknowledge the porous boundaries and especially the loose networks that constitute the three United Nations. Yet deciding who is responsible for what portion of the blame for failure or what contribution to success—what Robert Cox and Harold Jacobson long ago called "the anatomy of influence"[17]— is a necessary and increasingly complex task that requires identifying the strengths and weaknesses of numerous actors. The stage for the drama set by Claude's two United Nations has, over the last six decades, become increasingly crowded with other actors who play more than bit parts. At the same time, states are still in the marquee, national interests have not receded as the basis for decision making, and international secretariats serve these state masters. This book is mainly about what is wrong with these two United Nations and how to fix it. Readers wishing to learn more about the third UN will have to wait for another book.[18]

Organization of the Book

This volume has two parts—the first diagnoses what is wrong with the UN, and the second provides some prognoses for how (partially) to fix it. Throughout, readers should keep in mind John Godfrey Saxe's fable "The Blind Men and the Elephant":

> It was six men of Indostan, to learning much inclined
> Who went to "see" the elephant, though all of them were blind.
> The first approached the elephant and happening to fall
> Against his broad and sturdy side at once began to bawl,
> "This wonder of an elephant is very like a wall."

Another argues that the elephant is clearly like a spear, while another "boldly up and spake" that it is actually more like a snake.

Descriptions of the United Nations are equally wide-ranging and inaccurate. Political differences and contestation are inevitable and desirable in an institution with 192 member states and tens of thousands of staff members and soldiers. Analogous to the six men of Indostan, there is no consensus among scholars, governments, civil servants, journalists, non-governmental organizations, and others on whether the beast is really more like a wall, spear, or snake. Is the world organization the potential solution to pressing global problems or rather a pathetic reflection of the inability of human beings to attack the problems that threaten their survival and dignity?

The collective attempts to describe the animal create not an elephant, but a "theologic war." Analyses of UN affairs and recommendations about its future are similar in that narrow perspectives impede the perception that we are experiencing this elephant together. Hopefully, we can overcome at least some of the differences in perception by the final chapter.

The purpose in Part One of the book—"Diagnosing the Ills"—is to use the medical metaphor and spell out in four chapters my diagnoses of four essential shortcomings of the United Nations. Illustrations in each chapter detail one or more salient examples from the world body's three main substantive areas of work: international peace and security; human rights; and sustainable development. This subject template is maintained throughout, but the reader will find different illustrations for each of the main areas of work within every chapter. The same headings thus should not give the impression of redundancy but rather guidance to related substantive discussions.

It is impossible to be comprehensive, but well-chosen illustrations permit the reader to understand through specific cases the nature of the major challenges as well as the logic behind my diagnoses. The illustrations sometimes involve lengthy discussions and sometimes shorter vignettes. The UN's problems are interrelated, and many cases could be discussed under several headings, but here they appear where they most clearly highlight a particular diagnosis. I hope that this selective and inductive approach both helps make the overall analysis clear to readers while stimulating them to pursue in greater depth issues that move them.

The nature of this book series is to provide authoritative but succinct overviews, which explains why many of the illustrations are sketches rather than detailed case studies. A more in-depth treatment of cases would not have changed the argument but would have added to the length. The book unfolds more in the form of an essay than a detailed and documented tome; nonetheless, interested readers find additional sources to consult in endnotes and in the selected readings at the end of the book.

Chapter 1, "Westphalia, Alive But Not Well," starts our voyage with a look at the disconnect between the global challenges facing the planet and the United Nations, on the one hand, and the ways in which states base decisions on narrowly defined national interests, on the other. The interests of "major powers"—particularly the United States, as the most powerful—obviously influence and create obstacles to UN action, but they do not have a monopoly on such calculations. Smaller or poorer or less powerful states are just as vehemently protective of their sovereignty; they are, however, less able to influence outcomes.

Chapter 2, "North–South Theater," continues with an in-depth examination of the peculiar problems caused when states align themselves in rigid and counterproductive groups according to the artificial divisions between the industrialized North and the global South. Such groupings began in the

1950s and the 1960s as a way to create space for security diplomacy by the Non-Aligned Movement (NAM) and for economic negotiations by the Group of 77 (G-77) developing countries. These once creative voices are now prisoners of their own rhetoric, which generates barriers to conversations, diplomatic initiatives, and policy changes.

Chapter 3, "The Feudal System, or Dysfunctional Family," examines the structural problems arising from overlapping jurisdictions and the lack of coordination and centralized financing among UN agencies and bodies. The "spaghetti junction," otherwise known as the institutional organigram that appears in figure 1.1, suggests two possibilities: productive clashes over institutional turf and competition for resources, or paralysis. Both are less-than-optimal outcomes resulting from the structure of decentralized silos instead of more integrated, mutually reinforcing, and collaborative partnerships among the various moving parts of the United Nations.

Chapter 4, "Overwhelming Bureaucracy and Underwhelming Leadership," concludes Part One. This chapter looks closely at the widespread image of the second UN as a bloated and unproductive bureaucracy that is more part of the problem than the solution. While the stereotype is inaccurate in many ways, the nature of the international administration is certainly part of what ails the world body.

Extending the medical logic from problem identification and "diagnoses," Part Two—"Palliatives if Not Cures"—spells out how to mitigate these problems as well as how to point the way to a more ideal world in which the UN's institutional ills might be "cured." The diagnoses in Chapters 1–4 are mirrored by the prognoses in Chapters 5–8, using the same subject templates (international peace and security, human rights, and sustainable development). The "how to fix it" discussions are shorter because we have more illustrations of shortcomings than concrete examples of solutions. Nonetheless, steps in the right direction are highlighted as well as experiments that contain kernels of creative and worthwhile ideas that might be replicated in the future.

Part Two is thus not based on pious hopes for the UN-equivalent of a scientific breakthrough or miracle cure, but rather on specific and encouraging examples that could be repeated. They also suggest that substantial change is often possible. Nonetheless, this part's health regimen begins with the most difficult and least likely palliatives and moves toward the easiest. While a case could be made for taking the reverse approach, I wanted to end with what seems more do-able. Rienhold Niebuhr's "Serenity Prayer," the epigraph to this volume, is a reminder of the necessity to change what we can.

Chapter 5, "Redefining National Interests," begins with the spotty progress that has been made in recasting interests in terms of international responsibility and good global citizenship. In particular, it examines closely the emergence of the "responsibility to protect" (R2P) and other human rights norms that are making inroads in the fortress of state sovereignty.

Chapter 6, "Moving Beyond the North–South Divide," outlines the ways in which states on occasion have forged creative partnerships and overcome long-standing and counterproductive divides that too frequently hamstring international deliberations. Less posturing and traditional role playing is a prerequisite for the future health of the world organization.

Chapter 7, "Truly Delivering as One," looks at the numerous efforts, some successful and some not, to centralize authority and coordinate responses among UN agencies. Alternative strategies for funding the UN's budget are also examined. The extent to which palliatives are all that are politically feasible whereas cures are not raises the question as to whether any change of attitude and substantial change in approach toward international cooperation will result without a global catastrophe.

Chapter 8, "Reinvigorating the International Civil Service," highlights the need to rediscover the idealistic notions of the international civil service. It also investigates the possibility of recruiting a more mobile and younger staff and providing better career development for the twenty-first-century world organization.

The book concludes by considering the question "What's Next?" Readers may be tempted to jump ahead to an essay by a convinced multilateralist who is not a card-carrying member of the UN fan club. But they are encouraged to find out first what is wrong with the UN and how to fix it.

The old adage comes to mind—if the United Nations did not exist, we would have to invent it. So, why not use our analytical toolkits to repair it?

Part One

Diagnosing the Ills

CHAPTER ONE

Westphalia, Alive But Not Well

Many of the most intractable problems (ranging from pandemics to the proliferation of weapons of mass destruction) are transnational in scope; and addressing them successfully requires action that is not only multilateral (involving more than two states) but also global. The policy authority and resource capacity necessary for tackling such problems, however, remains vested in states rather than in the United Nations. Established in 1945 by sovereign states seeking to protect themselves against external aggression, the UN was not built to confront many of the challenges that face the world today. The disconnect between the nature of a growing number of problems and the nature of the UN goes a long way toward explaining the world organization's recurrent difficulties on many fronts and the often fitful nature of what essentially are tactical and short-term responses to challenges that require strategic transnational thinking and sustained global attention.

The logic of the system of world politics continues to reflect the basic principle of sovereign jurisdiction, which has its roots in the 1648 Peace of Westphalia. Only those rules consented to, and only those organizations voluntarily accepted, exist in interstate relations. Sovereignty, constructed to produce order and to buttress central authority within the state, also means that central authority over global society and interstate relations has necessarily remained underdeveloped. All territorial states came to be seen as equal in the sense of having ultimate authority to prescribe what "should be" in their jurisdictions; and sovereign equality is the most essential building block of the world organization as spelled out in Article 2 of the UN Charter (or constitution).

Interstate relations reflect what political scientists label "anarchy"—no overarching authority exists beyond that of individual states. In the history of international relations and despite the notion of the sovereign equality of states, of course, all sorts of unequal relations have existed and have even been formally approved. In this sense, the fact that the five permanent members of the Security Council (P-5) each possess the veto, follows many examples of inequality.[1] Indeed, the widespread exceptions and routine violations have led Stephen Krasner to characterize the notion of sovereignty as "organized hypocrisy."[2]

The range of views about the conceptual traction and inherent value of national sovereignty varies. Krasner appropriately identified four different varieties: international legal (or mutual recognition between formal juridical entities); Westphalian (or the exclusion of external actors from a given territory); domestic (or the ability to exercise control within a territory); and interdependence (or the capacity to regulate the flow of information, goods, services, money, people, or pollution across borders).

Whatever variety used by diplomats or scholars, there are two poles that characterize contemporary stances on the value of sovereignty. On the one hand, the most numerous are those who tightly embrace it—not only many Third World countries but also "new sovereigntists" in the United States and elsewhere in the West. On the other hand, there are those who embrace passionately the construction of human rights norms as a step toward breaking down the "protection" supposedly afforded to war criminals by national boundaries. In between, there are more ambivalent observers, including those who see the erosion of sovereignty by globalization as an inexorable development with pluses and minuses.

Not surprisingly, proponents of the main theories of international relations—realism, institutionalism, constructivism—also vary in their appreciation of the current value of state sovereignty and its relevance for global problem-solving. Readers who have plowed through this literature will recall that for realists, sovereignty is an unquestioned value and the only way to think about world politics and foreign policy. For liberal institutionalists, it is a given that can be accommodated by pursuing enlightened policies within intergovernmental organizations. And for constructivists (or ideationalists), sovereignty is contingent, and so its definition and content can be altered over time by individuals and states. In the interests of full disclosure, the author falls in the last camp.

National interests currently are the only widely acceptable basis for governments to make decisions, which explains the narrow (i.e., national and not global) calculations by major as well as middle and minor powers. The United States and, increasingly, China are the contemporary hegemons, but the United Kingdom and Brazil are hardly different in the way that they approach international decisions; going it alone is easier for the hegemons, but others follow the same decision-making logic. Sovereignty is thus the explanation for the current multilateral system as well as the explanation for why that system is in such dire straits. This chapter begins with an overview of sovereignty in the age of globalization before examining some contemporary illustrations of the resulting difficulties that inhibit addressing looming problems in international peace and security, human rights, and sustainable development.

State Sovereignty, Worldwide Challenges, and Interdependence

Individuals exist and are grouped into nations. Nations, in turn, are governed by states. And states have governments, sometimes elected and sometimes imposed. Sovereignty is an attribute of all states, which is exercised by governments, whatever their orientations or origins. What is frequently called "national sovereignty" is actually state sovereignty. Whether the citizens of a nation are sovereign refers to whether the state derives its legitimacy ultimately from popular will. This latter issue has, for a long time, been considered an interior or domestic question; foreign actors have no authority to pronounce on it—although friends and foes alike are continually subjected to pressures from foreign ministries.

Most states—but especially the younger ones that achieved formal independence as a result of decolonization beginning in the late 1940s and accelerating in the 1950s and 1960s—value state sovereignty more than supranational cooperation to improve security, protect human rights, or pursue sustainable development. Many African and Asian countries achieved independence after extensive and protracted nationalist struggles; the leaders of such efforts helped to establish new states and shape the founding principles of their foreign policies. The anticolonial impulse survives in the corporate memory of elites whose views sometimes fail to get a respectful hearing in Western policy and scholarly circles. Paternalism by the self-appointed custodians of morality and human conscience undermines the credibility of many Western powers who preach human rights and intervention. Ramesh Thakur points out that developing countries "are neither amused nor mindful at being lectured on universal human values by those who failed to practice the same during European colonialism and now urge them to cooperate in promoting 'global' human rights norms."[3]

Anyone with even the most superficial understanding of colonial history should be able to understand readily why independence is precious. Algerian president Abdelazia Bouteflika's remarks during the 1999 General Assembly capture this reality: "We do not deny that the United Nations has the right and the duty to help suffering humanity, but we remain extremely sensitive to any undermining of our sovereignty, not only because sovereignty is our last defence against the rules of an unequal world, but because we are not taking part in the decision-making process of the Security Council."[4]

Edward Luck has pointed to American "exceptionalism" and traditional skepticism about inroads on its authority within the UN that is every bit as intense as any Third World state.[5] As Richard Haass puts it, "Americans have traditionally guarded their sovereignty with more than a little ferocity."[6] China, too, argues that only the state, not outside parties, can determine what is best for its own people, whether in the realm of security, human rights, or sustainable human development.

The perpetuation of state sovereignty—the idea that each state has absolute authority over a given population and territory and should be free from outside interference—as the essential organizing principle provides obvious benefits within the international system. It affords newer, smaller, and less powerful states an equal legal footing and a seat at the international table with older or more powerful states. It also guarantees some order and predictability within what Hedley Bull and the members of the English School call "international society."[7] Indeed, they see state sovereignty as not only a functional but also a political value that allows national societies to make choices and keep international organizations accountable.[8]

Moreover, international cooperation exists as a result of agreements among sovereign states—letters are delivered, flights take off and land, trade grows steadily—but it falls far short of giving international organizations the wherewithal to override decisions by states that fail to abide by the terms of their agreements or that simply opt out. The agreement in the UN Charter not to use military force except with authorization from the Security Council or in self-defense, for example, is ignored with few consequences for those that do so.

Nevertheless, as the peoples and states of the world become more materially and morally interconnected, the need for more effective international management increases. Terrorism, HIV/AIDS, refugee movements, and global warming all pose threats that are global in scope and cannot be adequately addressed by states acting individually to protect only their own citizens or territory. In today's world of near instantaneous global travel, to halt the spread of an infectious disease within its own territory, a state must also expend a certain amount of energy and resources on preventing the spread of disease in other states. Some may view such action as a moral imperative, but it is equally a practical necessity.

As peoples and states become not just interconnected but interdependent (meaning that their relations become sensitive enough that their own welfare is substantially affected by the decisions of others), demands often increase for more robust international management, which causes notions of state sovereignty to adapt. Americans are interconnected with Hondurans concerning trade in bananas; but, Americans can do without the fruit or easily find alternate sources of supply. By contrast, in 1990 Americans were interdependent with Kuwaitis concerning trade in oil. As such, this relationship was far more sensitive because energy is a necessity for which alternate suppliers are not numerous and the rapidly rising costs of finding such a supplier would have caused a major disruption in American society and the world economy. As a result of interdependence, some issues that were formerly considered domestic and inconsequential have come to be redefined as international and significant because of the strength of transnational concerns of either a material or a moral nature.

Still, even in the context of interdependence, most states are reluctant to transfer authority to international organizations, and certainly to the United Nations. The George W. Bush

administration's 2001 ceremonial gesture to revoke its predecessor's last-minute signature of the Rome Statute establishing
the International Criminal Court (ICC) is a case in point.
Regardless of the fact that the court is in many ways the product
of American input and reflects American values, the United
States refuses to become a party, pointing to fears that joining
the court will result in a loss of sovereignty. While the remaining superpower may be able to provide a few global public
goods—for instance, protecting the Earth from an incoming
meteor—far more of them require action (e.g., acid rain) or
inaction (e.g., nuclear weapon testing or non-proliferation) by
all states.[9] As such, less rather than more narrow conceptions of
state sovereignty, and more rather than less cooperation, is
required in Washington and all other capitals.

International Peace and Security: Saving Succeeding Generations from War

For many observers, international peace and security is the
essence of the world organization's work. Indeed, emerging
from the ashes of World War II, the United Nations was
designed, unlike its defunct predecessor the League of
Nations, to have military teeth to back up collective decisions.
Going beyond the League's attempts to delay the outbreak of
war through the establishment of a set of procedures constituting a cooling-off period for those countries contemplating
the use of force, the international community of states undertook a new experiment to halt war by signing the Charter in
1945. Two world wars within two decades, the Holocaust, and
the advent of the nuclear age produced, temporarily at least,
sufficient political will to improve on the League of Nations, to
safeguard the peace that had been won at great cost. In the
inspiring words of the Charter's Preamble, the UN's role was
to save "succeeding generations from the scourge of war,

which twice in our lifetime has brought untold sorrow to mankind."

In spite of the initial unanimity, Cold War divisions between the West and the Soviet bloc quickly resulted in permanent members' overzealous use of their veto power, thus preventing the Security Council from acting to address threats to peace and security. The post–Cold War honeymoon in the late 1980s and early 1990s offered a brief glimmer of hope that the Security Council would be allowed to fulfill its mandate to restore and maintain international peace and security. But preoccupations with state sovereignty soon once again constrained the Security Council even though the use of vetoes diminished. The end of the Cold War thus ushered in neither the "end of history" nor the "end of geography" in any meaningful way,[10] but rather a widespread resurgence of sacrosanct notions of sovereignty, the foremost bastion of which remains the United Nations.

Following the events of September 11, 2001, there was a brief moment when the United States seemed to support a more robust role for the United Nations on the world stage. In its bid to win international support for its "war on terror," however, the Bush administration quickly squandered the global goodwill that the attacks had engendered. It surpassed even the vitriol of the Reagan administration in terms of its criticism of the United Nations and willingness to resort to unilateralism to pursue sovereign prerogatives. While paying lip service to the value of multilateral institutions, the *National Security Strategy of the United States of America*,[11] unveiled by the president in September 2002, was anything but a manifesto for international cooperation. This "my way or the highway" approach has subsequently colored all discussions about using force.

Many regarded the new doctrine, with its emphasis on preventive intervention, as a lethal threat to the principle of nonintervention, which in turn brought forth defensive responses from other states that sought to renew the principle of nonintervention rather than downgrade sovereign prerogatives in any way. The Bush doctrine "has had the effect of reinforcing fears both of US dominance and of the chaos that could ensue if what is sauce for the US goose were to become sauce for many other would-be interventionist ganders," according to Adam Roberts. "One probable result of the enunciation of interventionist doctrines by the USA will be to make states even more circumspect than before about accepting any doctrine, including on humanitarian intervention or on the responsibility to protect, that could be seen as opening the door to a general pattern of interventionism."[12]

The administration pursued a variety of unilateral measures in other spheres—such as opting out of the Anti-Ballistic Missile Treaty and treating with disdain efforts to mitigate global warming through the Kyoto Protocol. The administration seemed oblivious to what Joseph Nye calls the "paradox of American power"[13]—the inability of the world's strongest state to secure some of its major goals alone.

At the other end of the spectrum are failed states, a terminal illness within the Westphalian order.[14] The early 1990s witnessed a dramatic rise in the number of intrastate as opposed to interstate wars, prevention of the latter being the original motivation behind the UN's founding. These "new wars" are characterized by situations where battleground states have minimal capacity and their monopoly on violence is contested by internal armed opposition movements that pay no attention to internationally recognized borders. Many have central governments whose sole existence takes the form of UN membership and control of the capital or the main export industries. Although these states claim to be part of the Westphalian order, they bear virtually no resemblance to their strong and more cohesive counterparts.[15] They do not exercise authoritative control over populations and resources. At a territorial level, these states suffer from an "unbundling," a negation of their exclusive authority as states.[16]

The frequency of state-versus-state conflict has decreased relative to the upsurge in violence within states—in the 1990s, for instance, 94 percent of conflicts resulting in more than 1,000 deaths were civil wars.[17] While the actual number of domestic armed conflicts has diminished somewhat since then,[18] nonetheless for 2004 one source found 25 emergencies of "pressing" concern, 23 of which were civil wars.[19] The battlefields of new wars do not feature conventional frontlines. Instead, violence gravitates toward resources and economic opportunism for which borders are oftentimes meaningless.

The period beginning in the 1990s features varying degrees of state failure and fragmentation: the regional wars in western Africa (in Nigeria, Liberia, Sierra Leone, and the Ivory Coast), central Africa (concentrated primarily in the Democratic Republic of the Congo, Rwanda, Burundi, and Sudan), the splintering of societies and states in central Asia (Afghanistan, the Caucasus, and Kashmir), and the growing unrest in South America (Colombia at the moment but with other Andean countries such as Peru and Bolivia perennially on the brink). While interstate elements are part of the mix in these conflicts—historically, their origins or irritants may reside in an earlier interstate war—these new wars are fought locally (in neighborhoods, villages, and other subnational units) even if modern technologies make external connections easy and weapons suppliers plentiful.

The role and importance of the state has been a mainstay of social science since Max Weber wrote at the beginning of the twentieth century about the state's legitimate monopoly on violence and its authoritative position in society.[20] However, the emphasis here is less on theoretical groundings of the state than on the concrete implications of states under duress. States surviving in the netherworld of fractured order have been described in a variety of ways: "disrupted states" (Amin Sakil);[21] "shadow states" (William Reno);[22] "rhizome states" (Jean-François Bayart);[23] "quasi-states" (Robert Jackson);[24] "collapsed states" (I. William Zartman);[25] and "state death" (Tanisha Fazul).[26]

While each of these appellations has merits and contains insights, I prefer the more common vocabulary of a spectrum ranging from "weak" to "failed" states in order to understand the main characteristics that circumscribe central government authority in new wars—the UN's main business nowadays. The term "weak states" has been used by many scholars and policy analysts to emphasize how the power of states is encroached upon or effectively shaped by other actors. These other actors are mostly domestic, but pressure also emanates from international and transnational organizations such as the International Monetary Fund and transnational corporations. Internally weak states contend with armed nonstate actors as well as civil society and business interests.[27] Economic influences since the mid-1970s have also played a role—the slashing of state budgets, part of neo-liberalism's panacea, contributed to "weakness." Structural adjustment programs that decrease the ability of states to fund basic social services and institutions providing law and order undermined the already anemic strength of the most economically underdeveloped states.

The shorthand term "weak" tends to categorize states that do not measure up to Western role models in international political prestige, wealth, military prowess, and unity. States can be weak for one of two reasons, and sometimes for both.[28] First, they may lack the capacity to pursue national interests formulated by an effective leader or bureaucracy.[29] States may also lack the financial resources, technology, skill, population, or political capital to fulfill goals. Many states relied on outside support in the throes of the Cold War and have had no patron to fund or provide the maintenance of vital institutions since 1989. Some weak states have even turned to mercenaries to provide security.[30]

Second, states may not have the authority to make credible and binding decisions. When a state lacks local resources or those from abroad dry up, the popularity or even tolerance among local populations may disappear, and such states are therefore not perceived as legitimate. A lack of authority may further undermine capacity. Disdainful populations can be controlled through violence, fear, and other repressive measures. Yet the ability of the state to govern and manage the resources within its borders can be still further eroded in the process of trying to instill fear and repress dissidents, armed or not. Some states have ambivalent or hostile relations with the societies they supposedly govern, which is certainly a measurement of weakness.

"Failed state" has become a staple moniker since Gerald Helman and Steven Ratner coined the term in 1992 as Somalia disintegrated.[31] While "weak" illustrates various types of vulnerability and a range of capacities, "failed" implies that the illnesses in central authority are so grave as to be politically fatal. However, not all weak states fail (e.g., Mali), and some weak ones that collapse can make a comeback (e.g., Uganda).[32]

The ongoing images of mobs running amok in Mogadishu or Port-au-Prince suggest the emptiness of state sovereignty in Somalia or Haiti years after the outbreak of civil war and the deployment of UN missions. Rather than "anarchy" or "chaos," Mark Duffield's description of "durable disorder"[33] is perhaps more accurate. The same structures propelling economic globalization produce wealth and security in some parts of the world but may also create poverty and conflict elsewhere. In many such downtrodden areas, one sees an enduring quality to the instability. Such situations may be chaotic but do not necessarily comprise chaos. Robert Kaplan's apocalyptic views in *The Coming Anarchy* emphasize crumbling capacities, but there is often present a "malorder" in which a kind of rogue order is manipulated or concocted to benefit a particular group.

In the late 1970s, Hedley Bull described the return to overlapping authorities as a "new medievalism."[34] He argued that over time the gradual development of a society among states is crucial to international order, but late twentieth-century patterns of unraveling authority reversed this historical arrangement in at least some parts of the globe. More recently, scholars have drawn parallels between today's wars and those that accompanied European state formation. Jessica Matthews notes that the post-Cold War power shifts among states, markets, and civil society resemble the dynamics of the Middle Ages.[35] Mohammed Ayoob, drawing on Charles Tilly's work, goes so far as to argue against those who try to halt humanitarian emergencies by pointing out that armed conflict was an essential ingredient of European state making and that similar kinds of humanitarian disasters are the invariable by-product of comparable processes at work in much of the Third World.[36]

What is unfamiliar, however, is the central challenge to international peace and security. As Kal Holsti reminds us, "the major problem of the contemporary society of states is no longer aggression, conquest and the obliteration of states. It is, rather, the collapse of states."[37] In this context, failed-state analysis goes beyond the logic of weak states, emphasizing how fundamental flaws destine a state to implode. Failure stems not only from material pressures (specifically, a loss of capacities) but also from a conceptual shift away from sovereignty. I have already referenced Stephen Krasner, for example, who emphasizes sovereignty as a politicized social construct backed by the most powerful states that routinely ride roughshod over it.

Our ability to diagnose what's wrong with the UN thus may be distorted by inaccurate assumptions about a pre-Westphalian order in certain parts of the globe and a post-Westphalian one elsewhere. As a practical matter, the deinstitutionalization of sovereign central authorities means, at a minimum, a diminished role for international law. The UN Charter's emphasis on the sovereign equality of members is perhaps most puzzling in countries where a central government does not exist or is in charge only of the capital and one export industry. The fiction also is exposed when comparing countries like Norway with a per capita income of almost $40,000 and Sierra Leone with less than $600; or China with 1.3 billion inhabitants and Palau (the last UN trustee to have become independent in 1994) with 20,000 citizens.

The inability of a growing number of states to function in any meaningful way to guarantee the safety and well-being of their populations clearly illustrates why Westphalian sovereignty is not well. While reconstituting weak states is essential, treating traditional sovereignty as a cornerstone for the United Nations is a fundamental structural weakness in urgent need of replacement.

Human Rights: The ICC, Durban, and Protection

The shortcomings of sovereignty and the ill-health of the UN system can be illustrated for the human rights arena with several examples: the major powers and the International Criminal Court; American and Israeli reactions to the Durban conference; and protection's secondary priority. These too provide further illustrations of the chronic UN ailment.

The Major Powers and the ICC

The Bush administration's decision to "unsign" the Rome Statute establishing the International Criminal Court demonstrates graphically the degree to which even the world's most powerful states—whose sovereignty is clearly uncontested and unchallenged by the ICC—continue to resist the creation of meaningful international authority. Its objections to the ICC reflect fear of an unrestrained prosecutor; it contends that the court's procedures neither adhere to US Constitutional rights nor provide proper due process (primarily because of the lack of a trial by jury), and that the definition of the crimes over which the ICC has jurisdiction are too vague. These objections underpin the argument that the court infringes upon US sovereignty and could even limit the use of American military force.

The United States is hardly alone in rejecting the International Criminal Court. Some 90 states, including most North Atlantic Treaty Organization (NATO) members, may have accepted the Rome Statute and the ICC's jurisdiction and authority; yet other crucial states such as Russia, China, India, and Israel have thus far rejected the court.

Washington vigorously leads the opposition. Active opposition, however, has eased somewhat because its earlier efforts were so successful. It threatened states that accepted the court with dire consequences; and it sought to conclude new agreements with as many states as possible in which the signatories agreed not to turn over the other's citizens to the ICC. Countries that refuse to provide such immunity—referred to as "Article 98"— are subject to cuts in US aid and investment. Sometimes, as in Colombia, the United States has reduced military assistance in order to try to pressure a state into non-cooperation with the court. During 2002, it delayed deployments by UN blue helmets until the Security Council granted a one-year exemption, renewable, from the court's jurisdiction, for American soldiers.

The lengths to which Washington has taken its objections are striking. Already by 2005 no fewer than 100 countries had signed Article 98 agreements with Washington not to extradite US soldiers or citizens to the ICC.[38] In 2002, the Congress passed the American Servicemembers Protection Act—which critics dubbed "The Hague Invasion Act"—that authorizes the use of military force to liberate any American citizen detained by the ICC. Washington and triumphant Beltway lobbyists failed to appreciate the irony in coupling the authorization of military action to the name of the city so intimately linked since the late nineteenth century with international efforts to have the rule of law replace the law of the jungle—the Hague Conventions of 1899 and 1907, the Permanent Court of Arbitration, the Permanent Court of Justice, the International Court of Justice, and the International Criminal Tribunal for the former Yugoslavia before the ICC.

Washington's opposition to the court was more ideological than logical. For example, the prosecutor could not proceed with charges against a US citizen unless such proceedings had been approved by a special panel of judges of the court and no investigation was underway or planned in the United States—at least two layers of protection for US citizens. In addition, the Rome Statute specifies that the court will not exercise jurisdiction over the crime of aggression until it can be better defined, thus negating another US objection. Likewise, Washington's concern for its military personnel and its argument that the ICC failed to provide due process (the lack of a jury) also seemed hollow because US military courts do not include juries, and the United States routinely extradites individuals for trial to countries that it maintains adhere to due process but do not provide trials by jury.[39] In short, Washington was more interested in defending an absolute conception of state sovereignty and national independence than in thwarting largely fictional legal onslaughts against its citizens.

In 2005, the Security Council turned to the ICC for an investigation of genocide, war crimes, and crimes against humanity in Sudan. The United States could have vetoed the council resolution but abstained as the ICC's judgment was, ironically, viewed as useful in Washington. Perhaps previous talk by Republican officials about genocide in Darfur, combined with growing pressure for some kind of action, caused the Bush administration to temporarily suspend its ideological opposition to the ICC. Moreover, if we assume that US military personnel would not be introduced into Sudan—made clear during the February 2006 Security Council decision to augment and convert the African Union (AU) force there into a UN peace operation—US personnel were not liable to appear as defendants before the ICC. In addition, neither the United States nor Sudan had consented to the Rome Statute, which made ICC jurisdiction moot.

Durban Conference

Another example of sovereignty as an obstacle to global action was the United States' and Israel's strenuous objections to the way that UN High Commissioner for Human Rights Mary Robinson ran the 2001 Durban UN World Conference against Racism, Racial Discrimination, Xenophobia and Related Intolerance. The United States and certain other Western countries—which after the Cold War seemed to want the United Nations to be more assertive on human rights issues[40]—initially welcomed Robinson's assumption of the high commissioner post. However, the conference's treatment of Israel and Zionism brought her into disfavor in Washington and subsequently forced her resignation.[41]

Taking up the position of high commissioner in 1997, Robinson transformed the Office of the High Commissioner for Human Rights (OHCHR) from an almost invisible unit into an effective bully pulpit in defense of human rights. Her vocal criticism took in the policies of the United States, Russia, China, and Israel, among others. By the end of the 1990s and with Robinson's enthusiastic backing, a UN field presence for human rights had expanded to also include Cambodia, Central African Republic, Democratic Republic of the Congo, El Salvador, Gaza, Guatemala, Indonesia, Liberia, Malawi, Mongolia, Sierra Leone, South Africa, Southern Africa, and Southeast Europe. In the name of universal human rights, the UN was acting on matters that had once been considered domestic affairs. In addition to debates about human rights in New York and Geneva, the second high commissioner was trying to make a difference "on the ground."[42]

After Robinson had announced her intention to resign in 2000, Secretary-General Kofi Annan eventually persuaded her to extend her office another year, ironically to lead preparations for Durban. But Robinson increasingly ran afoul of sovereign member states. The United States (the recipient of criticism for its actions in Afghanistan as well as its support of capital punishment) and Russia (for its actions in Chechnya) both opposed her candidacy, and in 2002 her tenure as high commissioner ended.

Just as the United States had seen to it that Boutros Boutros-Ghali did not continue as secretary-general in 1997, so too Washington made clear that Robinson's high-profile discussion of human rights violations in places like China and Israeli-occupied territories did not coincide with US policies. In China, for instance, the United States had adopted a bipartisan policy of engagement with authoritarian Beijing, in which the issue of human rights was relegated to quiet diplomacy, not public pressure. Washington had long declined to seriously press Israel on its repeated violations of the Fourth Geneva Convention of 1949 regulating occupied territory, as affirmed by various UN agencies as well as the International Committee of the Red Cross (ICRC). Because Robinson was more committed to raising the awareness of human rights than to quiet diplomacy, she became an irritant not only to those states with serious human rights violations, but also to the United States. She was also a champion of socioeconomic human rights, which Washington rejected.

The final straw for Washington was the perceived way that Robinson ran the conference in South Africa in September 2001, which featured anti-Semitism in the attacks on Israel and Zionism by many Third World states and some NGOs. While there were certainly some very shameful moments at Durban, they would have been even uglier without Robinson's leadership; and her overall record in any case was beyond reproach.

Sovereignty Trumps Protection

The shackles of sovereignty are perhaps most apparent in the operation of the UN's main human rights machinery. Created in 1946, the Commission on Human Rights (CHR) functioned until 2006 when it was replaced by the Human Rights Council (HRC), which was supposed to be an improvement. The following discussion focuses mainly on the CHR's 60-year track record, but this past is almost certainly a prelude to the HRC's performance. The issue of human rights illustrates more clearly than any other the extent to which orthodox interpretations of state sovereignty remain a chronic ailment for the United Nations.

During the CHR's lifetime, many of the most egregious human rights villains not only were elected to the commission but spent most of their energy protecting their own performance from scrutiny by being on the inside. A number of governments, such as India and the Philippines, routinely opposed certain initiatives, preferring to elevate either solidarity among developing countries (and their collective desire to fend off criticism as unacceptable intervention) or the principle of state sovereignty over protection of human beings. Latin American countries, for instance, tried to shield more repressive Latin American states, including Cuba, from the commission's scrutiny and pressure.

While such a repressive government as Saudi Arabia was often given the nod by regional caucuses, the election of Libya as chair of the CHR in 2002 seemed to be the most egregious indication that sovereign states did what they wished, regardless of commonly understood human rights standards. Libya was put forward by the African caucus as president of the commission. Given Libya's dismal record on many civil and political rights, the African caucus emphasized equitable geographical representation and friendly relations rather than any reasonable interpretation of human rights performance. According to UN tradition, it was "Africa's turn" to hold the presidency of the commission, and Libya was elected over the protests of the United States and other Western governments.

For many states, especially in the global South, state sovereignty or cultural solidarity routinely trump UN efforts to protect rights. Indeed, election to the CHR was highly sought as one way to set the agenda and avoid criticism. After assuming the presidency, and contrary to promises of balance and integrity, the Libyan representative made predictably polemical speeches. Coming shortly after the United States' failure, for the first time, to be elected to the commission, the presence of Libya in the chair seemed especially galling.

Will the Human Rights Council—created in 2006 after earlier controversy in preparations for the September 2005 World Summit—be any different from its scandalous predecessor? The 53 elected members of the CHR in 2005 included Sudan at the same time its government was pursuing slow-motion genocide in Darfur, and Zimbabwe while it was bulldozing the houses of 700,000 suspected opposition supporters and rounding up journalists and other critics. The High-level Panel on Threats, Challenges and Change (HLP) recognized the CHR's "eroding credibility and professionalism" and that "states have sought membership of the commission not to strengthen human rights but to protect themselves against criticism or to criticize others." However, its recommendation was counterintuitive in dealing with the litany of embarrassments: universal membership instead of "only" one-quarter of the UN's member states.

The secretary-general, in his only serious dissent from the HLP's recommendations, went out on a limb and proposed that member states "replace the Commission on Human Rights with a smaller standing Human Rights Council." The World Summit's leaders argued about whether the new council might one day become a principal organ, like the Security Council and the Economic and Social Council, and review the human rights of all members, not just those selected for special scrutiny.

World leaders at the 2005 World Summit were unable to agree on the details of a replacement, but at least those present did "resolve to create a Human Rights Council" as a subsidiary of the General Assembly, which would not only create it but also decide its "mandate, modalities, functions, size, composition, membership, working methods and procedures."[43] The proposal that members be chosen by a two-thirds vote of the General Assembly was eliminated as well as the possibility that it might someday be transformed into a principal organ. Protracted negotiations continued until March 2006 when the General Assembly finally decided on the new council's mandate and composition. The first members were elected by the General Assembly in May 2006, and the council convened in Geneva for the first time in mid-June. A brief comparison is found in table 1.1.

Some were disgruntled because the mandate given to the new council was mainly promotional and involved no clear

Table 1.1: Member States of the Human Rights Council, Listed by Date that Their Three-year Mandate Expires			
2007	2008	2009	2010
Algeria	Brazil	Azerbaijan	Angola
Argentina	France	Bangladesh	Bolivia
Bahrain	Gabon	Cameroon	Bosnia and Herzegovina
Czech Republic	Ghana	Canada	Egypt
Ecuador	Guatemala	China	India
Finland	Japan	Cuba	Indonesia
India	Mali	Djibouti	Italy
Indonesia	Pakistan	Germany	Madagascar
Morocco	Peru	Jordan	Netherlands
Netherlands	Republic of Korea	Malaysia	Nicaragua
Philippines	Romania	Mauritius	Philippines
Poland	Sri Lanka	Mexico	Qatar
South Africa	Ukraine	Nigeria	Slovenia
Tunisia	United Kingdom	Russian Federation	South Africa
	Zambia	Saudi Arabia	
		Senegal	
		Switzerland	
		Uruguay	

Source: UN Human Rights Council website; http://www2.ohchr.org/english/bodies/hrcouncil/year.htm

protection role. Others were displeased because the number of members of the new council had decreased while others thought the body was still too large. And there was criticism that membership was subject only to a simple majority vote instead of the more stringent two-thirds requirement.[44]

It is too early to evaluate the performance of the Human Rights Council definitively, but the preeminence of sovereignty rather than human rights is already clear. The fact that the United States has chosen not to be a candidate was seen as an ominous sign, as was the election of such other human rights "champions" as China, Russia, Egypt, Saudi Arabia, Pakistan, and Cuba. For the first session in June 2006, hopes were high but results proved disappointing. The HRC condemned Israel nine times but no other country. Both Kofi Annan and Ban Ki-moon have questioned why the HRC could single out Israel but ignore Sudan, North Korea, and Myanmar. According to Nico Schrijver, "during its first year the Council faced more confrontations and polarization than even its discredited predecessor was used to experiencing during hot seasons."[45]

The universal periodic review (UPR) (see table 1.2)—a thorough scrutiny of all HRC member states during their three-year terms—was designed to be a key feature of the new institution. In April 2008, however, during the UPR Working Group's first session, a procedure for conducting reviews was decided, by which each country will be reviewed only once every four years. As terms are for three years and states are ineligible for re-election after two consecutive terms, a government facing review simply could not run for office. Furthermore, the involvement on a review team of government-appointed experts—probably the worst way to ensure an independent and objective evaluation—is still being discussed. The HRC seems more intent on not offending a country under review than on addressing human rights abuses.

Special "rapporteurs," or independent experts, have been used over the years to highlight the precarious human rights situation in particular countries, or cross-cutting themes in a number of countries (for instance, on summary executions or indigenous peoples). But the June 2007 session of the HRC voted to terminate the mandates for the special rapporteurs for Cuba and Belarus as part of an attack on transparency and a defense of sovereign prerogatives. Human Rights Watch, for one, expressed grave concern about the selection process for

Table 1.2: Human Rights Council, Universal Periodic Review Schedule

Human Rights Council Universal Periodic Review

	1st Session (2008)	2nd Session (2008)	3rd Session (2008)	4th Session (2009)	5th Session (2009)	6th Session (2009)
1	Morocco	Gabon	Botswana	Cameroon	Central African Republic	Côte d'Ivoire
2	South Africa	Ghana	Burkina Faso	Djibouti	Chad	Democratic Republic of the Congo
3	Tunisia	Mali	Burundi	Mauritius	Comoros	Equatorial Guinea
4	Algeria	Zambia	Cape Verde	Nigeria	Congo	Eritrea
5	Bahrain	Benin	Turkmenistan	Senegal	Vanuatu	Ethiopia
6	India	Japan	Tuvalu	Bangladesh	Viet Nam	Bhutan
7	Indonesia	Pakistan	United Arab Emirates	China	Yemen	Brunei Darussalam
8	Philippines	Republic of Korea	Uzbekistan	Jordan	Afghanistan	Cambodia
9	Argentina	Sri Lanka	Colombia	Malaysia	Uruguay	Cyprus
10	Ecuador	Tonga	Bahamas	Saudi Arabia	Belize	Democratic People's Republic of Korea
11	Brazil	Guatemala	Barbados	Cuba	Chile	Costa Rica
12	Netherlands	Peru	Israel	Mexico	Malta	Dominica
13	Finland	France	Liechtenstein	Canada	Monaco	Dominican Republic
14	United Kingdom	Switzerland	Luxembourg	Germany	New Zealand	Norway
15	Poland	Romania	Montenegro	Russian Federation	Slovakia	Portugal
16	Czech Republic	Ukraine	Serbia	Azerbaijan	The Former Yugoslav Republic of Macedonia	Albania

Source: Human Rights Council website, http://www.ohchr.org/EN/HRBodies/UPR/Documents/uprlist.pdf

Table 1.2: (continued)

Human Rights Council Universal Periodic Review

7th Session (2010)	8th Session (2010)	9th Session (2010)	10th Session (2011)	11th Session (2011)	12th Session (2011)
Angola	Guinea	Liberia	Mozambique	Seychelles	Swaziland
Egypt	Guinea-Bissau	Libyan Arab Jamahiriya	Namibia	Sierra Leone	Togo
Madagascar	Kenya	Malawi	Niger	Somalia	Uganda
Gambia	Lesotho	Mauritania	Rwanda	Sudan	United Republic of Tanzania
Qatar	Kiribati	Lebanon	Sao Tome and Principe	Palau	Zimbabwe
Fiji	Kuwait	Maldives	Myanmar	Papua New Guinea	Syrian Arab Republic
Iran (Islamic Republic of)	Kyrgyzstan	Marshall Islands	Nauru	Samoa	Tajikistan
Iraq	Lao People's Democratic Republic	Micronesia (Federated States of)	Nepal	Singapore	Thailand
Kazakhstan	Grenada	Mongolia	Oman	Solomon Islands	Timor Leste
Bolivia	Guyana	Honduras	Paraguay	Saint Vincent and the Grenadines	Trinidad and Tobago
Nicaragua	Haiti	Jamaica	Saint Kitts and Nevis	Suriname	Venezuela (Bolivarian Republic of)
El Salvador	Spain	Panama	Saint Lucia	Belgium	Antigua and Barbuda
Italy	Sweden	United States	Australia	Denmark	Iceland
San Marino	Turkey	Andorra	Austria	Greece	Ireland
Slovenia	Armenia	Bulgaria	Estonia	Hungary	Lithuania
Bosnia and Herzegovina	Belarus	Croatia	Georgia	Latvia	Moldova

the 41 human rights experts or working groups focusing on particular themes, such as violence against women and arbitrary detention, and on specific countries, including Myanmar (formerly Burma) and Sudan. In the future, these experts will be appointed from a published roster of "qualified candidates," but the selection process itself includes a disquieting decision-making role for a committee appointed by the council's regional groups—another recipe for sovereignty rather than human rights considerations to be the top priority.[46]

This discussion of human rights demonstrates how firmly the sovereign equality of states is entrenched. The central principles and main tenets from the Peace of Westphalia impede effective international action to protect human rights. How else can we explain across-the-board foot-dragging, even in the midst of mass murder and forced displacement in Darfur? Russia's and China's lack of enthusiasm for having outsiders consider problems in Chechnya or Xinjiang is no less in evidence than the United States' resistance to having the death penalty or Guantánamo reviewed. As former US Ambassador Morton Abramowitz and Pulitzer Prize winner Samantha Power quip: "Major and minor powers alike are committed only to stop killing that harms their national interests."[47]

Sustainable Development: The Environment Under Threat

This section on sustainable development examines the machinations surrounding the Kyoto Agreement and China's resistance to cutting greenhouse gas emissions as it prepares to surpass the United States as the world's biggest polluter. As was the case for both international peace and security and human rights, Westphalian sovereignty impinges directly on more robust action by the United Nations in protecting the human environment.

The Kyoto Protocol to the United Nations Framework Convention on Climate Change (UNFCCC) seeks to reduce global warming through the stabilization of atmospheric greenhouse gas concentrations. Knowing that the commitments set forth in the 1992 UNFCCC would not be adequate to address the issue of climate change, states engaged in a series of negotiations that eventually culminated in the drafting of a treaty in Kyoto, Japan, in 1997. The treaty works by obligating developed countries (those included in Annex I of the UNFCCC, consisting basically of the industrialized West) to reduce greenhouse gas emissions by 2008–12. Developing countries—or, non-Annex I countries, consisting basically of the global South—are not obligated, under the terms of the treaty, to reduce greenhouse gas emissions. However, they can benefit from the Clean Development Mechanism, which allows Annex I countries to receive emissions reduction credits in exchange for the establishment of reduction programs in non-Annex I countries. Developed countries can also receive credits for projects undertaken in developed countries and can—through what is called "emissions trading"—sell spare reductions, which are accumulated when a country reduces its emissions more than required, to other Annex I countries.

Though the United States played a significant role in negotiating and drafting the Kyoto Protocol, it is not a party to the treaty. Washington objects to the fact that only developed countries are required to cut emissions. Vice-President Al Gore symbolically signed the treaty in 1998, but it was never submitted by the Clinton administration to the US Senate for ratification. The George W. Bush administration—with its strong links to the oil and gas industries—later voiced strong opposition to the treaty. It refused to support any agreement that did not equally obligate all states—regardless of industrialization level—to cut emissions. In particular, the United States was adamant that it would not join any initiative that did not subject China, not included in Annex I under the Kyoto Protocol, to binding commitments.

As the world's largest producer at the time of greenhouse gas emissions, the US refusal—not only to become a party to the agreement but also to adopt any of its provisions—was a significant blow to the treaty's viability. Since ratification by at least 55 countries was required,[48] including Annex I countries accounting for at least 55 percent of their collective carbon dioxide emissions, for some time it seemed doomed. Eventually, the treaty was saved from collapse when Russia—which had initially declared it would not ratify the treaty, claiming that its cold climate could benefit from global warming—ratified it in 2004, allowing the treaty to meet the 55 percent threshold and resulting in its coming into force in 2005. As of early 2008, there are 175 states party to the treaty. Supporters argue that its value—in uniting the world to address the issue of global warming—is primarily symbolic. Critics, however, point out that without US support, the treaty is insufficient to tackle the problem of climate change. Time will tell about the treaty's impact. But sovereignty prerogatives and narrowly perceived national interests—in this case, those of the oil and gas companies supporting the Bush administration—often prevent effective UN action to address global issues.

Although at the time the Kyoto Protocol came into force the United States was the largest producer of greenhouse gas emissions, China is now poised to overtake—and by some estimates, has already overtaken[49]—the United States in the race for the title of "world's worst polluter." China's rise in emissions, fueled heavily by coal, is particularly worrying. Even though it is a party to the Kyoto Protocol, it is not obligated under the treaty to take any measures to reduce emissions. China has repeatedly deflected criticism of its policies by pointing the finger at developed countries, which it argues should shoulder the burden of reducing emissions. In June 2007, China unveiled a 62-page climate change report stating its intention to reduce its use of non-renewable energy and increase its use of renewable energy by 2010. It reiterated, however, Beijing's view that the primary responsibility for cutting gas emissions rests with developed countries. In view of China's size and relative power, there was as little outside leverage to change Beijing's aberrant policies as there was to change Washington's.

In December 2007, the UN Conference on Climate Change held in Bali was the setting for the most recent illustration of the unwillingness of states to face the dramatic consequences of global warming. Secretary-General Ban Ki-moon pleaded with delegates to "deliver to the people of the world a successful outcome." The conference's dramatic eleventh hour included tears from the head of the UN Climate Change Secretariat, and Papua New Guinea's open challenge to the United States: "If you're not willing to lead, get out of the way."[50]

After the deadline for reaching an agreement had passed, 187 states present (including China and the United States) unexpectedly resumed talks on the global effort to rescue the planet from climate change, which culminated in the so-called Bali roadmap—a two-year negotiation process to guide the establishment of a new treaty by 2009 to replace the soon-to-expire Kyoto Protocol in 2012. At the close of the conference, newspaper pieces with such titles as "We've been suckered again by the US. So far the Bali deal is worse than Kyoto,"[51] and "Answer to hot air was in fact a chilling blunder,"[52] accurately captured the disappointing outcome. While countries agreed to "green" technology transfer, funding for poorer countries, and "deep cuts" in greenhouse gas emissions, no clear goals or timetables were set.[53]

Deep concessions were made so that the United States would sign on, yet Washington still had "serious concerns" about the inadequacy of responsibilities assigned to developing countries,[54] while Russia, Canada, and Japan also objected to some of the agreement's key aspects. Meanwhile the G-77 and some NGOs were disappointed at the lackluster final text. Indeed, the ambassador of Grenada described the outcome as "so watered-down" that "there was no need for 12,000 people to gather . . . in Bali. We could have done that by email."[55] Clearly, sufficient action on this issue will be impossible without a change in approach toward traditional sovereignty.

Alive But Not Well

State sovereignty provides the fundamental organizing principle for international relations and for the United Nations. Solutions to transboundary problems—be they dealing with the conundrum of failed and failing states, the protection of fundamental rights, or climate change—cannot be found by allowing sovereigns to make decisions based on their own narrowly defined interests and then to opt out of agreements when they prove inconvenient.

Westphalian sovereignty is 360 years old, or 360 years young. This venerable institution remains a hearty enough virus. It is a chronic ailment for the United Nations, and perhaps a lethal one for the planet; a topic to which I return in Chapter 5.

CHAPTER TWO

North–South Theater

As decolonization unfolded in the context of the Cold War, beginning in the late 1940s and gaining speed during the 1950s and 1960s, former colonies generated two key bodies through which to articulate their security and economic interests vis-à-vis the major world powers—the Non-Aligned Movement (NAM) and the Group of 77 (G-77). Thus, in addition to the East–West rivalry, another rather rigid dichotomy was mapped onto the globe—the so-called North–South divide. While the East–West split disappeared with the implosion of the Soviet Union, the division of the world into camps representing the North and South has survived despite its increasing irrelevance in a globalizing world. Many parts of the UN system, even the most "technical" of its organizations like the World Health Organization or the Universal Postal Union, are still likely to reflect the simplistic division between the wealthy North and the less advantaged South.

On many key areas of UN concern, especially pertaining to sustainable development, the NAM and G-77 remain the only way to organize international debates and negotiations between industrialized and developing states. The North–South divide is counterproductive to the generation of norms and practices geared toward ensuring human security, in its broadest conceptual sense. However, a number of issues reveal that, when it is in the perceived interest of individual countries, developing states are willing to abandon Southern solidarity.

Conor Cruise O'Brien aptly described the United Nations as "sacred drama."[1] This chapter first provides an introduction to the strange (and inaccurate) geographical terms describing the main groups of countries and then examines how the various roles on the international stage and in the global theater are played by actors from the two major troupes, North and South.

UN Geography, Mathematics, and Lexicon

Amateur geographers among readers may have trouble without a special compass. During the Cold War, the "East" consisted of the Soviet Union and its allies in Central and Eastern Europe while the "West" consisted of the industrialized countries (North America, Western Europe, Japan, Australia, and New Zealand). These were also called the "Second World" and "First World," respectively, to contrast with what at the outset of the 1950s Alfred Sauvy first called the *tiers monde* (Third World). Whatever their actual hemispheric locations—Taiwan is nowhere (i.e., is not a member of the UN), and Israel is usually a member of the Western and "other" group—the "developed" countries of East and West constituted the "North," and the "developing" countries the "South." In more recent years the adjective "global" has been inserted in front of South.[2] "All terms used to denote countries needing 'development' have shortcomings," notes Maggie Black. "Axis descriptors—developing/developed, non-industrialized/industrialized, rich/poor—are crude and value-laden."[3] This may partially explain the continued popularity of "North" and "South," which have the fewest pejorative connotations.

To understand the North–South divide within the United Nations, it is helpful to go back to the beginning. The first visible manifestation was at the Asian-African Conference—the momentous political gathering held in Bandung, Indonesia, in April 1955. "It was the kind of meeting that no anthropologist, no sociologist, no political scientist would ever have dreamed of staging," wrote African-American novelist Richard Wright. It cut "through the outer layers of disparate social and political and cultural facts down to the bare brute residues of human existence: races and religions and continents."[4] The key figures at the conference were the giants of that first generation of Third World leaders: Indonesia's president and host of the conference, Sukarno; Indian prime minister Jawaharlal Nehru; and Egyptian president Gamal Abdel Nasser. Also present were Ho Chi Minh, leader of the Democratic Republic of Vietnam; Kwame Nkrumah, the future prime minister of Ghana; and, Zhou Enlai, foreign minister and prime minister of the People's Republic of China.

The original motivation for the Bandung conference was to find a way to steer between the Soviet Union and the United States within the confines of the United Nations. Specifically, many newly independent countries were fed up with the logjam resulting from their inability to secure membership of the UN, which had become enmeshed in the rivalry between the two superpowers. By 1954, no new members had been admitted since Indonesia in January 1950 because neither Moscow nor Washington would agree to permit a member from the other's camp to join; the veto was in evidence.

Eventually, the conference would lead to the formation of the NAM—representing those countries claiming to be aligned neither with the Soviet Union nor the United States—in the 1960s. Following the 1955 conference, the African-Asian Peoples' Solidarity Organization was founded at a meeting in Cairo, and then a more moderate group gathered in Belgrade in September 1961, at the First Conference of the Heads of State or Government of Non-Aligned Countries. Despite rhetoric, "most nationalist movements and Third World regimes had diplomatic, economic, and military relations with one or both of the superpowers."[5] Indeed, amateur

lexicographers might have problems in finding a commonsen-
sical dictionary entry for "non-aligned" that included such
Soviet lackeys as Fidel Castro's Cuba and such American ones
as Mobutu Sese Seko's Zaire.

Working in parallel with the NAM but concentrating on economic issues, another conglomeration of developing countries became known as the "Group of 77";[6] and here amateur
mathematicians require a special calculator. Established in
June 1964, the G-77 was named after two new members joined
the original 75 members (which included New Zealand) in a
working caucus that gathered to prepare for the first UN
Conference on Trade and Development. The numbers continued to grow, and New Zealand left. Although there are now
over 130 members, the label stuck.[7]

The crystallization of developing countries into a single bloc
for the purposes of international economic negotiations represented a direct challenge to industrialized countries.[8] The
Third World's "solidarity" resulted in cohesion for the purposes of early international debates. It meant that developing
countries were in a better position collectively to champion
policies that aimed to change the distribution of benefits from
growth and trade,[9] just as they were better able to create some
middle ground on security issues through the NAM.

The well-known divisions between East and West during the
Cold War have disappeared, but the United Nations continues
to struggle with member states that align themselves along
regionally defined ideological and economic divisions, especially the North–South axis. The predictable antics between the
industrialized North and the global South continue to impede
any sensible regrouping of the majority of voices, which should
change from issue to issue. As Stephen Lewis has lamented,
"Alas, man and woman cannot live by rhetoric alone."[10]

The fable about Indostan is helpful as a way to understand
this UN ailment. Dramatic and largely symbolic or theatrical

confrontations, rather than a search for meaningful partners, has become the usual way to proceed. With a push toward consensus as the operating principle—the preferred route for UN discussions—lowest common denominators are one way to have 192 states (the current UN membership) agree on a resolution, work program, or budget. The other is for each country to interpret a resolution in the way that it sees fit or to ignore programs that it dislikes.

International Peace and Security: Terrorism, Security Council Reform

This section discusses two crucial security issues: terrorism, which has been on the UN's agenda for decades; and the composition of the Security Council, the world body's preeminent security organ, which has preoccupied international deliberations since the ink was drying on the signatures penned to the UN Charter in June 1945.[11] The former issue demonstrates the extent to which North–South divisions have stifled conceptual consensus and consequently practical progress on combating a fundamental threat to international peace. The latter issue illustrates the substantive emptiness of the groupings when narrow interests trump collective ones. While much of the most recent debate on Security Council reform, centering on the 2005 World Summit and its aftermath, supposedly concerns divisions between the over-represented North and under-represented South, actual country positions have little to do with these categories.

Definitions of Terrorism
While the jury is still out regarding whether a paradigm shift in international relations took place after the tragic attacks of September 11, 2001, the topic of terrorism has clearly moved front and center, at UN headquarters and elsewhere.

UN discussions of the topic have for decades been bogged down by North–South bickering. There was and still is no agreed working definition of "terrorism"[12] thanks to two main sticking points: the first is captured by the expression "your terrorist is my freedom fighter"—that is, many developing countries justify armed violence by those fighting for national liberation; the second is whether "state terrorism" should be included in any definition agreed by member states—the use of force by Israeli and more recently US forces is, for many, to be mentioned in the same breath as the use of suicide bombers. The sticking points remain because of vacuous North–South disputes.

Significantly, the HLP confronted head-on these traditional stumbling blocks: "Attacks that specifically target innocent civilians and non-combatants must be condemned clearly and unequivocally by all."[13] The secretary-general chimed in: "the proposal has clear moral force."[14] Yet the final text from the 2005 World Summit contains no such clear definition of terrorism. For the first time in UN history, however, the heads of state and government agreed to "strongly condemn terrorism in all forms and manifestations, committed by whomever, wherever and for whatever purposes."[15] The final text eliminated earlier and clearer language asserting that the targeting of civilians could not be justified because the G-77 could not agree as a group to drop an exemption for movements resisting occupation.

On balance, the summit added momentum to the secretary-general's evolving counterterrorism strategy, which was adopted in September 2006 in General Assembly resolution 60/288. Whether or not the assembly "concludes a comprehensive convention on international terrorism" in the near future, as was hoped, the summit's clear condemnation of violence against civilians was a small step forward. The September 2006 resolution marked the first time that member states agreed to a framework since the issue came before the League of Nations in 1934. There is an ethical content, which contains the basis for a convention and places the UN near the center of the fight against terrorism.

Nonetheless, as a prerequisite for meaningful progress, there will need to be defectors both from the mindless support for "freedom fighters" in the South and from the mindless rejection in the North of a consideration of state terrorism. This is ironic, to say the least, as a group of experts pulled together by the Stanley Foundation argues: "There is a widespread feeling inside and outside of UN circles that global counterterrorism initiatives are primarily of importance to the 'Northern' states while, in fact, the majority of deaths from terrorism are South–South rather than South–North in nature."[16] Addressing this threat requires a holistic approach, not divisions into warring camps with empty and predictable outcomes.

Security Council Reform

From the outset, the clearest candidate for inaction and paralysis at the World Summit was the Security Council. In proposing reforms, both the HLP and Secretary-General Kofi Annan made tactical blunders by making changes in the council's numbers and procedures the *sine qua non* of their sales pitches. Of course, the Security Council reflects the world of 1945 and not the twenty-first century's distribution of power. Every potential solution, however, brings as many problems as it solves. And no amount of diplomatic theater can eliminate that reality.

The debate about the Security Council presents a microcosm of a perpetual problem: the UN is so consumed with getting the process right that it neglects consequences. Allowing the Security Council to expand into a "rump" General Assembly of two dozen or more members, as some demanded, would not stimulate activism by the body. The council would be too large to conduct serious negotiations but too small to represent the membership as a whole. None of the possible changes would foster decision making about the use of force in cases such as Darfur or the Congo—they would no doubt inhibit it.

The HLP proposed two alternatives for a 24-member council, an expansion from the current permanent five (P-5)—the United States, the United Kingdom, France, Russia, and China—plus 10 nonpermanent members elected to two-year terms. "Model A provides for six new permanent seats . . . and three new two-year-term nonpermanent seats . . . Model B provides for no new permanent seats but creates a new category of eight four-year renewable-term seats and one new two-year-term nonpermanent (and nonrenewable) seat." In both, the veto remains the exclusive prerogative of the P-5, and seats are divided among the major regional areas. Article 23 of the Charter never specified diversity as a criterion for membership but rather sought a willingness of council members to contribute to the maintenance of international peace and security. The HLP wished to revive the largely ignored criteria of financial, military, and diplomatic contributions as part of the selection and re-election qualifications of those aspiring to membership.

Everyone can agree that the council's decisions would have greater political clout and legitimacy if they had broader support. How to get to there from here has always been the conundrum. Significantly, no other previous blue-ribbon international group had ever tried to disguise their lack of agreement by presenting two options as a "recommendation." If the 16 individuals who composed the HLP in their personal capacities could not find a way to formulate a single way forward, how could almost 200 states and their parliaments? Even a single individual, namely the secretary-general, did not take a stand, urging "member states to consider the two options . . . or any other viable proposals."

Against a backdrop of anti-Japan street demonstrations, fueled in part by Tokyo's campaign to secure a permanent seat on the Security Council, China dealt a peremptory blow to the notion of expansion. Beijing told the General Assembly in April 2005 that it was unwilling to rush a decision. The next day, Washington echoed the sentiment with specific references to "artificial deadlines."

Nonetheless, three more options were put on the table in mid-July. Germany and Japan, ever more impatient about their roles as ATMs for UN budget shortfalls, joined forces with Brazil and India in the "G-4"—the "Group of 4" or, less affectionately, the "Gang of 4." They initially appeared willing to push for a showdown in the General Assembly in the hopes of a symbolic but Pyrrhic victory of 128 votes—that is, two thirds of the member states present and voting—on their proposal to add 10 new seats (four nonpermanent and six permanent, including the four for themselves and two for Africa).

Meanwhile, a group of their regional rivals—Argentina, Mexico, Italy, Pakistan, and South Korea among others—which had been caucusing for years as the "Coffee Club," rechristened themselves "Uniting for Consensus." Taking umbrage with the G-4's claim to permanent status, they proposed instead increasing Security Council membership to 25 by adding 10 new two-year nonpermanent seats with provision for re-election, but no new permanent members. Simultaneously, following a regional summit in Libya, African states proposed 26 council seats with six new permanent seats with veto power (including two for Africa, but without specifying among Nigeria, South Africa, or Egypt) along with five new nonpermanent seats, with two earmarked for Africa. At the same time, other options were also being floated, including a 21-member council with six longer-term, "double-digit" (that is, 10-year or longer) renewable seats, and a host of ways to alter working methods.

Because of insufficient support, the G-4 switched gears. They first dropped a demand for a veto but then sought to woo the 53 members of the African Union, which was still insisting that the veto be given to new permanent members. Late in July 2005, the foreign ministers of the G-4 met at UN headquarters with 18 counterparts from Africa to reconcile the irreconcilable. Shortly thereafter, African states met in Addis Ababa, where nine out of ten rejected the no-veto proposal. At that point, the secretary-general postponed any vote in order not to sink the coming summit ship totally.

In the end, the heads of state and government could only agree merely to "support early reform of the Security Council" and "continue to adapt its working methods." The cacophony, jealousies, and vested interests that had plagued this issue since the world organization's 50th anniversary in 1995 remained intact through the 2005 summit. And they have since—as they will for the foreseeable future. It is not clear, for instance, whether some of the most serious candidates will agree to take half a loaf: a permanent seat with no veto. While the G-4 backed off, Africans became firmer about no second-class permanent membership.

Moreover, it is not clear that Britain and France will accept the inevitable discussion of giving one permanent seat to the European Union, originally a possibility proposed for an initial 15-year review in 2020. It is also not clear that the United States will agree to consider a body with 24, 25, or 26 members. Washington's rare public pronouncements indicate a preference for at most 19 or 20 members, with perhaps two additional permanent seats. Nor is it clear that some of the main "losers" (including Italy, Algeria, Mexico, Pakistan, Canada, and the Nordic countries) will drop the very issues to which they have consistently objected, or whether Arab or

Central European states will agree to a formula that makes no specific allocation to them.

Most important, it is not clear how any of the recommended changes will improve the chances for reaching consensus regarding the use of force. "[T]he enlargement of the Security Council is the least urgent element in the reform proposals on the table," laments Venezuela's former UN ambassador, Diego Arria, who helped institute several innovations in the council's working methods in the mid-1990s. "[T]he opposition and divisiveness that it has generated worldwide guarantees that the council's composition will remain unaltered." Moreover, he emphasizes the importance of successful experiments becoming traditions rather than being formally codified, which is the usual view emanating from the South. For example, it would be a mistake to spell out any procedures for the Arria formula, which permits NGOs and other private parties to brief the council in informal sessions. Unlike philosophers who are worried when what works in practice does not in theory, Arria cited with respect the philosophy of former baseball hero Yogi Berra: "If it ain't broke, don't fix it."[17]

Diplomatic clashes over the last decade, however, have contributed to a permissive environment that facilitated the pragmatic modifications in working methods favored by Arria by opening up closed discussions to permit inputs from troop contributors and belligerents, briefings from UN officials, informal sessions with NGOs and experts, and first-hand exposure to missions. These have injected more openness, accountability, and diverse inputs into council deliberations. They have not removed the problem of decision making based on national interest, but neither would UN Charter amendments.

Will the inability to move ahead with dramatic reforms compromise UN credibility? No more than in the past. Will North–South groupings facilitate debate and agreement?

Clearly not. If coalitions for and against various reform possibilities contain members from every region and every level of development, the North–South split has very limited value as a structure for debates about Security Council reform as for other UN issues, as demonstrated in the following sections.

Human Rights: Zimbabwe, Universality

In the UN's human rights theater, as elsewhere, the *dramatis personae* are mainly states whose national self-interests dominate their performances. While international civil servants and NGOs are actively trying to improve publicity and accountability, nonetheless the limelight is on states whose behavior makes or breaks human rights codification and enforcement.

Various double standards and inconsistencies are well-documented in the Commission on Human Rights between 1946 and 2006—and have not been different in the Human Rights Council since then. The United States at times focused on rights violations in Cuba, but disproportionately to events actually taking place there, especially when compared to more serious rights violations in allied states like Guatemala and El Salvador.[18] Washington had long used human rights criticism as a political weapon to try to delegitimize the Castro government. Similarly, during the Cold War, the Soviet Union was openly opportunistic in the commission, using human rights as a weapon against such US allies as Augusto Pinochet's Chile but remaining silent about major violations of human rights closer to home—in the Soviet Union itself and in other communist bloc states. Human rights language was put at the service of ideological and strategic calculations in the global South as well. Most developing countries paid far more attention to violations by well-known pariahs—Israel, or the white-minority regimes of Rhodesia and South Africa—rather than to similarly egregious ones in Idi Amin's Uganda or Pol Pot's

Kampuchea. In short, many heads of state and government have their own versions of the quote attributed to US President Franklin D. Roosevelt about a Central American strongman: "Somoza may be a son of a bitch, but he's our son of a bitch."

The promotion of human rights is one of the key elements and organizing principles in UN Charter Articles 1, 55, and 56. While member states commit themselves to the promotion of fundamental protections, the concept of universal human rights remains contested. Developing out of the Western liberal tradition of "natural rights," human rights have often been labeled as "Western imperialism," and criticized for placing too much emphasis on the rights of individuals at the expense of communities. While this is not new—utilitarian theorists such as Jeremy Bentham criticized early proponents of natural rights such as John Locke and Thomas Hobbes for their pro- motion of individualism—the inability to move beyond a sim- plistic and ritualized North–South pattern is definitely a debilitating ailment, as the following discussions of Zimbabwe and universality demonstrate.

Zimbabwe's Ongoing Pain

A contemporary example of misplaced Southern solidarity can be found in South Africa's spinelessness in the crisis in Zimbabwe, including a refusal to react in the face of the "stolen election" of March 2008 as we go to press. At the helm since 1980—first as prime minister and, since 1987, as presi- dent—Robert Mugabe has been widely criticized for corrup- tion, massive human rights violations, harsh suppression of political opposition, mismanagement of land reform, eco- nomic policies that won Zimbabwe the dubious distinction of being "Africa's worst economic performer" in the UN Economic Commission for Africa's 2007 report, and the politicization of food aid that has resulted in mass starvation, internal displacement, and refugee flows into neighboring countries.[19] The World Bank and IMF have suspended loans; and major powers—such as the United States and EU—have implemented targeted sanctions and travel bans. Nonetheless, important African countries—including the continent's most prominent economic, military, and political powers, South Africa and Nigeria—have supported the Mugabe government's chokehold on the Zimbabwean people, presumably to maintain solidarity with one of the storied examples of anti-colonial and anti-imperial struggle.

Given South Africa's economic leverage in Zimbabwe, numerous Western countries have criticized South African president Thabo Mbeki for allowing the crisis to continue, and exerting no visible pressure on "Comrade Bob." Looking to the precedent for South African intervention in Zimbabwe set ironically by a white South African prime minister, John Vorster—who, in 1965, removed support for Rhodesia's (as Zimbabwe was formerly known) leader Ian Smith by threatening its trade routes—human rights groups have unsuccessfully to date called upon Mbeki to cut off electricity to Zimbabwe and impose blockades that would effectively cripple Mugabe's ability to govern unless he changes policy.

Whatever happens subsequently, Zimbabwe's beleaguered president managed for far too long to maintain the support of Mbeki and other African leaders by going on the offensive, attacking "Western imperial hypocrisy" and predictably calling criticism by human rights groups a tool of Western hegemony. At the inaugural session of the Human Rights Council in June 2006, Minister of Justice, Legal, and Parliamentary Affairs Patrick Chinamasa took double-speak to a whole new level when expressing Zimbabwe's expectation that the new council would "succeed in fostering a culture of genuine worldwide commitment to the promotion and respect for human rights," and would make it its business to "depoliticize the pursuit of human rights issues." In the next breath, he noted that accusations of human rights violations in developing countries were a pretext for "hegemonic control and interference in the internal affairs of those countries" and that local NGOs were funded entirely by developed countries in order to promote destabilization and "disaffection and hostility among the local population against their popularly elected government."[20] With friends of human rights like that, who needs enemies?

Universality

In 1948, governments were divided over the issue of universality while drafting the Universal Declaration of Human Rights. The West argued for the primacy of civil and political rights, which are also referred to as "negative" rights because governments have to refrain from attacking them. Meanwhile, the East stressed the importance of economic, social, and cultural rights, which are also called "positive" rights because governments have to initiate steps to ensure that they are implemented. The failure to reach consensus on this issue ultimately led to drafting two separate additional treaties in 1966—the International Covenant on Civil and Political Rights (ICCPR) and the International Covenant on Economic, Social and Cultural Rights (ICESCR)—that put more flesh on the bones of the Universal Declaration and created mechanisms for implementation, monitoring, and enforcement.

Perhaps an athletic image would help complement our theatrical one. To a large extent, within the UN until the late 1980s, human rights were an ideological football (or soccer ball), kicked back and forth in an international game between East and West. Western players wore the colors of political and civil rights, Eastern players those of economic and social rights. Depending on their political affiliations, Southern players actively joined one team or the other on the playing field, or cheered from the sidelines for whoever seemed to be in the lead. The international game was mainly a shouting match, with lots of attack and denunciation but little attention to the practical problems and issues that were often high on domestic agendas at the time, and that could have been ameliorated by sharing lessons and exploring new approaches. Only as the Cold War was beginning to thaw, and groups concerned with the rights of women and children entered the stadium, did the game and playing field change.[21]

Progress in human rights has, nonetheless, been nothing short of remarkable. The original idea has made substantial inroads into policy and legislation. Beginning in the 1980s, a surge of ratifications of human rights conventions occurred, along with increasing implementation of many measures and outrage over abuses. About three-quarters of UN member states have now ratified the ICCPR and ICESCR, as well as the Convention on the Elimination of All Forms of Discrimination against Women, a kind of international bill of rights for women. According to UNICEF, only the United States and Somalia have not ratified the Convention on the Rights of the Child, largely because of an unwillingness to renounce capital punishment or the recruitment of soldiers under 18 years of age.[22]

More recent challenges to the universality of human rights have come from part of the global South. The first is the concept of "Asian values"—the assertion that the continent's cultures value the well-being of the community over that of the individual and exhibit a natural respect for authority. The Asian values argument has been used to justify enduring authoritarian institutions despite trends toward greater political liberalization in many parts of the globe. The second is the "tradeoff" theory—that developing countries should be allowed to neglect human rights in their pursuit of development until they are able to "catch up" to the West. Invoking the relatively successful economic performance of countries such as South Korea, Singapore, and China over the past few decades, supporters argue that the suppression of political and economic rights is necessary for robust growth. The debate has played out in bitter exchanges between the North and South in General Assembly discussions, with those parts of the South that disagree very often reluctant to break ranks.

Sustainable Development: Stockholm, Rio, and Beyond

The fault-line in the debate about the human environment has mainly been along a North–South cleavage, virtually from the very outset of the international consideration of the issue. To appreciate the nature and extent of the current synthesis, one must look back to a conference held over three-and-a-half decades ago in Stockholm—the United Nations Conference on the Human Environment (UNCHE). It was during the preparations for this 1972 conference that a way was found to integrate development and environment. More specifically, at a meeting of experts in Founex, Switzerland, UNCHE secretary-general Maurice Strong probed the concept of "eco-development" that would serve as a foundation on which the sustainable development dialogue would be built. Although the Club of Rome and others had put forward notions about the nature of threats to the human environment, they did not carry the same force or impact as the Founex report.[23]

Under Strong's leadership, participants were able to bridge some important political divides, in particular the clash of interests between developing countries whose priority was economic growth and that of developed countries seeking the conservation of natural resources and protection of the environment. The confrontation was captured by India's prime minister Indira Gandhi, who opened the Stockholm conference by arguing that in the South "poverty is the greatest polluter."[24] By arguing that long-term development was necessary to combat the poverty that contributed to pollution, but that such growth also depended on dealing with shorter-term environmental problems, Strong was able to help bridge the North–South conceptual and political divide. He also suggested that the governments of industrialized countries sweeten the negotiating pot and help defray the costs of environmental protection in developing countries. The concept of "additionality," meaning to increase resources in order to apply them to a new problem rather than to subtract them from another use, helped overcome skepticism in the South.[25]

The issues had to be revisited. In 1987, an important conceptual breakthrough came with the Brundtland Commission's reframing the solution as "sustainable development."[26] Meanwhile, the preparations for and activities surrounding the 1992 UN Conference on Environment and Development (UNCED) in Rio de Janeiro, more commonly known as the "Earth Summit," far exceeded almost all normal conceptions of a conference, as did the extensive documentation.[27] In addition to the intergovernmental conference, which incorporated a summit meeting of heads of state and government during its final days, the Rio process included a series of related events, unparalleled in scope and sponsored by civic-based entities that together were referred to as the Global Forum. These parallel activities drew tens of thousands of participants and an estimated 200,000 onlookers. A record number of national governmental delegations attended the Earth Summit; and some 1,400 NGOs with approximately 18,000 participants were at the parallel Global Forum.

The "road to Rio," then, was long and arduous.[28] Participants were engaged in the preparatory process almost continuously for three years. Maurice Strong, who after 20 years was selected to serve again as secretary-general of the conference secretariat, repeated what he had said about the earlier UNCHE: "The process was the policy."[29] The process of building consensus was regarded by many participants as being just as important an outcome of UNCED as any set of declarations, treaties, or agendas. However, the process was not always easy. After three years of laborious and often tedious negotiations, the specification of timetables, qualitative and quantitative targets, and acceptable limits still eluded negotiators as they rushed to finalize agreement on the conventions, statements of principles, and plan of action.

Continuing North–South tensions also reflect competing worldviews that underpin multilateral politics more generally. While the North–South division has been broken down from time to time for the sake of international peace and security as well as human rights issues, it remains rigidly intact for debates about sustainable development because group positions so closely mirror the short-term perceived national interests of developing countries. Southern governments are skeptical of the Northern push to impose ecological imperatives on the global development agenda. From their myopic perspective, ozone depletion, hazardous waste pollution, and global warming are products of industrialization and overconsumption in the North. The priority to protect the environment at all costs, so the argument goes, comes at the expense of development in the South. Cooperation from developing countries has been conditioned on the North's willingness to atone and pay the bill for at least a percentage of previous environmental sins. If the North wants the active partnership of the South in redressing environmental problems, Northern donor governments should make available additional financial and technical resources.

North–South tensions were brought into particularly sharp focus during the debate at Rio over deforestation. Southern negotiators—led by the Brazilians, Indians, and Malaysians—resisted any incursion into the principle of sovereignty over natural resources. Similarly, tensions prevailed in drafting the Rio Declaration, which was to guide governments and nongovernmental actors in implementing the many provisions of Agenda 21. With its unmistakable flavor of compromise between negotiators from industrialized and developing countries, this declaration integrated many of the most important elements of the perspectives of both sides. Even as the rights to exploit resources within a state's geographical boundaries were reaffirmed, the responsibility of states to exercise control over environmentally damaging activities within their boundaries was also proclaimed. In addition, among the 27 principles embodied in the declaration was one stating that the cost of pollution should be borne at the source and should be reflected in product cost at all stages of production.

Two legally binding international conventions were incorporated in the larger Rio process. The Convention on Biodiversity requires signatories to pursue economic development in such a way as to preserve existing species and ecosystems. The Convention on Climate Change embodies a general set of principles and obligations aimed at reducing greenhouse gases. Due largely to the intransigent position of the George H. W. Bush administration, formal intergovernmental negotiations over the creation of these two legal conventions were inconclusive. The final documents represented "framework conventions." Although they designated general principles and obligations, precise timetables and targets were unspecified and subject to future negotiations over protocols—that is, additional treaties.

Agenda 21 is over 600 pages long and covers the gamut of issues. Although most of this text was agreed before UNCED, a number of problematic issues surfaced on the Earth Summit's agenda: biodiversity, biotechnology, deforestation, and institutional and procedural issues involving financing, technology transfer, and institutional arrangements for carrying out the action agenda. Some proved to be intractable and remained unresolved at the close of the conference. Foremost among them was how to generate the financial resources to implement the program of action and associated activities. Estimates varied; the calculations made by the UNCED secretariat put the price tag at well over $100 billion per year for the first decade alone. These figures reflected the massive bill for the shotgun wedding between development and environment during the Rio process.

Linked to the issue of financing was governance. Who decides when and how such resources are to be spent? Again, North–South tensions fueled the debate. The Northern negotiators, led by Washington, pressed to have all such financing channeled through the World Bank group. In that setting, the locus of control would be well established, with the G-8 possessing effective veto power. Also, the World Bank and the IMF tended to approach environmental protection through markets. The Global Environment Facility (GEF) was in place and could be expanded to encompass a broader mandate.

This proposed solution, however, was not acceptable to most Southern participants, who preferred a "more democratic" arrangement. They proposed the creation of a new "green fund," which would operate on more egalitarian voting principles than those in the Washington-based financial institutions. Most major Northern donors found this proposal wholly unacceptable. For them to commit significant levels of funding, some guarantee of control was required. A compromise was achieved to enhance the South's participation while retaining donor control. The GEF would be expanded and its rules altered to provide for decision making by consensus among equally represented groupings of donors and recipients. The governance issue was, at least temporarily, put to rest. But the matter of securing the requisite financial resources remains problematic, with only a very small fraction of funds actually mobilized. Moving ahead will, as elsewhere, necessitate moving beyond North–South theater.

Future Performances

The end of the Cold War allowed scholars and some diplomats to begin to look more objectively at alliances within the United Nations. But, as we have seen, many of the labels and mindsets from the former era remain although it is now commonplace to point out the economic, ideological, and cultural hetero-geneity among developing countries.[30] In the past, it was polit-ically more correct to speak of the Third World as if it were homogeneous, with little hesitation in grouping Singapore's and Chad's economies or Costa Rica's and North Korea's approaches to military affairs. If one probes a bit deeper and adds a dash of cynicism, the problem is that the governments of the powerful states in both the North and the South are com-fortable maintaining this fiction because it permits them to avoid any substantial democratization of international rela-tions. They embrace fixed roles and oppose any global demo-cratic means for dealing with most of the problems generated by globalization—the North because global democracy would challenge its privilege, and the South because global democ-racy would require local democracy.

On some issues—like emphasizing the importance of the General Assembly, where each state has one vote—developing countries demonstrate consistently common positions. In such instances, the North–South divide continues to be salient. Frequently, developing countries subdivide according to the issue before the UN: between radicals and moderates; between Islamic and non-Islamic; between those in a region and outside; between maritime and landlocked; between those achieving significant economic growth and those suffering from stagnation or decline. Even within the Western group, there have always been numerous differences, which have come more to the fore with the abrupt disappearance of East–West tensions. Divisions among and within all groups over the pursuit of war against Iraq in 2003 clearly illustrated this phenomenon.

So, where are we after so many performances? The artificial division of the world into a global North and a global South is a simplification; and, like all simplifications, it overlooks substantial parts of reality. If it is frequently the default option, it is so because no other template is readily available. The previous discussion suggests that the North–South division fits better in the case of sustainable development than in the case of peace and security or human rights. Such rigid categories are more helpful for diplomats hoping to write a clear and simple script than for analysts attempting to move beyond the paralysis and sterile confrontation that characterizes UN deliberations. I return to these problems in Chapter 6.

CHAPTER THREE

The Feudal System, or Dysfunctional Family

The generic label attached to the organizational chart of the entire United Nations is "system." However, this term implies more coherence and cohesion than is characteristic of the world body's actual behavior. Frequent reference is also made to the UN "family," which has the advantage of leaving ambiguous the extent to which the United Nations is harmonious or dysfunctional, united or divided.

Using its clearly non-imperialist credentials to midwife the birth of many developing countries and help establish political, administrative, and economic institutions in them, the United Nations took on the conceptual task of "development." A prolific and somewhat haphazard growth in the institutions of the UN system began soon after the pioneering reports on the development conundrum in the late 1940s and early 1950s: *National and International Measures for Full Employment*; *Measures for the Economic Development of Under-Developed Countries*; and, *Measures for International Economic Stability*.[1]

Consensus about a rationalization of structures and priorities is difficult, to say the least. With 192 member states and the expanded use of the UN as a platform to discuss anything to which the words "international" or "global" can be even tenuously applied, there is nothing that is not on the world body's agenda. Organizational relationships also reflect overlapping missions, competition for limited resources, and the desire to keep abreast of what is "popular" with donors. UN organizations are not unlike other institutions in that they may innovate to exclude rivals or to cooperate with them, operating within a wider "network" of market forces.[2] The competition within and among secretariats is a factor—sometimes helpful, sometime hurtful—in the production and application of ideas and the conduct of operations.

In speaking about the relationship between UN headquarters and the specialized agencies, readers should keep in mind the horizontal nature of authority in the UN system. "The orchestra pays minimum heed to its conductor,"[3] wrote Brian Urquhart and Erskine Childers. They pointed out the extent to which the UN is totally incomparable with the vertical and hierarchical structures of most governments. The heads of agencies are appointed by different bodies with different priorities and budgets; the agencies' headquarters are located around the world, and their leaders may even choose to skip "cabinet" meetings held a few times a year. Robert Jackson, in his customary outspoken and picturesque fashion, began the 1969 *Capacity Study* as follows: "Governments created this machine which is . . . unmanageable in the strictest use of the word . . . like some prehistoric monster."[4]

Modestly organized confusion is the result, an image of which, as used in this chapter, is one of feudal kingdoms (the individual organizations) and feudal barons (their executive heads). The coalition of state interests that oppose an integrated UN system has helped cripple it by maintaining this feudal structure of separate organizations. The silver lining is that the structure also means that, at any one moment, at least some of the organizations working on a single problem may be effective and competent. However, we can certainly do better than justify the continuation of the current system with that rationalization.

The analysis of the autonomous moving parts of the United Nations Organization and the UN system (including the Bretton Woods institutions) provides insight into another part of the diagnosis of what is wrong—the world body's extreme decentralization. Efforts to identify coherence inevitably will be frustrated.

Intersecting and overlapping responsibilities are obvious from a glance at the UN's organizational chart (recall figure 1.1), but what is less obvious is the absence of any meaningful hierarchy. The tidy organigram is misleading because the secretary-general is only *primus inter pares* (first among many). The organizational chart also does not indicate the geographical locations of the various parts of the world organization itself and of the UN system. The problems resulting from such dispersion are exacerbated by funding patterns (short-term and increasingly voluntary rather than longer-term and assessed or obligatory).

The UN system is the opposite of a top-down hierarchy, such as professional armed forces and most Fortune 500 corporations. Many textbooks begin with the observation that the world organization is not a world government. Moreover, what kind of sensible soldier or meticulous manager would design such a poor imitation with ministries that go begging for resources and are located in the following way: the Ministry of Education in Paris (UNESCO), the Ministry of Defense in New York (Security Council and Department of Peacekeeping Operations), the Ministry of Agriculture in Rome (FAO), the Treasury in Washington (the World Bank and IMF), and the Ministry of Environment in Nairobi (the UN Environment Programme, UNEP)?

Again, Saxe's elephant looks quite different when viewed by agencies themselves and by donors who embrace the system in spite of the silo-like character of individual institutions that add up to less than the sum of their parts. The lack of a central institution for internally displaced persons (IDPs), on the one hand, and the plethora of institutions active in trying to protect human rights in war zones and in development efforts for women and the environment, on the other, reflect the bureaucratic and centrifugal pressures of a feudal UN system.

International Peace and Security: Internally Displaced Persons

Perhaps no other issue better illustrates the number of disparate moving parts of the system—lacking any center—than the pressing problems of internally displaced persons. An in-depth discussion of the UN's approach to one of the most troubling results of contemporary wars provides a microcosm of more generic problems that are illustrated more briefly elsewhere in the chapter.[5]

The most reliable indicator of suffering in war zones is usually the number of "refugees"—that is, according to the text of the 1951 UN Convention on Refugees, persons who, because of a legitimate fear of persecution, flee across the borders of their country of origin. Physical displacement is *prima facie* evidence of vulnerability because people who are deprived of their homes, communities, and means of livelihood are unable to resort to traditional coping strategies.

When such people are forced migrants *within* their own countries, especially as a result of war, they often are even more vulnerable. Whereas international law entitles refugees to physical security and human rights protection in addition to assistance, no such guarantees exist for those who participate in an "exodus within borders."[6] Agencies seeking to help persons who have not crossed a border require permission, in fact, from the very political authorities who are responsible for the displacement and suffering in the first place.

Over the past two decades, the ratio of refugees to IDPs—that is, between forced migrants who flee across national borders and those who also flee violence but physically remain within their own countries—has seen a dramatic reversal. The number of refugees in 2007 was around 9 million and the number of IDPs considerably higher. Depending on who is counting, as many as 25 million people have been displaced by wars in some 40 countries (12 to 13 million in Africa, 5 to 6 million in Asia, 3 million in Europe, and 2 to 3 million in the Americas), and a similar or even greater number has been displaced by natural disasters and development projects.[7] When IDP data were first gathered in 1982, there was 1 IDP for every 10 refugees;[8] at present, the ratio is probably 3:1.

In 1992, UN Secretary-General Boutros Boutros-Ghali submitted the first analytical report on IDPs to the UN Commission on Human Rights (CHR) in Geneva. The commission, in turn but not without controversy, approved resolution 1992/73 authorizing him to appoint a representative to explore "views and information from all Governments on the human rights issues related to internally displaced persons." The CHR limited the scope for reporting to existing laws and mechanisms, possible additional measures to strengthen the application of such laws, and new ways to address the protection needs that are not covered by existing instruments. Nonetheless, many states were still uneasy with this potential intrusion into domestic jurisdiction, while many humanitarian agencies were leery about bureaucratic fallout and a negative impact on fundraising.

Shortly thereafter, Boutros-Ghali designated Francis M. Deng, a former Sudanese diplomat and a senior fellow at the Brookings Institution, to serve as the representative of the secretary-general (RSG) on internally displaced persons. Deng maintained his independent base and salary at Brookings, where his co-director was the US human rights advocate, Roberta Cohen. Together they directed a small secretariat, the Project on Internal Displacement (PID). The CHR consistently extended his mandate for two- and three-year terms until July 2004, when Deng's extension ran into UN time limits for such mandates; he was replaced by Walter Kälin, a Swiss professor whose title became RSG on the human rights of internally displaced persons.

At the outset of the 1990s, the number of IDPs and the changing nature of warfare suggested to watchful observers that what formerly had seemed a modest blemish on the international humanitarian system was an ugly structural scar. The fastest growing category of war-affected populations had, and still has, no institutional sponsor or formal international legal framework, leading Donald Steinberg to describe IDPs as "orphans of conflict."[9] Diminishing refugee populations continue to benefit from well-developed institutional and legal efforts by the UN high commissioner for refugees. Moreover, the anodyne lingo of "internal displacement" fails to convey the immense human suffering involved. IDPs lack food, shelter, and physical and legal security, and according to a Centers for Disease Control study, they could have death rates 60 times higher than non-displaced populations in their home countries.[10]

In theory, the creation of a new agency specifically mandated to respond to crises of internal displacement would have been a straightforward solution, but there was neither political support nor resources. The next best thing would have been to endow an existing agency with the mandate for IDPs. And finally, there was the possibility of enhanced coordination, the usual default setting within the decentralized UN system.

Given the similarity between the needs of refugees and IDPs, Deng and Cohen, as well as a number of other observers, considered UNHCR to be the best choice for the second option: "UNHCR plays the broadest role in addressing the problems of the internally displaced: it offers protection, assistance and initial support for reintegration."[11] Unlike other UN agencies and the International Organization for Migration (IOM), UNHCR was the best fit for the job because it had both a human rights and a humanitarian mandate. It also had a distinguished half-century of hands-on field experience in protecting and succoring uprooted people fleeing abuse by governments and insurgents.

UNHCR was divided. Some staff favored adding the internally displaced to their agenda. They pointed out that IDPs already substantially exceeded refugees in numbers, and that the agency on numerous occasions had helped IDPs because they were in "refugee-like conditions" and mixed with refugee populations. Others objected, arguing that the assumption of responsibility for persons in their countries of origin would alter the character of UNHCR and undermine its primary mission, to protect and assist refugees. These "refugee fundamentalists" tried to keep UNHCR's focus away from IDPs. They warned that any shift in emphasis would play into the hands, and was perhaps even driven by the interests, of asylum countries that sought to keep large numbers of potential refugees away.[12] And they feared that UNHCR's involvement with IDPs would lead to conflicts with host countries and jeopardize its refugee protection mandate—for example, a conflict with Khartoum over its IDPs could hurt activities in Sudan on behalf of Somali and Ethiopian refugees. In any case, the agency's efforts in the Balkans in the early 1990s certainly had mixed results, with the dangers of in-country protection obvious as refugees and IDPs were sometimes saved only to be executed later. Indeed, the massacre of some 8,000 men and boys in the supposedly "safe area" in Srebrenica in 1995 became a conversation-stopper on this topic.

UN High Commissioner for Refugees Sadako Ogata's ambivalence toward the IDP issue grew from events during the Gulf War. The 1991 crisis in northern Iraq and the mass exodus of Kurds led to a vast infusion of funds, enhanced exposure and visibility from the media, and praise from the United States (the main donor). At the same time, much of Ogata's staff was upset that the agency had lost its soul, while massive management problems hampered the overextended organization.[13]

The logical result of keeping IDPs away from the UN agency best equipped to deal with them amounted to callously shunting aside the obvious needs of the internally displaced in exchange for the dubious advantage of respecting mandate purity. It also pleased other institutions that wanted to keep open the possibility for their expanding operations by persuading funders to provide additional resources. Georgetown University's Susan Martin called the approach "morally bankrupt."[14] While the "containment theorists" (another way to describe the refugee fundamentalists) wished to avoid diluting UNHCR's mandate, one could make the opposite case—that by adopting the internally displaced, UNHCR could reinforce that mandate. The agency would be in a better position to defend asylum with potential host countries if they were effectively doing their utmost to prevent IDPs from migrating by good-faith efforts to assist and protect them in the home countries. For a competitor in the intergovernmental system, "international assistance has long been explicitly recognized by IOM member states to include assistance in countries of origin as well as outside them."[15] Why would UNHCR also not be in a better position to find creative solutions if the agency were working on both sides of a border?

The clash between UNHCR's organizational purists and IDP proponents—both within the agency itself and outside—perhaps explains why Ogata was so ambivalent. Moreover, she was apprehensive that taking on such a large additional burden might stretch the agency's financial and personnel resources to breaking point.

Substantive concerns, however, were not the most decisive factor. The bureaucratic objections of other UN organizations and NGOs killed the idea of putting responsibility for the internally displaced in the hands of UNHCR. After he took over from Boutros Boutros-Ghali as secretary-general in January 1997, Kofi Annan ordered a system-wide review of the world organization with special attention to humanitarian and human rights operations. He put in charge of the reform effort Maurice Strong, the Canadian businessman and old UN hand who had made his mark as secretary-general of two blockbuster UN conferences on the environment and as head of the Office of Emergency Operations in Africa. His penultimate draft of the proposals for reform recommended handing responsibility for internally displaced persons over to UNHCR, and an appendix even fleshed out the possibility of creating over the longer run a consolidated UN humanitarian agency.

Other UN agencies, especially UNICEF and WFP, as well as NGOs in the guise of their consortium InterAction, sensed a threat to their territory.[16] They feared that UNHCR would come to loom over them in size and authority in the rescue of major casualties from contemporary armed conflicts. The women who headed these agencies—Carol Bellamy (UNICEF), Catherine Bertini (WFP), and Julia Taft (InterAction)—yielded no ground in the battle with Ogata over organizational turf. Bellamy even managed to get the US Congress to pass legislation to protect UNICEF from reform.

Facing fierce opposition—backed by donors who preached coordination but had their own agendas as well, including protecting the territory and budget allocations of their favorite intergovernmental and nongovernmental organizations in quintessential patron–client relationships—Annan backed off. The final version of his 1997 reorganization consisted largely of repackaging the Department of Humanitarian Affairs (DHA) as the Office for the Coordination of Humanitarian Affairs (OCHA).[17] The quintessential old-wine-in-a-new-bottle routine meant that coordination was reaffirmed as the UN's mechanism of choice for dealing with urgent crises of internal displacement.

Eyes glaze over at the mere mention of "coordination" because it amounts to wishful thinking about improved effectiveness without the power of the purse to compel working together. Prospects for successful coordination depend on getting the main UN operational agencies that play a role with internally displaced persons (UNHCR, UNICEF, UNDP, WFP) and those outside the UN framework (ICRC and IOM and also the largest international NGOs) to pull together. Coordination thus depends on good faith and is entirely voluntary.

But no single agency is responsible for IDPs, and no legal statute guides state or agency behavior. Susan Martin explained her rationale for a new agency: "Accountability is the bottom-line. And no one is accountable."[18] Not one of the organizations responding to emergencies has the ability to meet all the needs of IDPs. But with proper overall guidance—or so goes the theory—they could respond effectively. In practice, "coordination lite" rarely works. As numerous NGO and UN staff remark: "Everyone is for coordination but nobody wants to be coordinated."

The UN is the logical choice for orchestrating international humanitarian responses. The 1991 General Assembly resolution 46/182 created the position of Emergency Relief Coordinator (ERC) and the DHA; but it gave a mandate only for assistance, not for protection. In many cases, protection is as critical as assistance, but ensuring security involves usurping a central function of state sovereignty. IDPs are a domestic human rights issue, and so repressive governments are unlikely to welcome international protection during a civil war.[19] In any case, there are few resources and no significant field presence. These gaps are very serious limitations for dealing effectively with IDPs.

The ERC, an under-secretary-general, has the same rank as the heads of UN organizations. He chairs the Inter-Agency Standing Committee (IASC)—the grouping of the main players within the UN and the UN system along with the ICRC, IOM, and representative coalitions of NGOs—and has control over its agenda. But he has neither a cadre of operational staff at his disposal nor the power of the purse and the accompanying authority to oblige agency heads to respect directives or even consensus decisions. Without either sticks or carrots, the most that the ERC can do is plead and suggest.

UN organizations are like feudal fiefs, symbolically operating under the authority of the secretary-general but with their own separate boards of directors and funders, jealously guarding their independence and taking cues mainly from funders. And secretaries-general are rarely, if ever, ready to give ERCs the kind of backing that they would require to coordinate agencies. The rapid turnover of early ERCs—three between 1992 and 1997—also further reduced the chances for leadership and effectiveness.

One of the IASC's first actions after it was set up in 1992 was to create an IDP task force, the first real institutional attempt at coordination specifically designed to respond to the IDP phenomenon. It brought together in ad hoc meetings representatives of the UN's major humanitarian and development agencies with other partners. Among the task force's initial actions was to recommend that the ERC be designated as the "reference point" for requests for assistance and protection in situations of internal displacement. But as originally constituted, the task force did not have the authority to discuss specific situations of internal displacement. In 1995, the task force recommended broadening its mandate to include not only the review of specific country situations but also the analysis of assistance and protection needs of IDPs and of national and international institutions to deal with them.

The task force was never able to fulfill this expanded mandate. A mixture of extreme caution and impulsive daring proved to be its undoing. It failed to make recommendations about specific situations in which UN agencies might become involved, as in Sierra Leone, which reportedly had one million internally displaced persons in dire need; or in the Great Lakes region of Africa, where a well-funded assistance operation for refugees existed alongside an under-funded and ill-coordinated response for IDPs.

But when Myanmar—a country with hundreds of thousands of IDPs whose government rejected any international oversight—was placed on its agenda for discussion, UN headquarters ordered the task force to withdraw the item lest it interfere with talks that the UN's Department of Political Affairs (DPA) was organizing in Yangon (formerly Rangoon). And when reports of IDPs being subjected to widespread abuses in Angola prompted the task force to propose a mission, both senior DHA officials and the staffs of operational agencies on the ground objected. Task force members complained that the task force's actions were too timid and too forceful. Some blamed its failings on its chair. The main difficulties, however, stemmed from the UN system's structural inability to come to grips with internal displacement.

In 1997, the IASC quietly shut down the task force and transferred the issue to the agenda of its working group, a senior to mid-level body charged with coordination of the UN's humanitarian and developmental operations. Deng was made a "standing invitee" of the IASC, where previously he was listed to attend only when issues involving the internally displaced were to be discussed. His inclusion in this forum provided a platform from which to broaden his and Cohen's campaign for integrating (or "mainstreaming") internal displacement into the work of all UN organizations. At the outset, IASC members looked askance at this new and unfamiliar item that raised the uncomfortable issue of protecting people within the borders of member states. Deng recalled one irony within this turf-conscious interagency forum: "Sometimes

UN agencies lagged behind the times and were unaware of the actual changes in government policies. Governments often complained to me of agencies' being behind the curve."[20] But gradually the working group came to accept internal displacement as a routine part of its discussions.

The result was, on paper, an impressive organizational chart for coordinating assistance and protection for IDPs. At its apex sat the ERC and DHA (OCHA after 1998), with a line running down to the IASC and its working group. From there lines ran to the right and left to the operational agencies and then down to the UNDP's resident coordinators in each country, who reported back up to the ERC. In 1998, at Deng's suggestion and with strong support from Sergio Vieira de Mello—the then newly appointed ERC who subsequently died in the August 2003 attack on the UN's Baghdad headquarters—the IASC directed its member agencies to appoint "focal points" (customarily mid-level UN officials) to facilitate collaboration. The resulting network of interagency focal points was to be coordinated in turn by a senior official in OCHA. This coordination mechanism led to the eventual establishment within OCHA of an interagency IDP network in 2000 followed by the Internal Displacement Unit in January 2002, which was upgraded to the Internal Displacement Division in July 2004.

Like many organizational concoctions, this one did not result in better performance. Field officials for the most part continued to do what they thought that their headquarters required, regardless of the needs of IDPs or the views of those sitting around conference tables in New York or Geneva. The resident coordinators sometimes tried to orchestrate country programs, and sometimes they did not.

When Richard Holbrooke, the US permanent representative to the United Nations, visited Angola in December 1999, he found the UN's so-called coordination mechanism sorely deficient. There were more than a million IDPs in camps, victims of Angola's long civil war. But for the most part, Holbrooke declared, they were "out of reach of the international community's assistance."[21] Not one to mince words, Holbrooke called the UN's programs in Angola "ill organized and unable to provide adequate support." He observed that "what's decided in New York or Geneva does not translate into real follow-up in the field, or vice versa. And the Office for the Coordination of Humanitarian Affairs, or OCHA, the organization entrusted with overall coordination responsibility, has neither the authority nor the resources to drive the system."[22]

Another possible approach was the "lead agency" arrangement. This method had worked elsewhere—indeed, UNHCR's performance as lead agency in the former Yugoslavia was one reason why many analysts and at least some agency staff wanted UNHCR to take over the mandate for IDPs,[23] and why Strong had proposed it in the draft of the 1997 reform. It consisted in conferring primary responsibility for IDPs upon a single agency in each major displacement crisis. The choice of an agency would reflect the specific needs of an affected population in a given crisis. If protection were paramount, UNHCR would play the main role. If material or development needs were the main concern, the job might be given to WFP, UNDP, or UNICEF.

Nonetheless, the lead-agency concept for IDPs never gained widespread acceptance within the UN system, although it was a de facto solution on occasion. OCHA considered it a challenge to its own authority to coordinate the actions of the various agencies. And it was joined by the operational agencies that saw such an arrangement as a back door for handing IDPs over to UNHCR.

To say that no institutional progress has been made would be an exaggeration. A variety of intergovernmental, regional, and nongovernmental organizations now routinely include IDPs in their plans, projects, and programs whereas at the beginning of the 1990s there was even a question as to whether IDPs were a special category. Important donors over time have focused more attention and resources on the phenomenon of internal displacement. As a result, ICRC as well as such major UN players as UNHCR, UNICEF, and WFP are obliged to publish reports to their governing bodies about how they are reorienting their programming. Donors allocate special funding for such efforts. UNHCR's revised guidelines on the protection of refugee women added IDPs to the categorization.

Yet to state the obvious, this haphazard institutional progress falls far short of what the size of the problem merits and what IDP advocates would have liked. The institutional foundation for protecting this type of war victim remains extremely wobbly. If the 2005 World Summit recommendation to double the allocation to OHCHR from the UN's regular budget over the next five years is implemented, perhaps the independent experts will receive more adequate back-stopping and funding, including oversight of IDP issues. But more important, the experimental "collaborative approach" used by the UN since 2006 continues to reflect ad hoc arrangements. It is simply impossible to compensate for the absence of a centralized UN presence.

A comprehensive outside evaluation of January 2004 damned in no uncertain terms OCHA's lack of strategic vision, but recommended a few years grace: "If, on the other hand, after a period of two to three years there is still no progress in the collaborative approach, the Unit [now Division] should be shut down—at that point it will have become a veil masking inherent failures of the system."[24] The notion that within a few years OCHA will improve the actual assistance and protection of IDPs calls to mind the characterization of second marriages by Oscar Wilde—as being triumph of hope over experience.

When UN mechanisms work—and we should not ignore the fact that many victims are fed, housed, and protected—it is because of good faith and compatible personalities rather than any coherent, centralized structure. Improving the actual performance of the international humanitarian system, as for other parts of the UN system, would benefit from fewer moving parts and more consolidation.

Human Rights: Atomized Humanitarian Protection

Continuing with the theme of human rights protection more generally will be helpful to our understanding of the implications of UN feudalism. Institutional concerns with turf have prevented the establishment of a central organization for IDPs. The same reflex against consolidation has led to a different manifestation of the same problem elsewhere. For humanitarian action—delivering emergency relief and protecting the human rights of war victims—there is not really a shortage but a surfeit of actors. The key problem is the lack of concerted action by a host of players within the UN system as well as a parallel universe of NGOs that function as UN subcontractors.[25]

The plethora of NGOs, whose numbers continue to grow, makes the combined UN–private humanitarian system ever more unwieldy. The enterprise is "atomized." Competitive individual units, rather than working as partners, often end up "defecting" from a common approach because it is in their perceived institutional interests to do so—though not, of course, in the interests of the victims of natural disasters, repression, and war.

Some of the growth in the last two decades reflects a creative adaptation to the crises growing from the new wars, but some of it simply reflects institutional expansion and empire building. And this reality frames the peculiar collective action problems of the new humanitarianisms. This section looks at the numbers and then takes a hard look at how coordination is preached versus how it is practiced.

To begin, there is a fundamental absence of longitudinal data regarding basic categories such as expenditure, income, number of organizations, and activities.[26] Nonetheless, there is evidence that the humanitarian sector has undergone significant change since the end of the Cold War—most noticeable in its population density, resources, and activities. There has been tremendous growth in the sheer number of humanitarian organizations.[27] How much? This depends on who counts and who is worth counting. Most surveys automatically include nonprofit relief agencies. Presently there are an estimated 2,500 NGOs in the humanitarian business, but only about 260 are serious players—based on a 2003 OCHA roster (which is no longer updated) that listed those active in humanitarian responses at the time. This figure excludes those NGOs not engaged in relief or the myriad mom-and-pop organizations that crop-up around specific emergencies. In 2001, the half-dozen or so largest NGOs controlled between $2.5 billion and $3 billion, or between 45 percent and 55 percent of total humanitarian assistance.[28]

A 2006 survey of US-based private voluntary agencies offers a reasonably good picture that typifies growth over the last 70 years in a number of wealthy countries. In 1940, at the start of World War II, there were 386 organizations, but the number dropped to 97 in 1945, 62 in 1950, and 57 in 1960. It began rising again thereafter—to 83 in 1970, 167 in 1980, 267 in 1990, and 436 in 2000.[29] Not only has the total number increased but so too have the dimensions of the largest among them. The dozen or so that represent the bulk of aid programming and personnel have all been in existence for some time.

In addition, dramatic crises often account for spikes in the numbers of smaller agencies on the ground. For instance, over 200 international NGOs were reported to have mailboxes in

Sarajevo and Kigali. The numbers of people working for the NGO component of the humanitarian sector grew by 91 percent from 1997 to 2005, while overall the international humanitarian system (if the UN system and the ICRC are also included) experienced a 77 percent surge in personnel.[30]

But even these figures may potentially undercount the number of aid agencies and personnel because of the tendency to focus on those based in the West. To some extent, this bias accurately reflects the origins of the bulk of resources and institutions. Yet there is also a very active relief sector in the non-Western world, most obviously in Islamic countries, the location for about half of the victims of wars since the beginning of the 1990s. There is more speculation than concrete knowledge; because of September 11, 2001, attention is directed less at understanding than connecting Islamic charitable organizations and terrorism.[31]

In addition to NGOs, of course, UN organizations are the most prominent actors. UNHCR and other aid agencies were born as humanitarian organizations. Other international organizations have for decades worked to foster development but are increasingly involved in relief and reconstruction, including UNDP and the World Bank, both of which have moved upstream toward operations in war zones rather than focusing on development further downstream. A similar dynamic exists for other non-disaster-oriented UN specialized agencies—for example, the WHO and UNESCO—whose almost nonexistent disaster programs have recently expanded to meet the new demand and availability of funding. Consequently, UN institutions that might not have counted as humanitarian in the 1980s are partially so today. There also has been a growth in the number of international and regional organizations whose primary responsibility is to coordinate assistance, including the European Community Humanitarian Aid Office, the UN's IASC and OCHA, and a host of coordinating mechanisms in the United States and Europe for NGOs (such as InterAction and the International Council for Voluntary Action).

States, for-profit disaster firms, other businesses, and various foundations are also increasingly prominent in the relief and reconstruction sectors and perform humanitarian functions. While the West continues to dominate the numbers, increasingly more governments are responding to disasters of all sorts. For example, 16 states pledged their support to Bosnia in the mid-1990s, most from the West; but a more diverse group of 73 came to the 2003 pledging conference for Iraq in Madrid, and an unprecedented 92 responded to the December 2004 tsunami. Such important non-Western donors as China, Saudi Arabia, and India have accounted for up to 12 percent of official humanitarian assistance in a given year; and their influence in certain crises—for example, Afghanistan and Palestine—is even more significant. As two researchers point out: "We know little about whether they follow the major Western states in their rationales for aid interventions, their policy priorities and their choice of response channel."[32] Nonetheless, the international system remains essentially a North American and Western European enterprise: "It works wherever it can in international society but is not really owned by all of international society."[33] In short, we understand surprisingly little about the population explosion of organizations that contribute to various forms of relief, but we do know that the task is becoming ever more complex.

There also are more financial resources than ever before. Recent trends show an increase in private contributions, but most impressive has been the growth of official (that is, governmental) assistance. Between 1990 and 2000 aid levels rose nearly threefold, from $2.1 billion to $5.9 billion—and in 2005–6 were undoubtedly over $10 billion.[34] Moreover, as a percentage of official development assistance (ODA), humanitarian aid rose from an average of 5.83 percent between 1989 and 1993 to 10.5 percent in 2000.[35] Over a longer period, total ODA has shrunk, but the humanitarian component has continued to grow. "From 1970–1990 humanitarian aid was less than 3 percent of total ODA," calculated a team from the Overseas Development Institute. "While ODA . . . as a whole has been declining as a share of donor countries' national wealth or Gross National Income (GNI), humanitarian ODA has been growing. In 1970 DAC [Development Assistance Committee] member countries gave 0.4 of a cent in humanitarian aid for every $100 in national income. In 2001 it was 2.3 cents."[36]

A few donors were responsible for much of this increase, and they also now comprise an oligopoly. In spite of its miserly performance at the bottom of the Organisation for Economic Co-operation and Development's (OECD) per capita ODA scale, the United States is the lead humanitarian donor by a factor of three; in 1999, for instance, its outlays to humanitarian organizations exceeded the total assistance of the next 12 largest Western donors. Between 1995 and 1997, it provided 20 percent of total humanitarian assistance, and in the following three years its contribution rose to 30 percent. The second largest donor collectively is the European Union, followed by the United Kingdom and several other European countries, Canada, and Japan.[37]

Language itself indicates how conceptual changes penetrate institutions or fail to do so. To the contemporary lexicon, humanitarian affairs has added "complex political emergency." This is a "humanitarian crisis in a country, region or society where there is a total or considerable breakdown of authority resulting from internal or external conflict and which requires an international response that goes beyond the mandate or capacity of any single agency and/or the ongoing UN country programme."[38] The UN's definition suggests that coordination is the most significant issue. The central problem is determining which agency should perform which function at which time on which stage. But with no central power of the purse and no wherewithal to compel compliance, effective collective action in this atomized system is the exception rather than the rule.

The reader should try to visualize the bevy of governmental, intergovernmental, and nongovernmental aid agencies that flock to emergencies along with other external actors. It is essential to try to keep in mind that the various decentralized categories of outside actors who arrive on the scene are composed of a confusing array of disconnected and diverse units. The label "IGO" fails, for instance, to capture the complexity of the European Union or the dizzying acronyms of the UN system—with the main abbreviations being UNHCR, UNICEF, WFP, UNDP, and OCHA. And the hundreds of international NGOs—some with budgets of multiple millions of dollars, others with financially trivial operations—are hidden behind the "INGO" label.

This reality suggests the extent to which calls for enhanced coordination are usually sung by a passionate chorus of bureaucrats, but actual behavior is accompanied by more tepid decibel levels that reflect administrative inertia and dominant economic incentives pushing in the opposite direction. As one perplexed former military officer summarized it: "the need for a concerted approach . . . contradicts the current independence of each responding agency and organization in an international response."[39]

The widespread euphemism referring to an international humanitarian "system" to describe the contemporary array of human rights protection and emergency relief efforts disguises the fact that agencies subscribe to different philosophies, have different cultures, and use different styles. The impact on a country in distress reflects the sum of individual actions rather than a planned, singular, and coherent whole. As indicated at the outset, a more apt image would be that of a dysfunctional international humanitarian "family."

The need to make better use of the many moving parts of international humanitarian machinery became an especially acute preoccupation in the 1990s because civilian humanitarian organizations interacted routinely in war zones with military forces. The modern efforts to improve UN leadership and coordination began in 1991 with General Assembly resolution 46/182, following the unacceptable humanitarian stumbling and confusion in northern Iraq after the first Gulf War. Almost two decades later, the charade continues. DHA was renamed OCHA; the notion of a humanitarian coordinator has been tried and mixed together with lead-agency and, more recently, cluster approaches; a variety of funding efforts have included the Consolidated Appeals Process, the expanded Central Emergency Response Fund (CERF), and the Common Humanitarian Funds. In the front offices of the UN, a cabinet-level Executive Committee for Humanitarian Affairs was begun along with several new attempts to organize and convene the Inter-Agency Standing Committee.

It is worth spending a moment in order to better understand the most recent experiment. The "cluster approach" resulted from the 2005 Humanitarian Response Review commissioned by the then ERC, Jan Egeland, largely in response to the immediate failures in Darfur but also the long-standing concerns about the unevenness and unpredictability of international humanitarian responses. In essence, a UN agency takes the lead in coordinating a particular sector and also acts as a "provider of last resort" if no other intergovernmental or non-governmental organization steps in for a particular activity or region: UNICEF for water, sanitation, and hygiene; UNHCR for shelter (IFRC for natural disasters); WHO for health; UNICEF for nutrition; UNHCR for camp management (and

IOM for natural disasters); UNDP for early recovery; UNHCR for protection (and UNICEF/OHCHR/UNHCR for natural disasters); WFP/UNICEF/OCHA for telecommunications; and WFP for logistics.

A number of problems arise with this cobbled together arrangement. One evaluation team notes: "The fact that the cluster system was 'designed' as a gap-filler and is being used as a system in itself creates inconsistencies and limits potential utility."[40] More obviously, NGOs are often dissatisfied with this UN-centric approach; and even more obviously coordination between and among clusters is still lacking.

The perceived need for coordination is continually felt and reinforced with unsuccessful, half-hearted experiment after experiment at reform. The necessity to have less waste and more impact within the humanitarian part of the system should be more urgent and compelling because so many lives are at stake in disasters. But the results are the same as elsewhere. The real problem is that everyone is for coordination so long as it implies no loss of autonomy. One practitioner who spent much of the last 15 years of his career in Afghanistan, Antonio Donini, draws distinctions among three broad categories of coordination within the United Nations:

- Coordination by command—in other words, coordination where strong leadership is accompanied by some sort of leverage and authority, whether carrot or stick.
- Coordination by consensus—where leadership is essentially based on the capacity of the "coordinator" to orchestrate a coherent response and mobilize the key actors around common objectives and priorities.
- Coordination by default—where, in the absence of a formal coordination entity, only the most rudimentary exchange of information and division of labor take place among the actors.[41]

Given the feudal UN system and the ferociously independent NGOs, coordination by command is clearly unrealistic, however desirable. The experience of the DHA under the best of circumstances—for instance, during the first six months after the Rwandan genocide, when agencies were especially sensitive to concerns over net impacts—could undoubtedly be described as coordination by consensus. The experience of its successor, OCHA, under the worst of circumstances—for instance, in the uncharted chaos of Liberia or Afghanistan—demonstrated the absence of meaningful coordination, and what little existed could accurately be labeled as coordination by default.

Some critics and practitioners are against hierarchy, believing it a recipe for mediocrity that would destroy some of the most productive parts of the UN system. Some of the hostility toward centralization and consolidation is philosophical—the devolution of decision-making power and administrative authority to the lowest level is seen as the way to promote democratic institutions. Some hostility involves a judgment about particular institutions—many see UNICEF and UNHCR as distinctive and effective contributors to relief and development whose performance would be diminished and dragged down to the lowest UN common denominator. For opponents, the tendency to emphasize centralization for cost-cutting reasons is short-sighted and likely to destroy some of the best features. Still others argue that UN coordination mechanisms constitute a hindrance rather than a help. Moreover, some ardent proponents of laissez-faire humanitarianism argue that a coherent strategy is unwise because it works against the magic of the market in which individual agencies pursue independent strategies but arrive at a sound division of labor. Perhaps individual creativity that spawns chaos is better than the damage from botched efforts at coherence? Is the process better self-regulated than poorly coordinated because one less layer of bureaucracy is preferable to one layer more? As no one is really in charge and no one can be sure what will work, so the argument goes, why not make the best of it rather than merely add a ceremonial layer?

However, throwing in the towel is unacceptable. There is an urgent need for fewer outsiders and for better orchestration among them when coming to the rescue. The feudal UN system is so disturbing because the world organization has a natural comparative advantage in pulling together all of the moving parts of the international humanitarian delivery system. Yet its own intra-system meandering and competition does not inspire enthusiasm from the other central players— the military, international NGOs, private contractors, and the ICRC.

No expression in the international public policy lexicon is more used and less applied than "coordination," but still it appears frequently in donor, UN, and NGO documents and discourse. They employ a host of other "soft" words (in meaning, not pronunciation) beginning with "C"—cooperation, cohesion, complementarity. These should be replaced by words that start with a hard "C" and have a meaningful edge— consolidation, command, control, and compulsion—or by one that starts with a soft "C" but that has a hard edge as well: centralization.

It is precisely such hard-content "Cs" that would improve international responses to war victims and protect human rights elsewhere. Collective action problems cannot be overcome while donors and aid agencies speak out of both sides of their mouths. Autonomy, not meaningful coordination, is the top priority of proprietary UN agencies and market-share-oriented NGOs. Crocodile tears shed by officials who lament waste and the lack of effectiveness should be replaced by serious efforts to forego financial and operational independence in the interests of human rights and the humanitarian enterprise and seriously addressing collective-action problems.

Sustainable Development: Institutions for Women and the Environment

The feudal ailment is, not unsurprisingly, characteristic also of development efforts, the bulk of the UN system's expenditures. Earlier, I described what Rube Goldberg could have designed for a "world government," the web of institutions each focusing on a substantive area often located in a different city from other relevant UN partners and with a separate budget, governing board, organizational culture, and independent executive head. If any more illustrations were needed of the problems with relying upon such structures for twenty-first-century problems, two come readily to mind: gender inequality and environmental threats. These issues require multi-disciplinary perspectives and efforts across sectors, not what the world organization provides.

Within the UN system, efforts on behalf of women and of the environment are located in a host of separate institutional kingdoms. Interestingly enough, as a follow-up to the 2005 World Summit, Secretary-General Kofi Annan convened a High-level Panel on UN System-wide Coherence in the Fields of Development, Humanitarian Assistance and Environment.[42] Its recommendations figure in a report aptly titled *Delivering as One*, but the chances of their successful implementation are about the same as those of the 1969 recommendations by Sir Robert Jackson. The prehistoric monster's DNA continues to thrive within the world body.

Institutions for Women

Lack of coordination and overlapping jurisdiction among multiple UN agencies has also hindered the UN's effectiveness at promoting women's empowerment, which has considerable ramifications for women and for the planet.[43] Such goals as reproductive rights; fair labor remuneration; access, participation, and representation in political institutions; and education are important ends in themselves but also have a direct impact on environmental sustainability and development. These concerns touch upon global threats, including overpopulation, the spread of HIV/AIDS, poverty, and pollution. In the words of the 1985 Nairobi Forward-Looking Strategy: "without the advancement of women, development itself will be difficult to achieve."[44]

Despite the gravity of women's issues, the UN lacks a central agency that can effectively work toward generating normative consensus and practical policies. Instead, responsibility is currently dispersed among several UN bodies—including the UN Population Fund (UNFPA), the Commission on the Status of Women (CSW), the UN secretariat's own Division for the Advancement of Women (DAW) as well as the Office of the Special Advisor to the Secretary-General on Gender Issues and the Advancement of Women (OSAGI), the UN International Research and Training Institute for the Advancement of Women (INSTRAW), and the UN Development Fund for Women (UNIFEM).

In spite of this long list of acronyms, readers should not assume that women's issues are at the top of the agenda or even well-resourced. As Rutgers University's Charlotte Bunch summarizes, "women specific work has largely remained marginalized, and the miniscule resources and power invested in it has plagued efforts to achieve implementation of the high standards repeatedly espoused on this topic."[45]

None of them—with the exception of UNFPA—comes close to qualifying as an agency with substantial resources and reach, to be mentioned in the same breath as UNICEF or UNHCR. Established in 1966 as the UN Fund for Population Activities with funding beginning in 1969, the name was shortened to the UN Population Fund after the 1994 International Conference on Population and Development in

Cairo. It is the world's largest international source of funding for population and reproductive health programs, working with governments and NGOs in over 140 countries on programs that help women as well as men and young people.

The CSW was established in 1946 as a subsidiary body of the Commission on Human Rights to be the UN's primary intergovernmental policy body on women. Its mandate is to prepare policy recommendations and reports for ECOSOC. Its impact is helped by drawing on NGOs, but the commission's resources are truly meager, and it only met every other year until 1987. The four UN world conferences on women (in Mexico City in 1975, Copenhagen in 1980, Nairobi in 1985, and Beijing in 1995) transformed in many ways the work of the CSW, which has met annually since 1987.

The DAW is the name of the UN secretariat's unit that provides substantive support for the CSW. Its work includes mainstreaming gender perspectives within the UN system as well as providing substantive and technical servicing to the Committee on the Elimination of Discrimination against Women.

The OSAGI resulted from a recommendation made at Beijing in 1995 that there should be a senior official taking a leadership role on gender mainstreaming and reporting directly to the secretary-general. The office also attempts to improve the status of women within the secretariat itself.

INSTRAW was established following the first World Conference on the International Women's Year in Mexico in 1975, and its operations moved to the Dominican Republic in 1983. Its research concentrates on technical issues (for example, attaching a specific value to women's household work). INSTRAW conducts training seminars and has elaborated training materials on gender and development.

UNIFEM also resulted from the Mexico conference and began as the Voluntary Fund for the UN Decade for Women in 1976 to promote what the decade's subtitle called "equality, development, and peace." It served as a catalyst for activities within the UN system and at the national level as well. In 1984, it became a separate operational entity and was renamed UNIFEM and associated with UNDP. In addition to headquarters in New York, it has 15 regional offices and is linked to UN development activities through UNDP projects at the country level in many developing countries.

UNIFEM has a mandate to support initiatives that benefit women and to bring women into mainstream development activities. It has focused on reducing feminized poverty and violence; reversing the spread of HIV/AIDS among women and girls; and achieving gender equality in democratic governance.[46] But it has failed to serve as an effective coordinating body for issues relating to women.

The High-level Panel on Coherence's 2006 *Delivering as One* identified the need for a more robust entity in the UN's "gender architecture" to deal with women's issues in a more structured and coordinated fashion:

> Three existing UN entities (UNIFEM, Office of the Special Advisor on Gender Issues, and UN Division for the Advancement of Women) will be consolidated into one enhanced and independent gender entity. It will have a stronger normative and advocacy role, combined with a targeted programming role. The gender entity will be fully and ambitiously funded. Gender equality will be a component of the One UN Country Programme, and remain the responsibility of all UN organizations.[47]

Most of 2007 was spent deliberating—not about the merits of strengthening the UN's work on women's rights and the consolidation of its gender architecture, but rather about who was going to get what and which person would head the new institution. The predictable result is that, as of this writing, no progress has been made, even if those close to the issue are hoping for more results in the near future.

Is the glass half full or empty? Charlotte Bunch answers: "On the one hand, there has been much progress since women first fought for their inclusion in the UN Charter; on the other hand, after sixty years of struggle, one could expect more as well from the world body whose power depends on its moral authority."[48] Part of the reason for the emptiness of the world organization's gender glass is the continued tolerance of separate, disparate, and feudal fiefdoms for the efforts on behalf of women instead of a passionate commitment to do what is necessary to consolidate and get the most for women from the United Nations.

Institutions for the Environment

What subject requires more pulling together of distinct perspectives than the human environment? This quintessential public good necessitates purposeful and collective action to slow and eventually reverse the continual depletion of non-renewable resources and the deterioration of the natural ecosystem. What's wrong with the UN's approach to environmental protection becomes clear when examining the overlapping and counterproductive jurisdiction between two key players, UNEP and the Commission on Sustainable Development (CSD). The former is a specialized agency and the latter an intergovernmental body, but neither has a critical enough budget or broad enough mandate to make a difference.[49] Both institutions emerged from global conferences, 20 years apart, in Stockholm and Rio.[50] As the reader will have realized by now, the default "solution" to international problems within the UN system is always to add—never subtract or consolidate—bureaucratic layers.

Perhaps UNEP's most important role is generating international norms and setting standards to protect the human environment rather than concrete projects to help improve air quality or protect forests or enforce norms on the books. The agency has played an instrumental role in the negotiations and adoption of a number of major international environmental conventions, including the Vienna Convention for the Protection of the Ozone Layer, the Convention on Climate Change, and the Convention on Biodiversity. Although UNEP does administer a few environmental projects, it is not primarily a project-executing agency in the sense of most other specialized UN agencies. Also, UNEP is not a source of financing—unlike UNDP, the World Bank group, and other multilateral funders. It does, however, disperse modest funds through its Environment Fund.

However, the waters surrounding UNEP's mandate were muddied further with the 1992 creation of the CSD and overlapping functions. As mentioned earlier, the General Assembly established the Commission on Sustainable Development to follow up the Earth Summit. An ECOSOC functional unit, it has 53 members and meets annually in New York to discuss clusters of thematic and cross-sectoral issues. The CSD is responsible for reviewing progress on Agenda 21, the Rio Declaration on Environment and Development, and the Johannesburg Plan of Implementation at the local, national, regional, and international levels. The Johannesburg conference reaffirmed the CSD's role as the forum for sustainable development within the UN system. The reader may wonder why exactly the CSD exists independently from UNEP, to which there is no logical reply.

Effective project implementation requires coordination at the operational level in the field. Although UNEP itself does not execute country programs, it supposedly cooperates with numerous other organizations in overseeing the implementation of projects that are supported by UNEP's Environment Fund. These projects are executed by "cooperating agencies" (that is, UN system agencies and bodies), primarily FAO, UNESCO, WHO, the World Meteorological Organization

(WMO), and the UN Center for Human Settlements, or Habitat (UNCHS). Other resources from this fund support project implementation by other intergovernmental organizations, NGOs, research institutions, and civic-based bodies (referred to in UNEP as "supporting organizations"). When projects also include UNDP sources, the UN resident coordinator serves as the primary point person for orchestrating the UN system's environmental activities in a country.

Overlapping jurisdiction adds a significant degree of complexity and ambiguity to UNEP's coordination functions, especially when its resources are in the first place so minimal in comparison with the dimensions of the problem and with those available from the World Bank or corporate coffers. Contributions to UNEP in 2006 totaled just $59.2 million, down $400,000 from the previous year.[51] In comparison, the World Bank's funding volume fluctuates from year to year but is currently about $10–15 billion. Its treasury has an annual volume of about $30 billion and an annual swap book total approximately five times that amount. The Bank manages $60–65 billion in global liquidity;[52] and, in fiscal year 2007 alone, it lent more than $2 billion to countries for environmental and natural resources management programs.[53] Meanwhile, in 2005 (the most recent year for which data is available), the US oil and natural gas industry's "environmental expenditures"[54] totaled $10.7 billion.[55]

The trend toward greater decentralization, regionalism, and involvement of civic-based entities in global governance complicates the already problematic task of making the UN function coherently, for the environment as elsewhere. In addition to its dwindling funds, a number of major donor governments prefer to bypass UNEP. As such, it remains a technical agency concentrating largely on environmental monitoring and assessment. UNEP's coordination of scientific information on ozone depletion, for instance, effectively makes it an expert lobby backing up diplomatic efforts to produce broad and binding agreement.[56]

So what can we reasonably expect UNEP to accomplish? The short answer is "little," certainly in comparison with the sweeping challenges of its mandate and the overwhelming menace of climate change. Many UN bodies are legally and practically autonomous; many of them were active in environmental work before the formation of UNEP and have access to far more significant technical and financial resources. Once again, the UN appears as the logical choice for coordination of the diverse array of institutional actors and arrangements. But UNEP has neither the authority nor the organizational wherewithal to coordinate the globe's network of critical institutions active in this arena.

1969 and Today

The obvious solutions to the dispersal of UN efforts and resources—consolidation and centralization—seem as obvious today as they were in 1969. At that time, Robert Jackson was given a task that resembled that of the 2006 High-level Panel on Coherence. The task of both reports was to alleviate the chronic disease of feudalism, but then as now it is seemingly impossible to transform the UN system to make it deliver as one.

Few reports have been discussed with as much praise, or as much venom as Jackson's *Capacity Study*. As Margaret Joan Anstee, who drafted the report with Jackson and later became the first woman under-secretary-general, recalled:

> The central thrust was the need for an integrated approach, the need for an end to fixed "agency shares" of the UN technical assistance "pie" in each country, the conviction that it shouldn't be the agencies or the headquarters who dictated the form of a program. We said, "Development is home-

made." There should be a country program and that program should stem from the needs of the country as seen by that country and should be integrated into, and synchronized with, the National Development Plan, where one existed. The Country Program, as an integrated whole, was a central pillar of the *Capacity Study*'s thesis, around which everything else was developed. It was a big break with the past, when UNDP assistance consisted of separate, unrelated projects, often "sold" by the specialized agency concerned, and unrelated to the country's own priorities . . . It should be one UN team with all its sectoral input as necessary, but geared to the country's needs . . . The basic philosophy of the *Capacity Study* was maximum centralization horizontally, with the UNDP exerting "the power of the purse" as the sole funder of technical assistance in the UN system, and maximum decentralization vertically down to the field level.

Anstee, never bashful, had especially strong views about why the report's recommendations were never implemented:

A main reason why the *Capacity Study* did not achieve its aims was that the power of the purse fell down and that, in the long run, was the downfall of UNDP. Many senior people in the UNDP opposed the study, among them Myer Cohen, in particular, and to some extent, Paul-Marc Henry because they also had their little fiefdoms . . . They were aided and abetted, of course, by the agencies . . . So, those same centrifugal forces that the *Capacity Study* had sought to curb within the UN system as a whole came to prevail within UNDP itself.[57]

The development economist Ignacy Sachs also was categorical about the UN's failure to establish a powerful central development agency as Jackson had recommended: "It is perhaps the most important failure at the institutional level for the United Nations that, on the pretext that everyone is concerned with development, the UN never even bothered to create a strong center capable of articulating and stimulating thinking about development."[58]

The approach of Jackson, known by friends and foes alike as "Jacko," was formed by his World War II experience as a naval commander in charge of solving logistics problems. Using the same direct approach, he attacked the willingness of the member states that pay the UN's bills to permit ongoing decentralization and waste. They put up with negative reactions of the kind that came in 1969 and continue today from UN officials' protecting agency turf. One of the UN's least bureaucratic officials, Brian Urquhart, points to the reasons why Jacko's sensible recommendations were tossed aside:

> He made a joke—well, he thought it was a joke—in the introduction of that report, saying, "As far as I remember, there were a number of dinosaurs and cavemen in the system." And Paul Hoffmann, who was the head of the Development Program among others, took violent umbrage at this, and rallied all of his fellow directors-general and others. It was ridiculous, because the *Capacity Study* was a perfectly sensible study, but, as so often happens, it was ruined by one sentence.[59]

The unwillingness to dismantle the UN's numerous feudal kingdoms remains a chronic illness. *Plus ça change, plus c'est la même chose.* (The more things change, the more they stay the same.) I return to this reality in Chapter 7.

CHAPTER FOUR

Overwhelming Bureaucracy and Underwhelming Leadership

While all bureaucracies share certain problems, the United Nations has peculiar difficulties, and the deterioration over time of its independence and competence is striking. In terms of leadership, the UN's top official is more "secretary" than "general,"[1] and other types of intellectual and operational leadership at all levels are circumscribed and more lackluster than is desirable.

Among the most serious difficulties faced by the world body are gender imbalance, recruiting, and retaining qualified staff due to such issues as geographical quotas, restrictions on spouse employment, and problems with the National Competitive Recruitment Examination (NCRE). Since this topic is poorly understood, even among specialists, this chapter begins with a short overview of the justifications for and the concepts behind the international civil service before illustrating its ailments with examples from international peace and security, human rights, and sustainable development.

International Bureaucracy

The second UN—the heads of UN organizations and their secretariats—consists of career and long-serving staff members who are paid through assessed and voluntary UN budgets. The possibility of constituting an independent group of internationally recruited people who are paid as much as the world's best civil service but whose allegiance is to the welfare of the planet, not to their home countries, remains a lofty but disputed objective.[2]

During World War II, the Carnegie Endowment for International Peace sponsored a series of conferences to learn the lessons from the "great experiment" of the League of Nations,[3] with regard to creating an international civil service—or administration or bureaucracy[4]—to attack international problems. This legacy was carried over to the UN, and Charter Article 101(3) calls for the "paramount consideration in the employment of staff" to be "securing the highest standards of efficiency, competence, and integrity" while paying regard "to the importance of recruiting the staff on as wide a geographical basis as possible."

A leading advocate for the second UN was the world body's second secretary-general, Dag Hammarskjöld, whose speech at Oxford in May 1961 spelled out the importance of an autonomous staff and dedicated civil service despite the fact that many thought this kind of "political celibacy" was "in international affairs a fiction." The most striking passage of his speech asserted that any erosion or abandonment of "efforts in the direction of internationalism symbolized by the international civil service . . . might, if accepted by the Member nations, well prove to be the Munich of international cooperation."[5] Hammarskjöld's speech was not Pollyannaish. His clarion call did not ignore the reality that the international civil service exists to carry out decisions made by states. But it emphasized that a UN official could and should pledge allegiance to striving for a larger collective good symbolized by the organization's blue-covered *laissez-passer* (essentially a UN passport) rather than defending the interests of the country that issues his or her national passport.

Setting aside senior UN positions for former high-level officials approved by their home governments belies the integrity of secretariats. Governments seek to ensure that their interests are defended inside a secretariat, and many have relied on such officials for intelligence. From the outset of the UN's existence, for example, the permanent members of the Security Council reserved the right to "nominate" (essentially to select) officials to fill the main posts in the secretary-general's cabinet. This procedure applies virtually everywhere to positions above the director level, and often below as well.

Beginning in the 1950s and 1960s, the influx of new member states following decolonization led states to clamor for "their" quota of posts in international secretariats, following the bad example set by the major powers. This resulted in a downplaying of competence and an exaggeration of the importance of national origins as the main criterion for recruitment and promotion. Over the years, efforts to improve gender balance have resulted in other types of claims, as has the age profile of secretariats.

While *ad hominem* as well as *ad feminem* comments are hardly the common bill-of-fare of scholarly analysis, nonetheless it would be helpful to list the backgrounds of just a few of the initial appointments made by Secretary-General Ban Ki-moon in early 2007, and let the reader determine whether appointment to senior-level positions in the UN reflects politics and connections more than competence. In my view, such practices are a major problem for the organization, its reputation, and its influence. Would any of the following have made a short list based on their qualifications and experience?

Recalling the findings of the Volcker Commission to create a better management culture, the ideal would be to have the secretary-general as chief diplomat and the deputy-secretary-general as manager of one of the world's most complex and challenging bureaucracies. The appointment as deputy-secretary-general of a former Tanzanian foreign minister, Asha-Rose Mtengeti Migiro, was puzzling. An African woman and a Muslim, she had extensive diplomatic experience in southern Africa and a PhD in law, but her management credentials and experience were hardly the basis for her selection.

And what of the appointments to the so-called UK and US posts? As the most senior humanitarian (emergency relief coordinator and under-secretary-general of OCHA), and as the UK's ambassador to Portugal and then France, John Holmes was selected. A close advisor to Tony Blair with substantial experience in Moscow and London, his exposure to the debris of human-made and natural disasters was remarkably absent from his résumé. Lynn Pascoe—the US Ambassador in Indonesia whose entire 40-year career was spent in Russia, the former Soviet Union, and Asia—had a distinguished diplomatic career but perhaps not the ideal qualifications to head the Department of Political Affairs, where the bulk of the work is in Africa and the Middle East. Their performances during the initial year of service—solid according to some insiders, lackluster according to others—are beside the point here. Senior officials should not have on-the-job training; they should be superbly qualified *before* being named.

Nonetheless, a basic idealism continues to animate the second UN. The likes of Ralph Bunche (the 1950 Nobel laureate for his work on the first armistice in the Middle East) and Brian Urquhart indicate that autonomy and integrity are not unrealistic expectations of international civil servants.[6] Today's professional and support staff number approximately 55,000 in the UN proper and another 20,000 in the specialized agencies. This number includes neither temporary staff in peace operations (about 100,000 in 2007) nor the staff of the IMF and the World Bank group (another 15,000). These figures represent substantial growth from the approximately 500 employees in the UN's first year at Lake Success and the peak total of 700 staff employed by the League of Nations.[7]

A 2000 report by the UN Joint Inspections Unit identified the need to address "work–life" or "work–family" issues

in order to increase retention of young qualified staff.[8]
Recognizing that the UN must find a way to decrease the
"steady outflow of young professionals through resignations,"
the report highlighted problems in three areas: delays in link-
ing candidates from the roster of those who successfully pass
the National Competitive Recruitment Examination to jobs;
job dissatisfaction among young professionals due to the organization's failure to rapidly integrate them; and a lack of support in aiding UN employees' spouses to find employment in
duty stations. Because an organization without young and
enthusiastic staff is moribund, the report states:

> Most young professionals enter the United Nations system
> with great expectations as to the nature of the tasks which they
> will be asked to accomplish. However, in several cases, insuffi-
> cient structures for the integration, orientation and develop-
> ment of staff restrict their ability to make a significant
> contribution to the work of their organizations, leading to
> rapid disenchantment. Limited lateral and upward mobility, as
> well as a general failure of management to provide enough
> support to young professionals and attention to their concerns
> and initiatives, can also lead to frustrations and separations.

These seemingly mundane issues are important to emphasize because people matter, for good and for ill. The second
UN does more than simply carry out marching orders from
governments. My argument thus takes direct issue with what
three observers—not Realists but sympathetic multilateralists
—consider trivial in comparison with the politics of member
states: "There appears . . . in the literature the curious notion
that the United Nations is an autonomous actor in world
affairs that can and does take action independent of the will
and wishes of the member governments that constitute the
organization."[9]

UN officials present ideas to tackle problems, debate them
formally and informally with governments, take initiatives,

advocate for change, turn general decisions into specific programs of action, and work for implementation. They monitor progress and report on this and related matters to national officials and politicians gathering at intergovernmental conferences and in countries in which the UN is operating.

None of this should be a surprise. It would be a strange and impotent civil service in any country whose staff members took no initiatives or showed no leadership, simply awaiting detailed instructions from the government in power. UN officials are no different except that formal decision makers are government representatives in boards meeting quarterly, annually, or even once every two years. With the exception of the Security Council, decision making and responsibility for implementation in most parts of the UN system, especially the development funds and specialized agencies, depends in large part on the executive head or staff members.

The recruitment, composition, rewards, retention, and performance of international civil servants are a substantial part of what ails the world organization. Most importantly, the quality and impact of the staff is a variable that can be altered far more easily, swiftly, and cheaply than the problems identified in the three previous chapters.

International Peace and Security: Oil-for-Food Scandal, Gender Imbalance

The UN's role in the maintenance of international peace and security was the original justification for its establishment. It remains, for many pundits and politicians, the *raison d'être* of the world body. Many persons have served the world organization with distinction and heroism since 1945, including Sergio Vieira de Mello and 21 other colleagues who lost their lives in Baghdad in August 2003, and the 17 UN staff who were killed in Algiers in December 2007. Indeed, the death of Dag Hammarskjöld in a suspicious plane crash while on a mission in the Congo in 1961 was a dramatic moment in UN history. Less dramatic but as indicative of dedication are the deaths of 244 other civilian staff members[10] and 2,431 soldiers[11] who had given their lives in UN service by early 2008. They are part of the reason for the award of the Nobel Peace Prize to UN peacekeepers in 1987 and to Kofi Annan and the secretariat in 2001. Nonetheless, there are serious problems as indicated by the oil-for-food scandal and gender imbalance.

Oil-for-Food Programme

In many ways the "scandal" of the Oil-for-Food Programme (OFFP) was overblown—member states were actually responsible for approving the bulk of the monies that found their way into Saddam Hussein's coffers and consciously overlooked "leakage" to key allies like Jordan and Turkey. Nonetheless, the basic sloppiness of the management of this politically visible and crucial assignment was lamentable. Operating in a country with hundreds of thousands of preventable deaths among children over the course of the 1990s, the UN is often seen as having played a role in exacerbating a dire humanitarian situation.

The OFFP was established in 1995 as a means of allowing Iraq to sell oil on the world market in exchange for humanitarian relief items—primarily food and medicine—to benefit ordinary Iraqis, who were suffering from the devastating effects of sanctions imposed by the Security Council after Iraq's invasion of Kuwait in 1990. The OFFP was regularly criticized as corrupt and inefficient, failing to address the basic needs of Iraqis while lining the pockets of corrupt Iraqi officials. In 2004, Kofi Annan appointed an Independent Inquiry Committee headed by the former chairman of the US Federal Reserve, Paul Volcker, to investigate the allegations. In

2005, the committee presented its report to the Security Council. The report stated that the conduct of the programme's executive director, Benon Sevan, had been "ethically improper" but stopped short of alleging that he had committed a crime. It also commented on allegations about misconduct on the part of Kofi Annan's son Kojo and criticized the absence of a substantial internal investigation once the potential conflict of interest had emerged.

The main details of most relevance for this analysis, however, related to an inattentive management system that was outmoded, inept, and quite out of its depth in administering a program of this size and complexity. The benefits of globalization, such as advances in communications technology, have seemingly passed the world organization by at the same time that the UN has moved at great speed from being largely a forum for discussions to having substantial military and civilian operations worldwide.

Secretary-General Annan named the first deputy-secretary-general in 1997. Rather than acting as an all-purpose stand-in for the secretary-general, this deputy should have a distinctly different job description. She should be an independent chief operating officer for the organization. In this way, the management buck would stop just short of the secretary-general, who should remain the UN's chief politician, diplomat, and mediator. The Volcker team proposed that the deputy, like the secretary-general, be nominated by the Security Council. Such a formality would be unwise as it would require amending the UN Charter—a hopeless task. But the objective is imperative and could be accommodated by having the Security Council informally approve the nominee—as part of the candidacy of a secretary-general—who would have "clear authority for planning and for personnel practices that emphasize professional and administrative talent over political convenience." Whether a purely administrative solution to an administrative problem would save the day remains a question, but without such changes there is no chance for significant improvement. The preface to the Volcker report contains language that could have been written by a Beltway neo-con: "The inescapable conclusion from the Committee's work is that the United Nations Organization needs thoroughgoing reform—and it needs it urgently."[12]

The oil-for-food findings are not an aberration; such problems are endemic to the institution in its current incarnation. Volcker later wrote: "The difficulties encountered—the managerial weaknesses, the failures to accept responsibility, the ethical lapses—are symptomatic of systemic problems running through the UN Organization." In looking beyond the crisis to the future, he continued: "Willing cooperation and a sense of legitimacy cannot be sustained without a strong sense that the Organization has both competence and integrity. It is precisely those qualities that have been called into question by the UN's administration of the Oil-for-Food Program."[13]

Gender Imbalance

One might have expected the UN to be taking the lead at integrating women into its workforce compared with other institutions, and faster than many of its member states. While efforts have been made to achieve an equitable gender balance in the world body, the rate of progress has been glacial.[14] Indeed, from the outset, women have had to challenge patriarchal norms and institutions, and much of their work on peace and security issues was separated from the UN's mainstream activities in its early years.

Eleanor Roosevelt, first chair of the Commission on Human Rights, was a pioneer, and in February 1946, in her "Open Letter to the Women of the World," she made a direct appeal for women to be involved in peace efforts, asserting that the UN provided a window of opportunity for them to do so.[15]

Some three decades later, at the first UN-sponsored world conference on women held in 1975 in Mexico City, governments signed the Declaration of Mexico, which proclaimed: "Women must participate equally with men in the decision making processes which help to promote peace at all levels."[16] That same year, the General Assembly called upon women to participate in the process of strengthening international peace and security in resolution 3519 (XXX).

At the beginning of the twenty-first century, however, women continue to be excluded from the front lines in this area, as illustrated by the paltry participation of women in UN peace operations at all levels. Table 4.1 shows the gender breakdown of military observers, staff officers, and contingent troops in 20 peacekeeping missions, as of January 2008. Overall, women account for only 2 percent of peacekeeping forces with 1,476 women out of a total 79,629 peacekeepers worldwide.

The current condition of women in the UN bureaucracy as a whole is disappointing. According to the Office of the Special Advisor on Gender Issues and Advancement of Women, the representation of women in the professional and higher categories in the UN system is only 36.9 percent. Only at the entry—P-1 and P-2—professional levels has gender balance been achieved. In the higher categories—D-1 and above— women make up only 23.7 percent of UN staff.[17] Moreover, in an arena with much flexibility—the appointment of special representatives of the secretary-general (SRSGs)—the results also remain poor. At the highest level—that of the secretary-general's special and personal representatives and envoys— statistics are not broken down by gender.[18] As US Ambassador Swanee Hunt stated: "Two female SRSGs and one female Deputy SRSG in 26 peacekeeping missions is indefensible; a list of dozens of qualified women has sat on the Secretary General's desk for years."[19]

Table 4.1: Gender Breakdown in Peacekeeping Missions, January 31, 2008

PK MISSION	Military Component											
	Military Observers			Staff Officers			Contingent Troop			Military Total		
	Male	Female	Total	Male	Female	Total	Male	Female	Total	Male	Female	Total
BINUB	8	0	8	0	0	0	0	0	0	8	0	8
MINURCAT	7	0	7	0	0	0	0	0	0	7	0	7
MINURSO	185	4	189	0	0	0	23	4	27	208	8	216
MINUSTAH	0	0	0	103	1	104	6831	131	6962	6934	132	7066
MONUC	709	28	737	0	0	0	16314	298	16612	17023	326	17349
UNAMA	15	0	15	0	0	0	0	0	0	15	0	15
UNAMI	7	0	7	0	0	0	223	0	223	230	0	230
UNAMID	218	2	220	273	1	274	6831	51	6882	7322	54	7376
UNDOF	0	0	0	38	4	42	988	15	1003	1026	19	1045
UNFICYP	0	0	0	45	2	47	771	41	812	816	43	859
UNIFIL	0	0	0	183	0	183	11836	436	12272	12019	436	12455
UNIOSIL	14	0	14	0	0	0	0	0	0	14	0	14
UNMEE	203	8	211	55	2	57	1403	3	1406	1661	13	1674
UNMIK	39	2	41	0	0	0	0	0	0	39	2	41
UNMIL	187	7	194	108	9	117	12977	197	13174	13272	213	13485
UNMIN	139	12	151	108	9		12977	197	0	139	12	151

Table 4.1 (continued)

PK MISSION	Military Component											
	Military Observers			Staff Officers			Contingent Troop			Military Total		
	Male	Female	Total	Male	Female	Total	Male	Female	Total	Male	Female	Total
UNMIS	519	18	537	178	5	183	8428	104	8532	9125	127	9252
UNMIT	32	0	32	0	0	0	0	0	0	32	0	32
UNMOGIP	43	0	43	0	0	0	0	0	0	43	0	43
UNOCI	178	9	187	88	6	94	7686	60	7746	7952	75	8027
UNOMIG	127	4	131	0	0	0	0	0	0	127	4	131
UNTSO	141	12	153	0	0	0	0	0	0	141	12	153
Total	2771	106	2877	1071	30	1101	74311	1340	75651	78153	1476	79629

Source: Peace and Security Section of the Department of Public Information in cooperation with the UN Department of Peacekeeping Operations, http://www.un.org/Depts/dpko/dpko/contributors/gender/2008gender/jan08.pdf

According to Devaki Jain, three aspects of the UN bureaucracy may explain the slow pace of change at the world body.
She writes:

> First, member states nominate candidates for secretariat
> posts. Informal networks of support from which women are
> often excluded operate to nominate men . . . Second, the prin-
> ciple of equitable geographical distribution . . . sometimes
> works against women candidates. A highly qualified woman
> from a member state that is oversubscribed according to the
> UN's complex calculus for geographical distribution will
> probably lose out to a male candidate from a member state
> that is undersubscribed . . . Finally, UN reform agendas
> sometimes work against the advancement of women.[20]

Cost-cutting measures designed to enhance efficiency may
lead to hiring freezes in upper-level positions, thus decreasing
opportunities for women's advancement. However, structural
problems alone cannot account for the inadequate progress in
achieving gender balance. As Jain asserts: "The world body has
much work to do before women assume their proper place
there—sixty years is a long time to wait. True reform will not
happen until the political will is created and activated to fully
bring women into the mainstream with equal privileges,
access to resources, and decision-making roles."[21]

Human Rights: Individual Courage and Institutional Cowardice

The performance of the UN civil service in the human rights
arena has been disappointing on too many occasions. It seems
justified to hold the international civil service to the highest
standards of consistency because international human rights
norms have been ironed out within the United Nations. The
standard bearer must abide by the standards that it has set for
the rest of the globe.

For instance, several recent cases of sexual trafficking and abuse by UN blue helmets suggest that important norms have been rather unevenly applied. Following widespread allegations of sexual abuse and misconduct—including trading money and food for sex and engaging in sex with minors—on the part of UN peacekeeping troops in the Democratic Republic of the Congo in early 2005, the UN instituted a number of system-wide reforms while downplaying the extent of the abuse. When similar allegations of sexual misconduct on the part of UN personnel surfaced later that same year in Burundi, Haiti, and Liberia, the UN was forced to acknowledge the widespread nature of abuse.

Secretary-General Kofi Annan adopted a "zero tolerance" policy toward offenders. The High-Level Conference on Eliminating Sexual Exploitation and Abuse by UN and NGO Personnel, convened in New York in December 2006, agreed to a UN-wide strategy to eradicate sexual abuse and exploitation. Nonetheless, reports of sexual misconduct by UN peacekeepers continued to surface in 2007 in the Ivory Coast.

Moreover, two cases of unacceptable administrative reactions to courageous human rights pleas indicate the lack of appropriate reactions from the highest levels of the United Nations. Perhaps the most searing was in the face of Rwanda's 1994 tragedy when the Canadian force commander of the UN Assistance Mission for Rwanda (UNAMIR), Roméo Dallaire, made repeated requests for assistance and authorization to try, even symbolically, to halt the fast-paced genocide.[22] His award-winning *Shake Hands with the Devil: The Failure of Humanity in Rwanda* recounts how his pleas to Department of Peacekeeping Operations (DPKO) headquarters for more combat troops and logistical support in the days leading up to the April 1994 genocide were denied.[23] Overseeing an initial force of about 2,600 (including 350 unarmed military observers) that was under-equipped and under-trained,

Dallaire made repeated requests for reinforcements—first a single battalion and later four battalions—that fell on deaf ears in New York and elsewhere. Instead, the UN ordered the UNAMIR force reduced to a token size as calculations by the major powers—particularly the United States, the United Kingdom, Belgium, and France—about reactions back home trumped human rights.

Arguing that a force of 5,000 could have prevented the genocide—probably an overly optimistic assessment according to other experts[24]—Dallaire's experience nonetheless illustrates how bureaucracy at the UN and lack of leadership among those in key positions thwarted decisive UN action. In the infamous exchange of cables in January 1994 (three months before the genocide began), for example, Dallaire reported to DPKO headquarters that the *Interahamwe*—meaning "those who work together," or the name of the Hutu paramilitary forces who eventually executed the genocide—were planning the extermination of Rwandan Tutsis as well as attacks on Belgian troops. Both predictions eventually transpired but met indifference from headquarters. When Dallaire informed his superiors in New York of his intention to raid the arms cache, he was ordered not to take any action for fear of embroiling the UN in armed conflict.

This is not the only such appalling example. The courageous calls by UN special representative to Sudan, Jan Pronk, for help to halt slow-motion genocide in Darfur met with similar silence from UN headquarters in 2004–6. Governments and the Security Council were collectively dragging their feet, as action would have required them to contribute financial resources and put boots on the ground. What is harder to understand was the lack of any hint of outrage from UN headquarters when Khartoum expelled Pronk as *persona non grata* in late 2006. As an especially outspoken advocate for peace within Sudan, he had unflinchingly reported on the violence against civilians perpetrated by government forces throughout his tenure as special representative. He was ordered to leave the country within 72 hours after posting information on his personal web blog about two incidents of Sudanese government defeat by rebel forces. Accused of displaying "enmity to the Sudanese government and the armed forces," Pronk unceremoniously returned to New York after Secretary-General Annan called him back for "consultations" ahead of the expulsion deadline and issued a statement saying that he was reviewing the request from the Sudanese government to remove Pronk from his post.[25] This lack of support from the UN's top official suggests an overly sensitive ear to the wishes of a sovereign state rather than to supporting the stance by his special representative who was trying to hold the government in Khartoum responsible for its reprehensible violations of human rights.

All bureaucracies have their ups-and-downs, and again the previous examples should not be taken to imply that there are not numerous instances of outstanding and courageous behavior by UN officials. But what is peculiar about the UN's human rights machinery is the visibility and extraordinary weight of the shackles of political correctness—measured in terms of what major and even minor sovereign states consider acceptable. The lack of independence by UN leadership is a critical weakness.

Sustainable Development: Politics Trumps Competence

In the past, the UN's performance in economic and social development has been degraded by political considerations that have taken precedence over competence. The person Ban Ki-moon selected as under-secretary-general to head the UN's Department of Economic and Social Affairs is Sha Zukeng, a

career Chinese diplomat with experience in multilateral negotiations but without exposure to development thinking and
practice. Again, while not gainsaying sterling contributions to
development by such intellectual stalwarts as Raúl Prebisch
and Helvi Siipila, and by operational ones such as Robert
Jackson and Margaret Joan Anstee, the selection criteria for the
position of under-secretary-general have too often been determined more by nationality than by qualifications and the ability
to do the job. Hence, politics gets in the way of selecting personnel and ultimately of optimum performance and impact.

Two of the most painful and well-known cases within the
field of sustainable development concern the egregious
incompetence of two sons of Africa, UNESCO's director-general from 1974 to 1987, Amadou Mahtar M'Bow, and the
FAO's director-general from 1976 to 1993, Edouard Saouma.
Some institutions are always headed by a national of the same
country—for instance, the World Bank by a US citizen, and the
IMF by a European—whereas others have positions that are
rotated among regions, including the UN secretary-general. In
M'Bow's and Saouma's cases, they were both elected because
it was "Africa's turn" at the helm of these organizations.

During the period that M'Bow led UNESCO, rampant mismanagement resulted in continual budget deficits. He was also
controversial due to his anti-Western bent—especially his and
UNESCO's hostility toward a free press as called for in the New
International Information Order. As a result, in 1984 the
United States withdrew from UNESCO in protest, followed by
the United Kingdom and Singapore in 1985. The withdrawals
resulted in a major loss of funding for the organization, and
many member countries breathed a sigh of relief when M'Bow
announced that he would retire as director-general in 1987.
Similarly, Saouma was lambasted by many, including the much-
publicized criticism by Graham Hancock in *Lords of Poverty*. His
corrupt and autocratic management practices, as well as his

rigid control of public information during his 17-year tenure as FAO director-general, became an embarrassment.[26]

For students of international relations and international organization, politics is, unsurprisingly, clearly of the essence; and so appointments can hardly be expected to be "above politics." However, when purely political considerations so clearly trump competence and independence regarding the appointment of senior personnel, both member states and "We the peoples" suffer from this illness.

Doing What Can Be Done

As the opening "Serenity Prayer" from the United States' most prominent twentieth-century theologian, Reinhold Niebuhr, suggested, I emphasize the secretariat because it can and should be changed. Renewing and reinvigorating the staff is critical as we move toward the second decade of the twenty-first century. If not the actual members of the UN secretariat, then who will care for the world organization and for the planet? The international civil service can and should be fixed, a topic to which I return in Chapter 8.

Part Two

Palliatives if Not Cures

CHAPTER FIVE

Redefining National Interests

Normative and geo-political remedies for the ailments resulting from the Westphalian system consist of calculations of
common interests and respect for international commitments. This prescription, of course, is not easy to swallow. The
logic is that democratic states have a long-term, rational, and
vital interest as well as moral responsibility to promote multilateral cooperation. Gareth Evans was Australia's foreign
minister in the late 1980s when he coined the expression
"good international citizenship."[1] This vision underpins, for
instance, Canada's human security agenda and the conviction
that there is a relationship between the provision of basic
rights and wider international security.[2] For advocates of good
international citizenship, the promotion of justice is key for
lasting order; often, however, they "must convince others of
their case, their competence, and their motives."[3]

The UN Charter clearly enumerates the need for calculations of common interests rather than narrower and purely
self-centered mathematics that stop at national borders and
entail only zero-sum games rather than win-win possibilities.
Persuading states of the logic behind trading their zero-sum
for a positive-sum perspective does, however, prove challenging, as does respecting international commitments. For
instance, redefining national interests so that eventually genocide will not be a policy option would seem to be in the interests of all, especially because three-quarters of UN member
states are signatories of the 1948 Genocide Convention.

Rather than ruined development investments, huge bills for humanitarian relief, and the use of military force to slow down violence, would it not make sense to act sooner rather than later? The answer is not as obvious at present as it should be.

Global governance—and especially the need to mobilize nonstate actors and their considerable energy and resources—is increasingly the frame of reference. There is also the need for a more active role for Europe and for the global South to balance the influence of the United States and China on the world stage. Moving ahead to redefine vital interests is a prescription for the UN's chronic ills resulting from the legacy of the Peace of Westphalia.

International Peace and Security: US Power, Regional Groupings

The original conception of the framework for the maintenance of peace and security in the UN Charter—complete with a Military Staff Committee and guaranteed robust responses by the major powers—was stillborn. The Cold War ensured the demise of that original vision of an institution with military teeth to back up collective decisions. After the Cold War, coalitions of the willing and regional organizations emerged with a UN subcontract to fill the gap and do the heavy lifting.

Even if we move away from a Westphalian world order, military force will remain in the hands of individual states. The fledgling effort in 2007 finally to come to the rescue of civilians in Darfur does not represent a "model" but does suggest a pattern of pooling resources—in this case, between the West and the African Union—to cope with the military anemia of the United Nations. After examining the extent of the US military, economic, and cultural role in the world, the need for Europe collectively to address military and political as well as economic problems becomes clear.

Raw US Power

In many ways, the High-level Panel on Threats, Challenges and Change and the 2005 World Summit were attempts, according to a host of diplomats, "to keep Washington in the tent." What exactly is the meaning of a collective security organization in a world so dominated by US power?

The introduction indicated the extent to which Washington's approach would be significant in this analysis. As will have become clear from the earlier chapters' examination of what's wrong, today represents an unparalleled multilateral and unilateral moment. If "unilateralism and multilateralism are best understood as two ends of a continuum,"[4] then what types of strategic considerations and which substantive issues would optimize the prospects for a "tactical multilateralism"[5] from Washington? That would be the place to start.

The sobering experiences in occupied Afghanistan and Iraq have highlighted the limits of American military power. So too, on a different scale, did Washington's decision to give up control of tsunami relief efforts to the UN in early 2005, after a slow start when a four-country team simply could not deliver a sufficiently coordinated response. Most Americans would acknowledge that when it comes to spotting, warning on, and managing international health hazards—for example, severe acute respiratory syndrome in 2003, avian flu more recently, and AIDS perennially—the World Health Organization is indispensable. The monitoring of international crime statistics and the narcotics trade, the policing of nuclear power, and numerous other important global functions, are based within the UN system. After the painful years of US unilateralism under the George W. Bush administration, it is hard to imagine that multilateralism and the United Nations will not become more appealing to the next and subsequent administrations.

Washington's short list for the UN should include not only post-conflict reconstruction in Afghanistan and Iraq but also fighting terrorism (sharing information and the fight against money laundering), confronting infectious diseases, pursuing environmental sustainability, monitoring human rights, providing humanitarian aid, rescheduling debt, and fostering trade. Ironically, President Bush's opening address to the World Summit on September 14, 2005 enumerated these very items.[6]

These kinds of concerns, however, have often been noticeably absent from Washington's recent public diplomacy and policies. Indeed, the United States seems to have become at best indifferent to the United Nations and at worst to have a penchant for weakening or even destroying the world body. The reality of US power means that if the UN and multilateral cooperation are to have a chance of working, and new concepts of national interests are to emerge, let alone flourish, then the globe's remaining superpower must be on board.

I hasten to recall a fact probably not in the minds of many readers when thinking about what ails the current United Nations—namely that the United States raced to be the first country to ratify the UN Charter, winning Senate approval on July 28, 1945. This was barely a month after the ink had dried on the signatures on the Charter for the 51 countries present in San Francisco. Moreover, we tend to forget that the United States was every bit as prominent on the world stage then as now.

Looking back on that "remarkable generation of leaders and public servants," Brian Urquhart remembers: "They were pragmatic idealists more concerned about the future of humanity than the outcome of the next election; and they understood that finding solutions to post-war problems was much more important than being popular with one or another part of the American electorate."[7] Could that same far-sighted political commitment and leadership dawn again? Indeed it must if a more collective sense of interests is to prevail internationally.

As former World Bank President and former US Secretary of Defense, Robert McNamara, and James Blight argue: "just as the ghost of Jacob Marley haunted Ebenezer Scrooge in Charles Dickens' *A Christmas Carol*, the ghost of Woodrow Wilson, whose presidency encompassed the whole of the First World War and its immediate aftermath, has haunted world leaders from his day to ours."[8] A new American administration in 2009, with a return to a more multilateral orientation, is certainly an essential part of the solution to what ails the contemporary United Nations.

Regional Groupings

An important element in the redefinition of global interests will be for other powers to be willing to bear more of the international military burden. Otherwise, what alternative is there to Washington's acting as the world's policeman?

The stark reality of US military hegemony in the contemporary international system will put a damper on peace operations unless Europeans invest more in an independent military capacity. There are now 27 members of the European Union, whose population of almost 500 million and gross domestic product of $16 trillion collectively rivals the United States. Yet to date, neither populations nor parliaments on the continent have demonstrated any willingness to contribute a fairer share of the Western defense burden or to reconfigure their forces to make them useful for international military operations.[9] Europe's continued free-riding and failure to develop a truly independent capacity—indeed, its military capabilities continue to decline vis-à-vis those of the United States—constrains bullish notions about multilateral peace operations.

Moreover, downsizing of the armed forces over the last 15 years has resulted in a supply of equipment and manpower insufficient to meet the demands of international operations. There are bottlenecks in the US logistics chain—especially in airlift capacity—that make improbable a rapid international response to a fast-moving, Rwanda-like genocide.[10] With half the US Army tied down in Iraq and a quarter of its reserves overseas, questions are being raised even about the US capacity to respond to a serious national security threat or a natural disaster like Hurricane Katrina, let alone minor "distractions" like Haiti or major ones like the Democratic Republic of the Congo.

To halt at least some conscience-shocking future cases of mass suffering or to stabilize other kinds of international conflicts, there simply will be no viable alternative to international military forces. There is some flexibility for action in minor crises. For instance, the prediction that major powers other than the United States would not respond at all with military force to a new humanitarian emergency after September 11, 2001 proved somewhat too pessimistic. A French-led EU force going into Ituri in summer 2003 halted an upsurge of ethnic violence and perhaps demonstrated to Washington that the EU could act outside of the continent independently of NATO. Furthermore, in early 2008, France led another such effort to keep the peace in Chad.

These efforts provide a faint glimmer of hope that an EU security identity could more substantially underpin future international military responses without the United States, at least for modest crises. *A Secure Europe in a Better World*,[11] the EU's summary of its defense priorities and future plans, lacks the crispness of its American counterpart. While spending on hardware falls considerably short of targets, the number of European troops deployed abroad has nonetheless doubled over the last decade and approaches the so-called

Headline Goals, which set targets for the European Union in terms of military and civilian crisis management. As two European security specialists have noted: "This incremental approach may move some way further yet, but it will come up against budgetary ceilings, against the unwillingness of some governments to invest in the weapon and support systems needed, and against the resistance of uninformed national publics."[12]

Perhaps the most robust indicator of a realignment of security interests among EU member states, from a focus on NATO to a more regional approach, is the creation of the European Rapid Reaction Force (ERRF). In 2000, the European Union announced that it would establish the ERRF, capable of being deployed within 60 days and remaining in operation for up to a year. Not a standing army, the ERRF is a multinational military force under the management of the EU. In 2003, the ERRF undertook its first mission in Macedonia, "Operation Concordia."

The EU has continued to take a more active role in the maintenance of peace and security in other regions as well. In December 2004, NATO passed the peacekeeping torch in Bosnia to the European Union Force in Bosnia and Herzegovina (EUFOR). Taking over from NATO's Stabilisation Force (SFOR), EUFOR's "Operation ALTHEA" deploys 7,000 military personnel (the same number as that deployed as part of SFOR) under a UN Charter's Chapter VII mission to "ensure continued compliance with the Dayton/Paris Agreement and to contribute to a safe and secure environment in Bosnia and Herzegovina."[13]

Europe is not the only region to have assumed a larger and more visible role in recent international peacekeeping efforts. In 2003, the newly renamed African Union (previously the Organization of African Unity) stepped up to the plate and sent troops to Liberia when the rest of the world refused to take action. Answering a call that the United States and other Western countries had ignored, the AU troops were able, virtually as soon as they deployed, to bring to an end the violence in Monrovia due to clashes between Charles Taylor's government forces and the Liberians United for Reconciliation and Democracy rebel forces.

In spite of notably inadequate logistics and firepower, the AU's efforts since 2005 in Sudan also highlight the shortcomings when the United Nations subcontracts with weaker regional organizations.[14] While such efforts have worked relatively well in the Balkans because NATO is well armed and well equipped, the AU's fledgling efforts in Darfur, like earlier ones in West Africa by the Economic Community of West African States (ECOWAS), are a different story.

Sudan undoubtedly presents as complex a multilateral challenge as is imaginable.[15] The UN has long been involved in trying to heal the North–South rupture (and the on-and-off violence dating from 1963), as has the AU in trying to manage the Darfur crisis (and the 200–400,000 dead and 2.5 million refugees resulting from what many call the "slow-motion genocide" that began in early 2003). The UN helped broker the January 2005 Comprehensive Peace Agreement (CPA) and fielded its UN Mission (UNMIS) to support the implementation of the CPA, assist with returns, disarmament, demobilization, and reintegration, and to protect civilians in imminent danger. Meanwhile, the AU Mission (AMIS) began in October 2004 and grew from 60 military observers and 300 protection officers to around 7,000 in late 2006 (the authorized strength was 6,171 soldiers and 1,560 police). The AU provided the troops and the West the logistics and finance, but clearly the presence of 7,000 poorly equipped and commanded troops in an expansive area (Darfur is almost the size of France) was insufficient for the task at hand.

After fighting worsened in the summer of 2006, the Security Council in August approved resolution 1706, which called for a new 17,300-troop UN peacekeeping force to supplant or supplement the poorly funded and ill-equipped AMIS. Sudan strongly objected to the resolution, saying it would view the UN forces in the region as the equivalent of "foreign invaders," and to demonstrate its mettle Khartoum began a major military offensive.

The long-planned exit by the AU and turnover to the UN became something else: an agreement in principle in July 2007 by Security Council resolution 1769 for a hybrid UN–AU Mission in Darfur (UNAMID). The collective waffling, reflecting an unadulterated respect for Khartoum's sovereign prerogatives, was baffling even by UN standards. Khartoum's pleas found sympathetic ears in some council members (including China with its oil interests, Russia with arms-sales interests, and developing countries with sovereignty preoccupations). A threat of further sanctions was deleted while the authorization to use force to protect civilians had an ambiguous reference to the responsibilities of the government that is waging war against those civilians. Khartoum "accepted" the resolution but claimed that UNAMID's use of force would be conditioned by government prerogatives. The AU president suggested that there would be no need for non-African troops, but finding 7,000 troops was hard enough let alone 20,000 soldiers, 4,000 police, and $2.5 billion annual funding; and key logistics and funding are still missing.

As of this writing in early 2008, the jury is out concerning the political will and ability of the UN's member states to make good on their long-overdue commitment to protect civilians in Darfur. And, were the force ever to be deployed, it will be too little far too late. Indeed, in a new affront to the UN's ability to maintain a truly multilateral effort, Khartoum rejected an offer by Norway and Sweden of a joint 400-strong engineering unit for UNAMID. Sudan President Omar al-Bashir also objected initially to UN plans to incorporate soldiers from Nepal, Thailand, and Scandanavian countries into the peace mission.[16]

Whatever happens in Darfur, African militaries need considerable help with equipment, training, and financing if they are to bear the burden of peace operations on the most volatile of continents. Agreement about continental upgrading, however, exists more at a rhetorical than a real level. For instance, the African Standby Force—with multidisciplinary (military, police, and civilian) brigades from five subregions —is supposed to be in a position to deploy in 30 days for peacekeeping operations and in 14 days for robust intervention. The planning phase was supposed to have been completed by mid-2005 but still has not. Africans have identified subregional headquarters and pledged troops, but so far these do not exist other than on paper, and the hub of the oversight unit in Addis Ababa essentially consists of the chief of staff. The wealthy Western donors and Russia, the so-called Group of 8 (G-8), agreed in 2004 to expand the global capacity to maintain the peace, but too little investment in such capacities in Africa has taken place, as the performance in Darfur amply illustrates.

State sovereignty remains the central organizing principle of the international system, but its content will have to change if what ails the UN is to be attenuated with regard to future international peace and security. Without efforts to move beyond narrow state interests—such as training and equipping Africans to keep the peace on their own continent even if they stop far short of one-for-all and all-for-one collective security—the United Nations is doomed to remain on the margins rather than central to the solution to global security problems. The same generalization applies to human rights, to which we now turn.

Human Rights: R2P, European Court, Protection Machinery

What it means to be sovereign has changed dramatically since the creation of the state system in 1648, and particularly so in the last 65 years. Although the UN Charter—in Article 2—affirmed the primacy of state sovereignty, the United Nations quickly became the "engine of human rights."[17] The UN Charter was followed in quick succession by the 1948 Universal Declaration of Human Rights and a number of other human rights treaties, including the 1948 Genocide Convention, the 1951 Refugee Convention, and the 1966 Covenants on Civil and Political Rights and on Economic, Social and Cultural Rights.

The rapid development and expansion of the human rights regime, fueled by the work of the UN and the proliferation of NGOs in the second half of the twentieth century, challenged traditional state sovereignty. In particular, the work by Francis M. Deng, the representative of the secretary-general on internally displaced persons from 1992 to 2004, served to recast "sovereignty as responsibility"—a novel notion for states because for some time irresponsible repression and abuse was seemingly acceptable as long as it did not move beyond the border. Beginning in 2007, Deng continued his re-definitional efforts as the UN special representative for the prevention of genocide.

This history is reminiscent of early social contract theorists' conceptualization of sovereignty as based on popular legitimacy—the consent of the governed. Likewise Deng emphasized states' responsibilities to their citizens. In an address in Germany, Deng explained how he had always dealt with the ever sensitive issue of sovereignty in meetings with senior government officials, in a way which has potential for the present discussion of how to fix what ails the UN in the human rights arena:

> Sovereignty is not a way of closing doors against the international community. In this world of intense interaction and interdependence, sovereignty is to me a positive concept, which stipulates state responsibility to provide protection and assistance for its people . . . Given an appropriate level of comfort, one can even add that the best way to protect sovereignty is to discharge the responsibilities of sovereignty and to call on the international community to assist in carrying out these responsibilities.[18]

The Security Council determined that human rights repression in Iraq in 1991 threatened international peace and security, that the breakdown of order within Somalia in 1992 was a proper area for UN enforcement action, and that the dire situation in war-torn Bosnia from 1992 to 1995 was such that all states and other actors were entitled to use "all measures necessary" to provide humanitarian assistance. Situations similar to these were formerly considered within the domestic jurisdiction of states. But the reality inside Iraq, Somalia, and Bosnia—and more recently in Rwanda, Haiti, Albania, Kosovo, and East Timor—came to be redefined as being of proper international concern.

In these cases, the principle of state sovereignty yielded to a transnational demand for the effective treatment of pressing human rights problems. This section discusses the most important illustration of such an expansion, the "responsibility to protect" (R2P), as well as the expansion to include individual (not just state) complaints in Europe, and the inclusion of nonstate perspectives in intergovernmental debates.

R2P

The "responsibility to protect" civilians trapped in the crosshairs of violence emerged as a mainstream concern[19] as part of the growing demand for an effective transnational management of pressing problems—in this case, of human-made humanitarian disasters.[20] Major states show no desire to let an independent UN official like the secretary-general make the key decisions about use of force or other important responses. Legally speaking, the Security Council or NATO may have taken a decision to use force or levy sanctions over matters essentially internal to a state, but in political reality it was certain member states taking such decisions and backing them with resources.

No idea has moved faster in the international normative arena than the catchy title for the 2001 report from the International Commission on Intervention and State Sovereignty (ICISS). The basic idea of the R2P doctrine is that human beings sometimes count for more than the narrowest interpretation of state sovereignty enshrined in UN Charter Article 2. As Kofi Annan graphically told a 1998 audience at Ditchley Park, a conference center in England, "state frontiers . . . should no longer be seen as a watertight protection for war criminals or mass murderers."[21]

Over time, a blurring of domestic and international jurisdictions has taken place, which became more evident in the 1990s with the willingness to override sovereignty by using military force to save threatened populations. The rationale grew from Deng's "sovereignty as responsibility" to help internally displaced persons and Annan's "two sovereignties" prior to the R2P.[22] As a result, the four characteristics of a sovereign state (territory, authority, population, and independence)—spelled out in the 1934 Montevideo Convention on the Rights and Duties of States—have been complemented by another: a modicum of respect for human rights. While this convention has not been officially renegotiated, for all intents and purposes the human rights content of sovereignty has changed.

The normative logic of R2P underscores a state's responsibilities and accountabilities to domestic *and* international constituencies for its human rights performance. Accordingly, a state would be unable to claim the prerogatives of sovereignty unless it meets internationally agreed responsibilities, which include respecting fundamental human rights and providing life sustenance to its citizens. Failure to meet such obligations would legitimize involvement and even military intervention by the society of responsible states. The content of sovereignty has thus been redefined to be more inclusive of the rights of individuals.

As suggested by paragraphs 138–9 of the 2005 World Summit decision, future policy debates and actions will be framed by *The Responsibility to Protect*, which since its publication in December 2001 has been greeted by largely positive reactions including academic reviews.[23] As just noted, the basic idea behind R2P doctrine is that human beings sometimes trump state sovereignty. Former *New York Times* columnist Anthony Lewis described it as "the international state of mind,"[24] and even one of its harshest opponents, Mohammed Ayoob, admits its "considerable moral force."[25]

The ICISS identified only two threshold cases, namely large-scale loss of life and ethnic cleansing, whether underway or anticipated. Humanitarian intervention should be subject to four precautionary conditions: right intention, last resort, proportional means, and reasonable prospects of success. And finally, the Security Council is the preferred decision maker.

The ICISS pushed out the normative envelope in three ways. The first appears in the report's opening sentence insisting that sovereignty also encompasses a state's responsibility to protect populations within its borders. Even committed advocates of human rights and robust intervention now see state authority as elementary to enduring peace and reconciliation and recommend fortifying failed, collapsed, or weak states. This realization does not reflect any nostalgia for the national security state of the past, but a realistic appraisal of a new bottom-line.

The second ICISS conceptual contribution of relevance for this discussion consists of moving away from the rights of outsiders to intervene toward a framing that spotlights the rights to protection of those who suffer from war and violence. Abandoning the picturesque vocabulary shifts the fulcrum away from the rights of interveners toward the rights of affected populations and the responsibilities (if not legal obligations) of outsiders to protect them. The new perspective prioritizes the rights of those suffering from starvation or systematic rape and emphasizes the duty of states and international institutions to respond.[26] Rather than authorizing states to intervene, R2P specifies that it is shameful to do nothing when conscience-shocking events cry out for action. With state sovereignty less sacrosanct today than in 1945, Richard Haass proposes a sound bite for a new sovereignty bumper sticker, "Abuse it and Lose it."[27]

The third ICISS contribution concerns the framing of responsibility not only to react in the face of mass-atrocity crimes but also—indeed, perhaps most importantly—to prevent reaching a stage when military force is required, and also to rebuild societies after intervention. The spectrum of the responsibility to protect thus spells out a logic that is more acceptable to opponents of outside military force because everything must be done to avoid the use of such force—but, in the face of mass murder and ethnic cleansing, it is acceptable as a last resort.

Amidst extremely modest achievements,[28] the September 2005 World Summit provided the latest endorsement for this emerging norm, which has progressed more quickly than many had thought possible.[29] As José Alvarez tells us, "traditional descriptions of the requisites of custom—the need for the passage of a considerable period of time and the accumulation of evidence of the diplomatic practices between sets of states reacting to one another's acts—appear increasingly passé."[30]

R2P suggests that consensus-building can sometimes take place around even the most controversial issues and with opposition from the strangest of bedfellows—at the World Summit, the United States and the Non-Aligned Movement. The summit's final text reaffirms the primary roles of states in protecting their own citizens and encourages international assistance to weak states to exercise this responsibility—which has led some to criticize it as "R2P lite."[31] At the same time, it also makes clear the need for international intervention when countries fail to shield their citizens from or, more likely, actively sponsor genocide. State sovereignty is no longer accompanied by the license to kill.

The NAM will undoubtedly continue to recite its ritualistic rejection of the so-called right of humanitarian intervention, and much backsliding will continue by Third World countries trying to deny there was any consensus on the summit text's paragraphs 138 and 139. Political will remains problematic—as Darfur and the Congo clearly demonstrate, and as Myanmar and Zimbabwe hint. And the threshold for military intervention remains high—not merely the existence of substantial human rights abuses but crimes of a mass nature such as genocide, war crimes, crimes against humanity, and ethnic cleansing. However, the proverbial new bottom-line is clear: when a state is unable or unwilling to safeguard its own citizens and peaceful means fail, the resort to outside intervention, including military force (preferably with Security Council approval), remains a distinct possibility.

That international military force for human protection remains a policy option represents significant new middle ground in international relations. It also indicates how the definition of what constitutes state sovereignty, perhaps the most chronic and life-threatening ailment of the present UN system, can be altered to move beyond the narrow confines dictated by the Westphalian order. It provides an illustration of the type of redefinition that is required to fix the United Nations.

European Court of Human Rights

Traditionally, states have been the only recognized subjects of international law, in a clear attempt to ensure that their narrow definitions of national interests, not the perceptions and definitions of individuals wronged, dominate international deliberations about human rights. Debates within the United Nations have usually replicated this pattern, but an important departure has taken place within Europe. There is no evidence of such a development at the United Nations, but the European precedent is another example from an intergovernmental context and can be cited as relevant for what ails the world organization.[32]

The European Convention on Human Rights and Fundamental Freedoms defined a set of civil and political rights. The European Commission on Human Rights served for a time as a collective conciliator, responding to state or private complaints to seek out-of-court settlements. The European Court of Human Rights existed to give binding judgments about the legality of state policies under the convention.

All states in the Council of Europe bound themselves to abide by the convention. In a profoundly far-reaching precedent, all governments allowed their citizens to have the right of individual petition to the commission, a body that could then—failing a negotiated agreement—take the petition to the European Court of Human Rights. And all states eventually accepted the supranational authority of the court. Its judgments holding state policies illegal were voluntarily complied with by members. This European regime for human rights functions through international agencies made up of independent individuals rather than state officials—although there are also committees made up of national representatives.

In the mid-1990s, the Council of Europe's members progressively accorded individuals standing to sue in the European Court of Human Rights without having the commission represent them. Thus, an individual would have almost the same legal status—or in legal jargon, "personality"—in the court as a state. Persons came to acquire both substantive and procedural rights.

In fact, the international protection of civil and political rights under the European Convention generated such a large number of cases that, to streamline procedure, the commission was dissolved. Individuals were allowed to proceed directly to a lower chamber for an initial review of the admissibility of their complaints. If they meet procedural requirements, individuals can move on to the substantive phase, basically on an equal footing with state representatives.

The details of the European situation merit scrutiny because they show that "muscular," supranational, and effective protection of human rights is possible in international relations when there is sufficient political will. Unfortunately, the European situation also shows how far the United Nations has to go before it can provide the same sort of human rights regime. Popular and state commitment to the serious protection of human rights is much greater in Europe than in other regions. There are fledgling regional human rights regimes, in the Western Hemisphere and Africa, but they do not equal the European record. These efforts at moving beyond the state to the individual in Europe, at least, point the way for the United Nations.

Changes in Human Rights Machinery

Double standards by states have traditionally operated side-by-side with the more principled work of human rights NGOs that participate in UN proceedings—in fact, the task of redefining sovereignty comes close to asking states to act more like NGOs than governments. The need to treat abuse and repression of individuals anywhere in the same manner is the hallmark of the best NGOs but a tall order for most governments.

Between 1946 and its last session in June 2006, there was some procedural progress inside the UN Commission on Human Rights to be more inclusive of private perspectives. Indeed, NGOs played a more significant role in Geneva in the CHR than on other issues or in other UN institutions. NGOs focused their efforts there and increased their numbers as well as influence. By the 1990s, large numbers of NGOs were active in all phases of proceedings.[33] The end of East–West conflict meant that a number of former communist states became champions of human rights and often teamed with NGOs in the commission. Controversies and foot-dragging by some governments could not halt the growth and use of thematic procedures and country-specific investigations called for by NGOs.

Over time the commission dealt mostly with civil rights such as freedom from racial discrimination, torture, forced disappearances, summary execution, and arbitrary detention. This might be seen as a bias stemming from the priorities of Western states and NGOs, and from developing countries aligned with the West. Nevertheless one could hardly disagree that such civil rights are fundamental to any reasonable and effective global human rights agenda.

The voice and weight of NGOs in Geneva is an important precedent. Great care needs to be taken, in fact, to ensure that the role of NGOs does not diminish in the new Human Rights Council. The so-called reform of the scandalous Commission on Human Rights with the creation of the HRC in 2006 falls short of Kofi Annan's vision of a "society of the committed."[34] Although hardly a model for fixing what is wrong with the United Nations, some advances may have resulted (see table 5.1).

Table 5.1: Features of the Human Rights Council Compared with Those of the Commission on Human Rights
• Subsidiary organ of the General Assembly rather than of ECOSOC
• Membership reduced from 53 to 47
• Election by absolute majority of all members: 97 out of 192 instead of 28 out of 54
• At least three sessions totaling no less than ten instead of one single six-week annual session
• Possibility of special sessions in urgent cases
• No permanent members (two consecutive terms at most)
• Suspension of membership by two-thirds majority of General Assembly
• Universal periodic review
• Right of NGOs to speak

Source: Nico Schrijver, "The UN Human Rights Council: 'Society of the Committed' or Just Old Wine in New Bottles?," *Leiden Journal of International Law 20*, no. 4 (2007): 817.

While the modest reduction in numbers and the simple-majority election procedure in the HRC were disappointing in relationship to earlier possibilities, nonetheless other measures might help. One advance was the actual election campaign, which was designed to discourage the worst human rights offenders from being candidates. Rather than backroom horse-trading, there was a more open election process. As a result, certain countries (e.g., the United States, Sudan, Libya, Vietnam, Syria, Nepal, Egypt, Zimbabwe, Uzbekistan, North Korea, and Belarus)[35] did not bother running, and others had to agree to place their own records on the table as part of the campaign. This approach could help attenuate the worst aspects of egregious human rights violators' shielding themselves from criticism by serving on the HRC. Their sovereignty, in short, provides less cover than in the past. Moreover, the General Assembly, with a two-thirds majority vote of those present and voting, can suspend the council membership of countries that are in fundamental breach of their human rights obligations.

The fact that the new council meets at least three times a year for ten weeks (rather than once for a few weeks) was a step forward in terms of making human rights an ongoing UN agenda item, as was the agreement that all members would be subjected to "universal review"—that is, no state elected to the HRC could opt out of having their human rights records scrutinized. That all members might themselves during their three-year, non-renewable terms be subject to an evaluation of their own records was a potentially powerful symbolic indication, which was set aside in a 2007 compromise. There had even been some speculation that the United States was not a candidate in 2006 in order to avoid scrutiny of such high-profile embarrassments as Guantánamo and Abu Ghraib.

Progress has been made with the universal periodic reviews. At least it has now been agreed that all states' records should be open to independent review and not shielded by claims of sovereignty. Thus, 192 member states have been scheduled for review, starting with Morocco in 2008 and ending with Moldova during the HRC's 12th session in 2011. The reviews will be done by peers, although the OHCHR will assist in compiling relevant information and documentation provided by the state concerned, treaty bodies, and other relevant stakeholders, potentially including NGOs and independent experts. The universal periodic review, however, remains state-oriented, while the method of work "reflects a co-operative and somewhat soft approach."[36]

Governments also agreed in September 2005 to strengthen the Office of the High Commissioner for Human Rights. It is staffed by professionals who have, among other tasks, been establishing human rights centers in troubled countries such as Cambodia, Guatemala, and Nepal and assisting special rapporteurs working on such thematic issues as torture. The summit document calls for doubling the budget of the high commissioner's office to permit recruitment of "highly competent staff."[37] The OHCHR's regular budget for 2006–7 did indeed increase by 18.2 percent from the previous biennium budget, revealing movement toward fulfilling summit goals. In addition, voluntary contributions increased by $17 million.[38] The expansion of independent professionals to improve UN monitoring efforts seems likely to be a reality by 2010.

Making more room for independent voices—be they from nongovernmental organizations or the secretariat—in challenging outmoded sovereigns would represent a fundamental alteration in the way that states view their prerogatives within the United Nations. In addition, another challenge is to build an international consensus behind policies that address the underlying cause of human rights deprivations, and that defend basic rights whenever they are threatened—a substantial redefinition of sovereignty's content. In terms of preventing future disasters, the redefinition of sovereignty should also include addressing many of the root causes of deprivation, which is a development task.

Sustainable Development: Health and Pandemics

How would a post-Westphalian notion of national interests influence approaches toward sustainable development? In many ways, *past* approaches to health issues hold powerful lessons for how to approach today's and tomorrow's challenges.[39] In this case, we can learn from the UN's earlier history—as William Faulkner once wrote of the American South, "The past isn't dead. It isn't even past."

The elimination of smallpox is perhaps the most spectacular illustration of why moving beyond narrow conceptions ultimately will better satisfy national interests. For more than

3,000 years smallpox was a scourge of mankind, feared for its high fatality—often 10 percent of all deaths each year—and for the pockmarks that disfigured those who survived. Edward Jenner, an English country doctor, discovered vaccination in 1796, and the spread of vaccination led to a marked decrease in the toll of smallpox in industrial countries. Yet, the disease continued almost unabated in Africa, Asia, and Latin America. In the 1960s, some 2 million people were estimated to be dying of smallpox every year.[40]

In 1953, the WHO's first director-general, Brock Chisholm, made an unsuccessful attempt to persuade the World Health Assembly, the WHO's governing body, to undertake a global program for smallpox eradication. Five years later, a Soviet delegate persuaded the WHO to accept responsibility for a global program—but only minimal funds were provided. The organization itself was preoccupied with a major and eventually unsuccessful effort to eradicate malaria, and many were skeptical about the feasibility of smallpox eradication, especially in Africa.

In 1966, the World Health Assembly agreed on an Intensified Smallpox Eradication Program (ISEP)—though still with doubts about its success. At that time, the entire staff numbered just over 3,300 persons, and only about 150 professionals were available to oversee smallpox programs in more than 50 countries.

Once started, the program advanced rapidly. A strategic plan concentrated on mass vaccination campaigns, using freeze dried vaccines quality assessed by special teams. A surveillance system was set up to detect and investigate cases and contain outbreaks. Three principles were critically important. All countries would need to participate, with some form of regional and global coordination. Programs would need to be flexible and adapted to the specifics of each country. And ongoing research, in the field and the laboratory, would be needed to evaluate progress and solve problems as they arose.

By the early 1970s, smallpox was on the retreat. A surveillance containment strategy was developed, sending flying squad teams wherever a possible case was discovered. The squads would make a diagnosis, identify and vaccinate all contacts, and swiftly contain the spread of infection. By 1975, the number of countries where the disease could still be found had fallen from 30 to 3—India, Bangladesh, and Ethiopia. By the end of the year, the last case of variola major, the most serious form of the disease, was reported in Bangladesh.

Attention then turned to Ethiopia, where the last case was reported in August—but not before nomads had carried the disease across the border into Somalia, where an epidemic occurred in mid-1977. In October, the last case was finally reported in Somalia. Three years later, the WHO declared victory. The total cost of the 11-year effort had been around $300 million, one-third of which came from international sources and two-thirds from the countries affected. The total cost was the equivalent at the time of three fighter-bombers. Because of eradication, the world now saves at least $2 billion each year by avoiding the purchase of smallpox vaccine, administration (including applying international health regulations), and related costs. This is certainly one clear economic way to measure the importance of redefining sovereignty to include fighting diseases far afield with as much vigor as diseases closer to home. Most of the savings have occurred in the budgets of industrialized countries, which have been able to avoid the upfront investment costs of vaccination and smallpox health regulations.

The eradication of polio, inspired in part by the successful experience with smallpox, is underway. The vaccines invented by Jonas Salk (1955) and Albert Sabin (1962) made it possible—with adequate resources and international cooperation that ignored national boundaries—to come close to extinguishing this disease. Some 150 countries have reported no case for three or more years. Efforts underway by WHO and UNICEF may soon conquer polio.

Tragically, efforts to tackle HIV/AIDS have been different; and they reflect a narrower and backward-looking vision of sovereignty. Of course, the absence of an AIDS vaccine makes the case incomparable, but even so the basic international approach differs from that taken with regard to smallpox and polio. Instead of seeing common threats and attacking them regardless of the location of illness, the approach is piecemeal and oriented toward narrow national conceptions of interest. Today, in 16 countries, all in Sub-Saharan Africa, more than one adult in ten is infected with the HIV virus. In seven of those nations, one in five actually carries the deadly virus. In Botswana, 36 percent of adults are infected, in Zimbabwe 25 percent, in South Africa 20 percent.

The world is gradually becoming more conscious of the magnitude of the problem. "We are at the beginning of a pandemic, not the middle, not the end,"[41] the director of the White House Office of National AIDS policy stated. Alas, the possibility of vaccination is too late for the 35 million people now living with HIV and AIDS, and for the many who will follow. Indeed, the number of new infections is estimated at 15,000 a day, and growing. The United Nations set a goal of cutting new infections by 25 percent by 2005; that objective was not met, but even attaining it would not have stopped the toll from doubling and doubling again. Early in 1986, the World Health Organization still regarded AIDS as an ailment of the promiscuous few. It was Jonathan Mann (who died tragically in a plane accident in September 1998) who convinced the WHO's director-general, Halfdan Mahler, that AIDS was not merely another infectious disease. It flourishes in, and reinforces, conditions of poverty, oppression, urban migration, and social violence. Mann was put in charge of a special program on AIDS. However, after Mahler's retirement in 1988, the WHO's AIDS program was slashed by the new director-general, Hiroshi Nakajima. Mann resigned in protest and pursued his crusade from Harvard University.[42]

By 1990, the sense of urgency about AIDS in industrialized countries had begun to wane. New drugs and other preventive measures meant that AIDS was no longer seen as the same threat to the West as it had been earlier—again, myopia appeared as concerns stopped at the border. At the same time, it is hard to overlook the incompetence of ministries of health in many developing countries whose leaders denied the existence of the problem and refused to cooperate even in data gathering. The WHO was laggard in elaborating the promising start but was not the only UN agency to cut its AIDS programs. At UNICEF, the health division fought from 1992 to 1994 in order to avoid involvement in AIDS.

Finally, by the middle of the 1990s, donor governments began to push for the creation of a joint UN–AIDS program, which was established in January 1996. However, the participating organizations cut back sharply on the resources and the personnel they devoted to AIDS. World Bank loans dropped from $50 million to less than $10 million; WHO spending dropped from $130 million to $20 million; and UNICEF's from $45 million to $10 million.

In the summer of 1998, Gro Harlem Brundtland became the WHO's director-general. In her first two *World Health Reports*,[43] her evaluation of the state of health in the world emphasized tobacco and tuberculosis rather than AIDS. In 1999, HIV/AIDS surpassed all other causes of death in Africa, a fact unmentioned in the text of Brundtland's 1999 report. In a secretariat of more than 2,000, only a handful of WHO professionals work on AIDS.

In January 2000, US Vice-President Al Gore articulated Washington's position before the Security Council, which was addressing Africa's social instead of security ills: "Today, in sight of all the world, we are putting the AIDS crisis at the top of the world's agenda. We must face the threat as we are facing it right here, in one of the great forums of the earth—openly, boldly, with urgency and compassion."[44]

To date, then, the HIV-AIDS pandemic—and the near misses with SARS and avian flu—have reflected a different approach from that of smallpox and polio. Of course, the clarity of understanding regarding the virology and epidemiology of smallpox was a precondition for its eradication. Nonetheless, the early embrace of cooperation and transnational interests, rather than going it alone on a national basis, also was essential. The HIV-AIDS story is one of waking up after the disaster has struck and of proceeding with minimal international cooperation.

The cure is a more inclusive notion of sovereignty. But even making modest inroads to include enlightened self-interest would constitute a substantial palliative to what ails the United Nations.

CHAPTER SIX

Moving Beyond the North–South Divide

Overcoming the North–South dichotomy, and generating new partnerships that transcend the confines of these simplistic categories, is of the essence. In the previous chapter, one remedy for what ails the UN was moving beyond traditional Westphalian understandings of national interests. Here, the medicine is equally hard to swallow for long-time UN hands. Benedict Anderson's well-known "imagined communities" also is a term that could apply equally to large groupings of states, which no less ferociously defend their constructed identities than do individual countries or nations.[1] There have been occasions, however, when the barriers between the North–South camps have been breached. They portend other types of coalitions of the willing that might unclog deliberations within the United Nations.

International Peace and Security: Landmines, Human Security

In the late 1990s, an intriguing alternative pattern for diplomatic negotiations took place for an important disarmament issue. This section examines the constellation of like-minded states—from both the North and the South—and NGOs that formed partnerships and triumphed in the face of hostility from some major powers. The Ottawa Process that brought about in 1997 the convention banning antipersonnel landmines is a prominent case of new partnerships that cross anachronistic categories.

This section also examines the changing notion of security. It traces the shift from a state-centric to an individual and broad-based conceptualization, which has united parts of the North and South in support of what has become known as "human security."

Ottawa Treaty to Ban Landmines

The 1997 Nobel Peace Prize was awarded to the International Campaign to Ban Landmines (ICBL), led by Jody Williams. It always makes for good journalism to associate a single face with a move forward in international relations. However, the problem of landmines mobilized a very diverse group of countries across the usual North–South divide, as well as global civil society under the leadership of the World Federalist Movement and the usually reticent International Committee of the Red Cross.

What was there about this issue that broke down the typical divisions? The indiscriminate use of antipersonnel landmines —especially in the late Cold War for the armed conflicts in Afghanistan, Kampuchea (Cambodia), and Angola—led to a ghastly number of deaths and amputees. Moreover, the presence of these munitions also impeded enormously complicated post-conflict transitions and peace-building. Yet many states and many belligerents viewed antipersonnel mines as war-fighting essentials. Meanwhile, nonstate actors normally have little lobbying leverage in areas of military policy and national security, and they tend to be allergic to working with governments.

With the end of the Cold War, movement on this issue suddenly seemed possible. Launched originally in 1992 by six NGOs—Handicap International, Human Rights Watch, Medico International, Mines Advisory Group, Physicians for Human Rights, and Vietnam Veterans of America Foundation—the ICBL was formed to advocate a comprehensive ban on the production, export, and use of antipersonnel landmines. Through conferences and campaigning events organized world-wide, the ICBL rapidly expanded its membership, not only mobilizing grassroots activists and public opinion but also effectively lobbying a wide range of sympathetic governments.

In spite of US opposition, an eclectic mix of lesser powers moved ahead and managed to have the Landmines Convention signed in December 1997. Don Hubert tells us why: "While much of the credit for the successful banning of land-mines has deservedly gone to the ICBL and to NGO advocates, the success of the campaign can be explained only through an examination of three other sets of actors: the International Committee of the Red Cross, the United Nations, and key governments."[2]

There are many lessons to be learned from this case, but the most important one for our purposes is that the coalition of like-minded states—including Canada and South Africa, France and Burkina Faso—ignored the usual boundaries between North and South and focused instead on substance.[3] Canada and its energetic foreign minister Lloyd Axworthy led the "Ottawa process," but the UN was an important player and legitimating force; and breaking down the barriers of the UN's negotiating blocs was essential to advancing debate.

Human Security

Another issue that unites parts of both the North and South is the notion of human security, which focuses on the security of individual human beings, in contrast with the national security of the countries within which such individuals live. In 1999 Juan Somavía, who now heads the ILO, questioned "why it seems to be more urgent for the United Nations to act when someone is killed by a bullet than when someone dies of mal-nutrition."[4] Although the UN was designed to halt bullets and foster international peace and security, human security differs in two respects from what was foremost in the minds of the Charter's framers. First, it reorients discourse on security away from the state toward individual human beings and their communities. Second, it broadens the scope of analysis and policy beyond classical military concerns and engages a much broader range of threats (from the domestic political through the environment and economy to health).

The need to broaden definitions was given a conceptual boost when a visible US foreign policy expert and former Pentagon analyst, Princeton's Richard Ullman, pointed out in a 1983 issue of the journal *International Security* that traditional concepts were framed "in excessively narrow and excessively military terms."[5] Since that time, a human focus has entered the critical security studies literature and has been reflected in the statements of liberal states and international organizations.

There may be as much division in the academic world as among member states regarding human security. In a set of essays on the topic in a 2004 issue of *Security Dialogue*, Ramesh Thakur praised the multidimensional quality of human security and recommended that "realists . . . should get real." Don Hubert—then in Canada's Department for Foreign Affairs and who had worked with Lloyd Axworthy in making his government a champion of the concept—scratched his head and wondered about the value of analytical hair-splitting in light of the demonstrated policy relevance of the concept of human security in banning landmines and establishing the International Criminal Court: "One might have thought that it was only French philosophers who rejected concepts that 'worked in practice, but not in theory.'"[6] At the same time, another Canadian, Roland Paris, in a critically acclaimed article, dubbed the notion "hot air."[7]

In spite of the controversy over the concept's intellectual and policy traction, North and South found common ground at the

1995 Copenhagen World Summit for Social Development, which focused on the *problématique* of human security. This meeting represented a landmark shift by governments toward a people-centered rather than a state-centered framework for social development as well as for peace and security.[8]

One way to unite what otherwise might be contending parties in discussions on human security is "mainstreaming": a compromise framing of essential issues that moves states beyond North–South theatrics to a middle ground. That is, instead of arguing that important new priorities require new institutions and posts, existing institutions can be reoriented and existing resources reallocated around new priorities. For instance, gender mainstreaming is an approach to promote equality that involves "ensuring that gender perspectives and attention to the goal of gender equality are central to all activities—policy development, research, advocacy/dialogue, legislation, resource allocation, and planning, implementation and monitoring of programmes and projects."[9] While incorporating a gender perspective into all levels of programming makes good sense, it is arguable whether mainstreaming by itself can achieve gender equality.

Oxford's Neil MacFarlane and Yuen Foong Khong have analyzed in depth the impact of this concept: "We may be a long way from utopia, but we are also a long way away from the unchallenged dominance of the state as the principal referent of security."[10] They argue that the discourse on human security has two valuable dimensions: questioning the traditional focus on the state in the security studies literature and focusing instead on the threats to individual human beings; and widening the discussion of "threat" beyond violence to include economic, environmental, and other dangers. The first has been useful in sensitizing the UN and member states to the protection needs of individuals and communities affected by conflict and in arguing that the sovereign rights of states depend in some sense on their capacity and willingness to ensure the physical security of their citizens. The latter seems less helpful. As MacFarlane and Foong Khong argue, "it is not obvious what additional analytical traction one gets from redefining human development or health or environmental issues as security issues."[11]

Human Rights: Universality in Vienna, the Rome Statute

The issue of human rights has often divided the planet rather than uniting it. The 1948 consensus between the North and South around the Universal Declaration of Human Rights existed temporarily and mainly because the "South" at the time consisted mostly of Latin American countries politically close to the United States and philosophically aligned with the West. Over time, North–South divisions regarding human rights have become less distinct. The Vienna conference and the signing of the Rome Statute demonstrate the increasing convergence of views among developed and developing countries in this issue area.

Universality in Vienna

I have mentioned the cross-cutting hostility toward the responsibility to protect, including from countries that would benefit. Perhaps an even clearer illustration of the necessary breakdown of unified fronts that do not reflect real interests but rather the value of theater was the affirmation of the interdependence and indivisibility of human rights at the 1993 Vienna World Conference on Human Rights.[12] The first global UN gathering on human rights since the 1968 International Conference on Human Rights was plagued by disagreements over the universality of human rights. Three regions of the global South—Asia, Latin America, and Africa—had held preparatory meetings prior to the Vienna conference. The Asia regional meeting, held in Bangkok between March 29 and April 3, 1993, issued the "Final Declaration of the Regional Meeting for Asia of the World Conference on Human Rights," which essentially declared that human rights were culturally relative—that is, that rights only existed specific to certain cultures, regions, and countries. A small number of African and Middle Eastern countries also threw down the cultural relativist gauntlet—"universal" human rights were thinly disguised "Western" values.

In the end, however, intense pressure from NGOs, in particular women's rights groups from across the planet, resulted in the bold assertion that "the human rights of women and of the girl-child are an inalienable, integral and indivisible part of universal human rights."[13] With the global South split, the Vienna Declaration and Programme of Action was adopted, reaffirming the universality, indivisibility, and interdependence of human rights, with a special emphasis on the rights of women. Essentially, the North was joined by two-thirds of the South to reaffirm the wisdom of the original 1948 decision. Ironically—considering the fact that the United States rejects the idea of economic and social rights as human rights—Washington played a leading role in pushing for the reaffirmation of universality.

Another key issue discussed at the World Conference was the need to increase the visibility of human rights in the United Nations, especially by creating a post of UN high commissioner for human rights. A minority of the Non-Aligned Movement—consisting of Islamic countries in North Africa, the Middle East, and parts of Asia—joined forces but were unable to hold sway when pro-rights NGOs and the North were joined by more supportive and pro-rights NAM members from Latin America and Africa. The result was the creation of the post that was filled by José Ayala Lasso (from 1994 to

1997), followed by Mary Robinson (1997–2002), the late
Sergio Vieira de Mello (2002–3), and Louise Arbour (2004–8).
The budget, while still derisory given the nature of the problems, has almost trebled (to about 2.25% of the total UN
budget), and the office has been strengthened somewhat, if
still inadequately for the task, in both headquarters and the
field.[14]

Rome Statute

Earlier, we encountered the group of reluctant or hostile countries, led by the United States, that have not only failed to ratify
the 1998 Rome Statute establishing the ICC but also have
actively tried to sabotage this international legal step forward.
Nonetheless, over the past decade, a broad-gauged coalition of
NGOs has worked in tandem with like-minded states across
the North–South chasm. As a result, the ICC has proven to be
more robust—and to have implemented its mandate faster—
than many had initially predicted.

The court came into being on July 1, 2002 when the Rome
Statute entered into force with the requisite 60 ratifications.
By the time of Madagascar's ratification on June 1, 2008 there
were 106 state members of the ICC allied in permanent efforts
to prosecute individuals for genocide, crimes against humanity, war crimes, and crimes of aggression. Another 40 countries have signed but not ratified, though a number of
important states (including China and India) have done neither; and, symbolically, the United States and Israel have both
taken what previously had been an unthinkable legal step—in
2002, they revoked their signatures.

The ICC can prosecute offenses committed after July 1, 2002
but only when a crime is committed on the territory of a state
party or by one of a state party's citizens, or when a case is
referred to it by the Security Council. While the non-signatories
are uneasy about jurisdiction, the court complements rather

than replaces national legal systems and can act only when national courts are unwilling or unable to investigate or prosecute crimes. With its headquarters in The Hague and led by Chief Prosecutor Luís Moreno-Ocampo, the ICC has opened investigations into the situations in Northern Uganda, the DRC, and the Central African Republic upon the requests of those countries' governments, and into the situation in Darfur upon the request of the Security Council; two suspects are in custody and awaiting trial.[15]

How did this precedent-setting organization get off the ground? Answering this question is especially important because of the deep hostility from the globe's most powerful country.[16] Given its traditional role as standard-bearer for human rights, many find Washington's position hard to explain, except in terms of an almost mindless ideological opposition. Indeed, the United States originally led the charge in the 1948 General Assembly to establish such a permanent court following large-scale atrocities against civilians in World War II and the war crimes trials in Nuremberg and Tokyo; and also it was an active participant in negotiations leading up to the draft of the Rome Statute in 1998.

In the wake of the end of the Cold War, the idea of an international court was again championed and received an additional push after the establishment of the ad hoc International Criminal Tribunals for the former Yugoslavia and for Rwanda.[17] The scale of atrocities—in Europe and in Africa—demonstrated the need for international justice in the 1990s just as they had earlier. And the shortcomings in the ad hoc tribunals (including costs and the burden of evidence) demonstrated the need for creating a permanent court that could also act as a deterrent for future thugs.

By the middle of the 1990s, governments across the North and the South as well as NGOs had formed coalitions to lobby for the creation of what would become the ICC.[18] This "like-minded group" began with the modest hope of achieving some kind of consensus at a preliminary diplomatic confer-ence in Rome in July 1997. When the official UN Conference of Plenipotentiaries on the Establishment of an International Criminal Court—known informally as the "Rome Conference"—convened a year later, the 60-country like-minded group represented a formidable and persuasive coalition that joined forces with the 700 members of the NGO Coalition for an International Criminal Court. The momentum was such that the actual formal Rome conference in 1998—which, unlike the landmines treaty, was negotiated under the auspices of the United Nations—moved toward a decision in spite of strong opposition from several members of the P-5. Afterwards, the signature and ratification process also moved on a fast track.

The need to set aside country-group cookie-cutters becomes clear when examining these two tough cases involving the high politics of international security. Progress resulted specifically from ignoring the theatrical and automatic ideo-logical divisions of North and South. While no two campaigns are identical, the efforts to agree on the Convention on Landmines and the ICC reflect two tactical advances: the agreement to move ahead without universal support; and a broad-based working coalition of NGOs and states from both the North and the South. Rather than digging the chasm deeper and wider, like-minded partners found ways to build bridges. As Teresa Whitfield notes, a host of small and "ad hoc, informal, issue-specific minicoalitions of states or intergov-ernmental organizations that become involved in and provide support for resolving conflicts and implementing peace agree-ments [have] become a critical element of an incipient system of post-Cold War global security governance."[19]

Analogously, an expert group assembled by the Stanley Foundation in June 2007 to discuss counterterrorism made a recommendation on this fraught security problem: "Narrow the gap of understanding between the G-8 and G-77 on substantive issues."[20] Nonetheless, David Malone and Lotta Hagman explain why this remains so implausible: "The political ecology of the UN, and especially of the General Assembly, often seems stuck in the past, with North–South polemics all too often paralyzing action . . . threaten[ing] the UN with irrelevance and redundancy."[21]

This section argues that it is necessary to find different roles, different actors, different scripts, and different stages in order to move beyond the empty North–South theater that often paralyzes action on human rights. The results-oriented negotiations on landmines and the ICC suggest the benefits of a more pragmatic and less ideological approach to international deliberations and that such reorientations are not impossible.

Sustainable Development: Millennium Development Goals, Global Compact

The reader may recall that the North–South debate began in earnest during preparations for the 1964 UN Conference on Trade and Development, which resulted in UNCTAD's becoming for many years the surrogate secretariat for the G-77.[22] Before the nail was driven into the coffin of the so-called North–South dialogue in 1981, the confrontation between the two had reached new heights with the establishment of the New International Economic Order (NIEO) in the mid-1970s. This effort—the most controversial among many—to develop new relationships between North and South emerged in the aftermath of the dramatic quadrupling of oil prices during 1973–74. This led to a major shift in global income toward OPEC countries and away from both industrial and developing countries without oil—the latter sometimes nicknamed the "NOPEC countries."

The proposals to establish the NIEO were a shopping list of grievances and not a single idea to level the economic playing field for the developing world. Yet, the NIEO served to focus debate on a wide range of ideas put forward since the early 1960s by developing countries. Whatever their feasibility, they encapsulated the passionate call to change international economic relationships that privilege industrialized states.

However, "entrenched interest, national hubris, ideological divisions, and mindless militancy all played their part," as Mahfuzur Rahman wrote about the NIEO's demise. "The idea of a new international economic order has long ceased to be a matter of serious discussion . . . [but] the story is worth recounting, if only to ponder the limits of international cooperation."[23]

In 1972, UNCTAD initiated the Charter of Economic Rights and Duties of States, which was formalized at the 1974 regular session of the General Assembly as resolution 3281 (XXIX). In 1975, the French government launched the Conference on International Economic Co-operation (CIEC) as a way to continue the dialogue but with fewer countries (25) than the entire UN membership. This continued under the appellation of "North–South dialogue," and there were also the so-called global negotiations in a series of UN contexts (often called the *dialogue des sourds*, or dialogue of the deaf) until the collapse of the discussions in 1981 at a conference in Cancún, Mexico.

The so-called lost decade of development in the 1980s was characterized by stagnation and in some cases a reversal of progress made in previous decades. The bargaining position of the South as a bloc diminished, with a number of countries suffering from unsustainable debt burdens resulting from the ramifications of the oil crisis and in need of assistance from the Northern-dominated Bretton Woods institutions. IMF/World Bank intervention, however, came with a heavy price tag. Orthodox structural adjustment programs called for the slashing of state budgets, privatization of state-owned industries, and liberalization of trade, which had considerable adverse social impacts. By the end of the decade, gaps between and within countries had increased.

While the UN as a whole remained "behind the curve,"[24] two UN agencies made a considerable contribution to reconceptualizing development—UNICEF and UNDP. These agencies challenged the IMF/World Bank's narrow pursuit of enhancing national growth often at the expense of the populations subject to neoliberal strategies. The early 1990s represented the beginnings of mainstreaming human concerns into structural adjustment programs.

While the theatrical value of South-versus-North confrontation continues in most debates, barriers came down during the Millennium Summit when heads of state and government agreed to eight major goals (and 18 targets): eradicate extreme poverty and hunger; achieve universal primary education; promote gender equality and empower women; reduce child mortality; improve maternal health; combat HIV/AIDS, malaria, and other diseases; ensure environmental sustainability; and develop a global partnership for development.

The 18 targets are fairly specific, quantifying what should be achieved by 2015. However, the eighth goal, relating to the formation of a global partnership for development, has no target, which would have implied obligations for developed countries —clearly a sticking point with some governments and especially Washington.

By not going to the mat in 2000 over this issue, developing countries found growing support for the goals among numerous donor countries and, perhaps more importantly, a focus for development aid. Moreover, the World Bank and the IMF joined in the consensus instead of remaining aloof from UN priority-setting—a significant departure from previous efforts to keep a safe distance.[25] The *Human Development Report* of

2002 and of 2003 emphasized strategies toward implementation. The reinforcement of the Millennium Development Goals (MDGs) was a major theme at the September 2005 World Summit, which became the largest ever (over 150) gathering of heads of state and government.[26]

Columbia University's Michael Doyle worked for Kofi Annan at the time and recalled how the secretary-general "was able to use his authority to convene the Bank, the IMF, and the OECD and stop the bureaucratic battle over what development means. The MDGs became a set of criteria for what development meant. The goals did not eliminate the bureaucratic conflicts, but at least got development policy focused on a similar target."[27]

Another issue that helped bring fresh air into the theater in the 1990s came to the fore when the UN and its associated agencies began to pay more attention to the role of women and gender in development.[28] Building on the work of feminist economists, UN agencies such as UNCTAD, UNDP, UNICEF, and UNIFEM, along with the World Bank and the IMF, began to research how men and women are positioned differently in the world economy, and in poverty. Under particular scrutiny were the gendered effects of structural adjustment programs on women in countries experiencing economic crises. By examining how the policies of governments and multilateral institutions affect the everyday lives of women, strategies could be developed to avoid some ill-effects and unintended consequences.

For example, the World Bank and the IMF have modified their policies such that structural adjustment loans can now be used, in part, for the alleviation of poverty and not just for market reforms. Furthermore, the World Bank now considers gender equality as fundamental to economic development and to poverty reduction. While the inclusion of women and gender issues on the development agenda has obvious benefits, it also complicates North–South relations in that conceptions regarding the status of women and their rights are markedly different—with some countries in the South being far closer in outlook and aspirations to the West than the more conservative countries of Asia and the Middle East.

At the 1995 Fourth UN World Conference on Women in Beijing, the traditional confrontation between North and South was replaced by a coalition of like-minded women pushing for priorities that united rather than divided them. These were often distinct from the public position of the member states issuing the visas that allowed them to get together. Although gender equality had nominally been one of the World Bank's objectives since the 1970s, it was the Beijing conference that catalyzed the Bank's increased attention to the issue. Attended by 189 governments and some 2,000 NGOs, the conference ended with the adoption by consensus of the Beijing Declaration and the Platform for Action, which outlined an agenda for women's empowerment.

The 2001 so-called Monterrey Consensus is also cited as a pertinent example of international development cooperation enabling partners from the North and South to move to common ground rather than to remain in separate trenches. In 2001, countries agreed at a conference in Monterrey, Mexico, that governments of developing countries had an obligation to reform themselves for the purpose of economic efficiency, while those in developed countries had an obligation to provide meaningful assistance for that improved process of development. The Monterrey Consensus attempted to reconcile the need for structural/market reforms and the need to authoritatively redistribute some of the wealth of the rich North to the impoverished South. Instead of sterile confrontation, the two camps sought common ground.

The administration of George W. Bush followed in 2002 with the announcement of a new Millennium Challenge

Account (MCA) of foreign assistance to the poorest countries. Recipient countries would have to meet certain criteria dealing both with economic effectiveness and good governance. The MCA would not be a multilateral arrangement, but rather would be administered by an independent corporation of the United States—the Millennium Challenge Corporation. Congressional appropriations for the MCA, however, have consistently fallen short of the administration's budgetary requests by about half. Given the restrictive nature of funding criteria, very few of the world's poorest countries are able to qualify for assistance. In the words of Jochen Steinhilber, "MCA funds are in effect reserved for the 'happy few,' that is, for those countries with the least pressing development problems."[29]

Washington's promises have not materialized to the extent imagined during the "truce" by the South. While the data is unclear—indeed, expenditures have increased for the 16 countries for which Millennium Challenge Compacts have been approved[30]—the importance of the discussion is to suggest that traditional postures and rigidity need to give way to more flexibility. Interests—national and international—rather than preconceived ideologies need to guide coalitions in their negotiating strategies.

Another tendency that would be diminished by moving beyond the uniform consensus sustaining the North–South facade is the kitchen-sink approach to agenda setting. In order to get all states—in the North and in the South—to take seriously a discussion or an operational effort, the typical procedure is to include something for everyone. This approach necessarily condemns deliberations to retrace steps over well contested ground rather than spending time on priority items or seeking new solutions to age-old problems. This is certainly part of what ails the United Nations.

There are, however, cases where new approaches have been tried with some success. For instance, the World Summit on

Sustainable Development (WSSD) followed the Monterrey session from August 26 to September 4, 2002. Coming 10 years after the Earth Summit in Rio, the WSSD in Johannesburg represented an attempt to reinvigorate the priority attached to sustainable development activities in the wake of deepening poverty and environmental degradation. New targets were set, timetables established, and commitments agreed. As the UN website for the Johannesburg Summit 2002 made clear, "there were no silver bullet solutions . . . no magic and no miracle—only the realization that practical and sustained steps were needed to address many of the world's most pressing problems."

The summit reflected a new more pragmatic approach to conferencing and to sustainable development more generally —a dialogue among major stakeholders from governments, civil society, and the private sector. Instead of concentrating primarily on the production of treaties and other documents, participants focused on the creation of new partnerships to bring additional resources to bear.

Another way to move beyond traditional roles is to bring new partners and counterparts into conversation. The Global Compact represented a most radical departure from previous UN orthodoxy—the fool's errand of international regulation of transnational corporate behavior favored by the South—toward an active engagement with the private sector. More than 3,000 companies in two-thirds of the UN's member states have signed on to a framework of 10 core principles to guide best business practices in such areas as the environment, human rights, and labor rights. Predictably, these efforts to move beyond orthodoxy have brought knee-jerk criticisms from many die-hard countries of the South, and from some NGOs, that the UN has lost its soul and gone pro-capitalist.[31]

When the Global Compact was launched in 1999, there was an opportunity to add to the policy clout of the UN by mobilizing the private sector to promote UN goals. Although it is strictly voluntary and based on self-assessments, nonetheless the Global Compact has become a useful device for promoting good corporate governance and responsibility. A key person who turned that idea into a reality was John Ruggie, now at Harvard University but at the time working for the secretary-general on policy issues. He explained:

> The first purpose underlying the compact was mobilizing the private sector to make a difference on development, on human rights, on environmental protection, and labor rights. The second purpose was that the very act of reaching out to the private sector would position the UN as an institution that was friendly to the more conservative powers—that is, the U.S., the Europeans, the Japanese—because it engaged with private enterprise. Previously, the UN had been regarded as an enemy of private enterprise.[32]

The Global Compact is predicated on the assumption that development, especially for poorer developing countries, cannot occur through governmental or intergovernmental means alone, even when augmented by NGOs. Neither can it occur through unbridled market forces alone. Creating local, national, and international enabling environments is essential, and a broad-based partnership involving all relevant "stakeholders" is required.

Unsurprisingly, not everyone is happy with the new coalitions. The role of the private sector remains controversial— their basic concern being the bottom-line rather than common interests. But certainly, if the UN is to begin to reflect the complexity of actors necessary to address global problems, the for-profit sector's resources and energy dwarf those of non-profit NGOs. The Global Compact placed transnational corporations at the center instead of the periphery of UN discussions—in spite of decades of negative views emanating from the South— and brought NGOs into the picture to measure best practices.

Some argue that the closer association with the market represents a "maturing" of the United Nations, while others assert that it amounts to a "selling out" or a "blue-washing for capitalism."

The jury is still out. By aggressively building an array of partnerships with civil society and a few thousand firms from the private sector, the UN is moving in largely uncharted international waters and cannot rely on the compass provided by North–South orthodoxy. Whether the concrete benefits for development turn out to be substantial remains an open question. However, what is clear is the need to move beyond the sterile performances guided by tired script-writers from North and South that virtually guarantee a poor and hackneyed production, and ultimate failure.

CHAPTER SEVEN

Truly Delivering as One

Too much analytical, political, and emotional energy and effort to reform the United Nations have been directed at the highly visible Security Council. Yet it is perhaps even more important to take a hard look at the way in which more typical and widespread operational activities are structured and at the people who carry them out.[1] This chapter addresses prescriptions for the UN's structural problems while the following one does so for its human resources.

The title for this chapter borrows from a report of November 2006, presented by outgoing Secretary-General Kofi Annan, but also signed by the then incoming Ban Ki-moon. The central question is what it might take to have a UN system truly *Delivering as One*.[2] In diagnosing the world organization's ills, Chapter 3 spelled out the reasons for the continuing lack of implementation of this recent overview—which were pretty much the same as for the *Capacity Study* of 1969. Here our task is to explore how the United Nations system could work more coherently and effectively in specific efforts to foster security, human rights, and sustainable development.

Donors need to insist upon more centralization—the single most essential change for the world organization—rather than permitting, to paraphrase Mao Tse-tung, a hundred flowers to bloom in the form of decentralized UN efforts. Greater centralization almost took place with the reform of 1997 in the humanitarian arena; and the spirit of this reform was the driving force behind the 2006 proposals from the High-level

Panel on Coherence. If donors were to put their money where their mouths are, the kinds of consolidation that are routinely called for would come closer to reality.

International Peace and Security: Rapid Reaction, Central Emergency Response Fund

Although not an example of a human-made disaster, such as the ongoing humanitarian crises in the Congo and Darfur, it is useful to begin this section with an exploration of efforts to respond to the December 2004 tsunami in the Indian Ocean. The UN-led response demonstrated global action to meet a security threat that transcended national borders as well as internal UN boundaries. It vividly illustrates a rare coming together of a well-coordinated international operation and the need for a more coherent response to similar disasters.

The earthquake that caused the tsunami was measured at 9.3 on the Richter scale. The second most powerful earthquake since 1900, it displaced billions of tons of overlying ocean water traveling at speeds of up to 500 miles per hour. The tsunami hit Indonesia 30 minutes after the earthquake, and the coasts of Thailand, Sri Lanka, and India about another half-hour later. The destruction of buildings, roads, and infrastructure was disastrous, and the tsunami killed more people than any other in history—estimates go up to 280,000. Tens of thousands of people went missing, and more than one million were displaced. Ten countries in South Asia (Indonesia, Sri Lanka, India, Bangladesh, Myanmar, Thailand, Malaysia, Maldives, the Seychelles, and Singapore), and three in East Africa (Somalia, Kenya, and Tanzania), suffered substantial losses and damages.

The response from a constellation of relief organizations, national governments, militaries, and private individuals around the world demonstrated what US Congressman Jim

Leach called "competitive compassion."[3] Unlike in many other crises, however, the response involved not a "scramble"[4] for resources (perhaps because they were so plentiful) but a sensible centralization of international efforts. An overall response network (states, IGOs, and NGOs) was in place, but the creation of the tailored network for the tsunami required negotiating a structure among existing groups as well as procedures to incorporate others that joined. Operational NGOs such as the International Federation of Red Cross and Red Crescent Societies (IFRC), Oxfam, CARE, Médecins Sans Frontières (MSF), World Relief, World Vision, and Habitat for Humanity International are just some of the transnational NGOs that responded immediately. The UN system—especially through the WFP and UNICEF—was also particularly active. While the UN itself was not the main avenue of implementation, the world body was the main institution coordinating response efforts, and its moral authority served to enforce compliance by naming and shaming non-cooperative actors.

The initial aid from Western countries was inadequate but grew quickly as information became available about the magnitude of the disaster. For example, by the middle of January 2005, the European Union had spent $30 million, and had pledged $132 million in short-term aid and $455 million for long-term reconstruction.[5] This was in addition to the amounts that individual European governments had spent and pledged. The corporate world contributed as well, and over $3 billion came from individuals. Neither the tsunami nor the response network respected borders, as states joined IGOs and NGOs in aggregating and channeling funds to recipients in the region.[6]

While criticism was leveled at poor management of relief funds (accompanied by fears that long-term support would dwindle), the basic goal of averting a second crisis and the accompanying human suffering was achieved. Yet could the response have been even better? And could the largely decentralized responses in war zones be improved by a similar type of centralized, top-down coordination?

In 1991, the General Assembly authorized in resolution 46/182 a new position of under-secretary-general for emergency relief (or emergency relief coordinator, ERC), to head up what was then a new Department of Humanitarian Affairs. But this official, however well-intentioned and adept, still operates in a milieu in which public and private agencies resist central control over their independence of action and fundraising. Donor states have expressed growing concerns about this "non-system," and in the early 1990s issued the following statement: "We commit ourselves to making the United Nations stronger, more efficient and more effective in order to protect human rights" and call for an "improvement in the UN system . . . to meet urgent humanitarian needs in time of crisis."[7]

But decisive change for the better has not materialized; in fact, the changes have been mainly cosmetic—including a name-change for the DHA, which became the Office for the Coordination of Humanitarian Affairs in 1998, the first reform by the then new secretary-general, Kofi Annan. A proposed and sensible centralization of all humanitarian efforts—combining UNHCR, UNICEF, WFP, and the then DHA—was abandoned at the last minute when donor governments backed down, and separate agencies argued that the sky was falling.[8]

A tiny bureaucratic step was taken toward more coherent coordination. As mentioned earlier, the ERC chairs the Inter-Agency Standing Committee, which includes major UN and non-UN humanitarian actors. This body strives to facilitate interagency analysis and decision making in response to humanitarian emergencies. Also, in his role as a UN under-secretary-general, the head of OCHA serves as convener of the

Executive Committee for Humanitarian Affairs, which is a cabinet-level forum for coordinating humanitarian policies within the UN. However, the potential relevance of more centralization for all crises was illustrated in the aftermath of the 2004 tsunami when ERC Jan Egeland prodded many donor countries that eventually contributed billions of dollars for tsunami relief in the largest relief operation in history. He also managed to cajole the system and NGOs to behave instead of going their own way as is the standard operating procedure. OCHA again shifted into high gear in response to the 2005 earthquake in Kashmir that left approximately 30,000 people dead and millions more homeless.

For armed conflicts and the public emergencies stemming from them, the politics of providing relief to civilians is more complicated than for natural disasters. Aiding and protecting war victims may be close to impossible, depending on the security situation and the stance of the government or political authorities involved. Outside assistance and protection may be viewed—correctly in many cases—as strengthening the "enemy's hand" (either the government or the armed opposition, depending on one's perspective). Food aid, for instance, may not seem like neutral assistance but rather a means to strengthen the opposition, either by providing resources or by freeing up other resources that can be devoted to making war rather than feeding supporters.

By law and by tradition, the ICRC coordinates international relief in interstate wars on behalf of the International Red Cross and Red Crescent Movement. The 1949 Geneva Conventions for victims of war, supplemented by the 1977 Protocol I, give the ICRC a preferred position for this task. The Security Council has affirmed the rights of civilians to international assistance in such wars, and belligerents have a legal duty to cooperate with neutral relief efforts. Protocol I states clearly that starvation of civilians is not permitted in warfare and that belligerents are not permitted to attack objects vital to the survival of the civilian population.

Two of the countries affected by the tsunami were embroiled in ongoing armed conflicts—Sri Lanka and Indonesia. In Sri Lanka, where a ceasefire had been in place between the Sinhalese government and the separatist Tamil Tigers, this natural disaster provoked a striking degree of cooperation from belligerents in the delivery of aid, sheltering survivors, and handling dead bodies. This accord broke down as the government tore up the ceasefire early in 2008. Meanwhile, in Indonesia, the Free Aceh Movement declared a unilateral ceasefire, which Jakarta observed as well. The government opened Aceh to foreigners, and the region became a key staging ground for relief efforts. In these cases, the needs of victims superseded the political goals of belligerents, at least in the short term. Indeed, in Indonesia cooperation led to an agreement that still holds.

As discussed in Chapter 1, however, belligerents in civil wars often do not adhere to the laws of war. Violence against civilians is often integral to the strategic aims of warring factions, and cooperation with relief organizations is hardly common practice. Alongside outright killing are widespread practices of forced displacement, starvation, mass rape, and mutilation—hardly an environment conducive to the effective delivery of aid. Meanwhile, aid workers themselves have increasingly become targets of violence.

Further complicating cooperation is the fact that aid agencies themselves have conflicting standard operating procedures in war zones. In some situations, a military presence is necessary to protect civilians from violence and to establish security so that humanitarian assistance can be delivered to beleaguered populations, but this very association with soldiers can appear to the other side as if humanitarians are part of the problem. Perceptions can be more important than intentions.

A Rapid Reaction Capability

The bulk of the expenditures for international peace and security revolve around what in 2007 were some 100,000 blue helmets and a budget of $5.3 billion,[9] a figure that may jump again in 2008 for as many as 130,000 blue helmets. The fact that these military and police personnel are lent by member states and remain under national authority and control makes change and reform a unique challenge for the United Nations.

The inability of the United Nations to halt genocidal violence, in Rwanda in particular, brought renewed attention to the idea of a UN rapid reaction force. Although a standing Military Staff Committee was originally envisioned when the United Nations was created, Article 47 of the UN Charter—which incorporated this idea—never became reality, largely due to opposition from the P-5.

Over the years, countries such as Canada and Norway have raised the idea of a lean and autonomous UN rapid reaction military capability that would provide the secretary-general with a contingent that he could deploy quickly in response to a pressing need or request—like, for example, the one from General Roméo Dallaire in April 1994 in Rwanda. In 2000, interest was rekindled when Representative Jim McGovern introduced Bill 4453 in the US Congress, which called for support for the creation of a 6,000-person UN Rapid Deployment Police and Security Force. Unfortunately, though he introduced a similar bill in 2001 (HR 938), neither came to fruition.

In 2005, Emergency Relief Coordinator Jan Egeland announced his desire to establish a rapid reaction force of 100 aid workers, another proposal that went nowhere.[10] Most recently, a group of scholars have come forward to support the idea of a United Nations Emergency Peace Service composed of 12,000–15,000 personnel of various backgrounds ready to be deployed in case of emergency.[11]

Although none of these initiatives has borne fruit thus far, and the financial and logistic constraints remain daunting, the creation of such standing capabilities would undoubtedly increase the UN's legitimacy and reinvigorate the organization. Indeed, the Commission on Global Governance proposed such a military capability because "Governments are understandably reluctant to commit troops rapidly for UN action, particularly in civil wars and internal conflicts."[12] Perhaps someday this sensible notion will actually be implemented. While not being yet a reality, and thus unlike other precedents discussed here, it is mentioned because the need is so obvious and significant governments have explored the possibilities. Indeed, the idea was originally floated by the first secretary-general, Trygve Lie.[13]

Central Emergency Response Fund

While a standing security force has not yet become a reality, there has been some progress with centralizing funding. Seeking to ensure that the UN would be able to react better to future disasters, in December 2005 the General Assembly established the Central Emergency Response Fund (CERF). It began operations in 2006 and aims to promote early action and response to reduce loss of life; enhance response to time-critical requirements; and strengthen core elements of humanitarian response in under-funded crises.

Managed by the ERC on behalf of the secretary-general, and funded through voluntary contributions from member states and private entities, CERF is intended to serve as a standby fund available to be used either for rapid response in the first 72 hours of a crisis or in response to under-funded emergencies. Designed as a reserve fund of $500 million—$450 million in grant money and another $50 million in loans—CERF has come up short thus far, with pledges and contributions for 2007 totaling $346 million.[14] Some countries have been criticized for not contributing and others for contributing trivial amounts.

But the fund is a step in the right direction. Core funds are controlled centrally by the ERC whose institutional interest lies in spending them in the fastest and most efficient way possible by relying on other agencies. The separation of fundraising from fund-disbursements (OCHA is not operational) means that incentives are provided to a central administrator to make the most of limited resources, not increase his or her own operational domain.

Human Rights: Funding Central Activities

Since the end of the Cold War, the United Nations has continually sought to centralize the activities of its disparate human rights bodies. In a speech at the United Nations just after the adoption of the Universal Declaration in December 1948, Eleanor Roosevelt predicted that "a curious grapevine" would spread the ideas contained in the Declaration far and wide.[15]

In December 1993, the General Assembly established a chief vintner, a UN high commissioner for human rights. Julie Mertus writes: "The idea, however, that human rights enforcement would be facilitated by placing broad authority in a single individual can be traced as far back as 1947." She goes on to summarize:

> One of the important innovations stemming from the creation of the Office of the High Commissioner for Human Rights is the creation of a streamlined process for requesting and receiving technical assistance in the field of human rights. Instead of involving other parts of the UN (as the previous procedure required), the whole matter remains within the purview of the OHCHR.[16]

Another notable achievement, furthering the goal of delivering as one, is the OHCHR's creation of the Rights-based

Municipal Assessment Programme (RMAP) in Bosnia and Herzegovina. The RMAP seeks to implement a rights-based approach to development, to integrate "the norms, standards, and principles of the international human rights system into the plans, policies and processes of development."[17] As such, it recognizes the interrelatedness and indivisibility of human rights and development and represents an attempt to operationalize the human rights framework. Problems are identified in each municipality through the use of rights-based assessments—based on human rights norms and standards—and then addressed under the guidance of human rights principles, such as "participation, accountability, non-discrimination, and empowerment," using municipality-specific indicators against which progress can be tracked.[18]

The UN has also sought resources through the establishment of voluntary funds to which governments and private donors can contribute to help bridge the gaps between UN allotments and priority program costs. While inadequate, these funds attempt to earmark money specifically for priority human rights activities; and implementation is based on need, not agency pull with favorite donors. Four trust funds for such activities currently exist: the Voluntary Fund for Victims of Torture (established 1982); the Voluntary Trust Fund on Contemporary Forms of Slavery (established 1991); the Voluntary Fund for Indigenous Populations (established 1985); and the Trust Fund for the International Decade of the World's Indigenous Peoples (established 1995). Each is administered by the secretary-general and is governed by a five-member board of trustees.[19] This kind of independent financial arrangement—it is the secretary-general who decides, not donor governments—is essential; and such resources should be augmented.

The OHCHR under Mary Robinson also launched other new initiatives to raise funds. In 1999, the position of senior fund-raising officer was created within the OHCHR, and in 2000 the OHCHR initiated a global annual appeal to encourage more predictability, activities, and planning. Also in 2000, the OHCHR's Voluntary Fund, which was created in 1993 to support the office's activities, began making annual appeals. The OHCHR has benefited from an increase in funding from the annual $5–6 million spent during the 1990s to a steady annual budget of $55 million since 2000.[20]

Pooling resources in a central fund is a healthy alternative to decentralized resource mobilization. The latter necessitates scrambling for funds and protecting turf rather than pursuing measures that take seriously need and capacity.

Sustainable Development: Bringing the Bretton Woods Institutions into the Fold, the Peace-Building Commission

The UN country office has, since the establishment of the UNDP's system of resident representatives, sought to establish a central UN pole in each country. In their transmittal letter to the secretary-general, the three co-chairs (the prime ministers of Pakistan, Mozambique, and Norway) of the panel that produced *Delivering as One* reiterate the crying need to "consolidate existing entities wherever necessary, and to eliminate unnecessary duplication and competition in UN operations." In making that obvious plea, they assert that substantial efforts at consolidation are necessary in order "to overcome the fragmentation of the United Nations so that the system can deliver as one . . . [and be] more than the sum of its parts." As the "Executive Summary" points out: "[T]he UN's work on development and environment is often fragmented and weak. . . . Cooperation between organizations has been hindered by competition for funding, mission creep and by outdated business practices."[21]

Two illustrations suggest feasible steps in the right direction for greater centralized control, financing, and decision making to implement sustainable development projects. It will be helpful to examine the attempt to pull the Washington-based financial institutions closer to the UN, and also the establishment of the Peace-Building Commission (PBC).

Bringing the Bretton Woods Institutions into the Fold

A greater integration of the international financial institutions (IFIs) and UN organizations is needed for development policy coherence. By far the largest players within the UN system are the Bretton Woods institutions, which have always operated independently. Attempts to bring the UN's programming closer to the World Bank and the International Monetary Fund—*de jure* parts of the UN system, but *de facto* totally separate—have been on the agenda for years.

At the World Bank, protecting the environment has increasingly been viewed as a legitimate part of its approach to investing in development. Over the years, considerable pressure was exerted by NGOs and others that helped bring about the organization's "greening."[22] In 1991, the Bank joined with UNEP and UNDP to create the Global Environment Facility (GEF), through which Bank funding was combined with UNEP and UNDP programming. The GEF provides grants to developing countries for environment-related projects and facilitates networking and cooperation among donors. It operates in four main issue areas—protection of the ozone layer, international waters, biodiversity, and climate change—and is charged with working with other UN agencies, regional development banks, and bilateral donors in integrated technical assistance and investment projects.

While under-resourced, the GEF represented a clear recognition of the relationship between development and the environment along the lines that had been so controversial in the run-up and immediate aftermath of the 1972 UN Conference on the Human Environment in Stockholm. As we saw earlier, at the 1992 UN Conference on Environment and Development in Rio de Janeiro, states voted into being a new UN coordinating organ, the Commission on Sustainable Development, that incorporated ecological concerns and sustainability. The CSD was weak in legal authority, and hence weak in practical coordination. Building on the precedent of the GEF suggests a way to bring the Washington-based financial institutions into the fold, with parts of the UN system to which they are supposedly integral. The World Bank group and the IMF are represented by a dotted line in the UN organizational chart because they are not really part of the system. Nonetheless, given the incoherence of the UN proper and its specialized agencies, it is absolutely essential to truly "delivering as one" that the weight and resources of the Bretton Woods institutions be brought to bear upon the UN system.[23]

Since 1980, the donor community has channeled growing resources to the Washington-based international financial institutions and increasingly followed their lead for policy advice and programmatic actions. This focus on the IFIs has frequently led to a serious neglect of UN organizations and their priority projects, leaving them marginalized because of inadequate funds. UN contributions have been neglected in key areas where the Bretton Woods institutions have pursued policies that were either wrong or too narrow—for example, on structural adjustment programs. A better balance is required between the World Bank, the IMF, and the United Nations—in policy leadership, as well as in funding and support for national and international actions. Stronger roles for the regional development banks and the regional commissions should also be part of a new cohesion.

The recent past offers some cause for optimism, relating to the adoption of the MDGs in 2000 and of the Poverty Reduction Strategy Papers (PRSPs) at the country level. The Bretton Woods institutions, the donor community, and the United Nations are cooperating better within countries. This important step forward toward "delivering as one" is, however, frequently overshadowed because UN agencies lack the resources and capacity to make the desired and feasible contribution to the partnership. Innovative financing could help mitigate the situation, but there is no substitute for more generous support, with fewer strings attached, from governments to the UN system.

Peace-Building Commission

One of the few concrete steps taken by the September 2005 World Summit was the decision to establish the PBC and its supporting office, along with a new fund specifically geared to elicit more coherence from UN partners in their collective efforts to move beyond conflict and begin a process of sustainable development.[24] The need to restore broken states along these lines was clearly a growth industry during the 1990s; equally clear was the incoherence of UN efforts to pick up the pieces after the conflicts that led to such breakups. The secretary-general's High-level Panel on Threats, Challenges and Change was unequivocal:

> In both the period before the outbreak of civil war and in the transition out of civil war, neither the United Nations nor the broader international community, including the international financial institutions, are well organized to assist countries attempting to build peace . . . What is needed is a single intergovernmental organ dedicated to peacebuilding, empowered to monitor and pay close attention to countries at risk, ensure concerted action by donors, agencies, programmes and financial institutions, and mobilize financial

resources for sustainable peace . . . Similarly, at the field level, many different elements of the United Nations system and the broader international community engage in some form of peacebuilding, but they work too slowly and without adequate coordination. Effective coordination is critical.[25]

The decision to establish the PBC in spring 2006 was a step in the right direction toward improving UN efforts to prevent any relapse into violence in war-torn countries recovering from armed conflict. The PBC's mandate is to propose integrated strategies for post-conflict peace-building, ensure predictable financing for recovery, draw international attention to peace-building, provide recommendations and information to improve coordination, and develop best practices requiring the collaboration of a variety of actors.

The PBC has an Organizational Committee comprised of 31 members: 7 from the Security Council; 7 from ECOSOC; 5 of the main financial contributors to the United Nations; 5 of the top military contributors to the world organization's peace operations; and 7 elected by the General Assembly to redress geographical imbalances that may result from the other selection criteria. The Peace-Building Commission also includes country-specific committees, which tailor programs to include country representatives and relevant contributors in each case.

The World Summit Outcome document also requested that the secretary-general establish a Peace-Building Support Office (PBSO) within the secretariat, whose qualified staff are to assist and support the PBC as well as advise the secretary-general. The PBSO also oversees the Peace-Building Fund (PBF), established by Kofi Annan in 2006 with a target of $250 million. By February 2008, deposits have reached about $200 million, and its total portfolio is approximately $256 million. The aim of the fund is to provide initial support for peace-building efforts and "kick start" donor investment in long-term recovery. If managed effectively, the fund has the potential to reduce the duplication of efforts and waste and enhance coordination among financial sources because the power of the purse is to make decisions centrally. Thus far, it has disbursed $35 million to Burundi and Sierra Leone, the two countries on which the PBC has focused attention in its first year of operation.

The PBC, however, is not without its shortcomings. It is a subsidiary body of both the General Assembly and the Security Council, which exacerbates reporting problems. Its functioning depends on cooperation among the main UN organs. Moreover, like most UN entities, it is an advisory body, rather than a decision-making body, and lacks enforcement mechanisms. As one analyst notes, "the advisory nature of the PBC—coupled with the stipulation that it 'shall act in all matters on the basis of consensus of its members'—seems at odds with the very concept of the body assuming the final responsibility for peacebuilding."[26] Moreover, since there appears to be some overlap between the PBSO and the activities entrusted to the DPA and DPKO, there is the potential for turf battles.

Nevertheless, the creation of the PBC, PBSO, and the PBF is an important step toward enhancing the coordination, efficiency, and effectiveness of post-conflict peace-building efforts financed and supervised by the United Nations.

Fighting Centrifugal Tendencies with Centralized Funding

In addition to the establishment of trust funds and initiatives such as CERF, new funding possibilities and alternative resources from the private sector have often been proposed in order to overcome traditional impasses in UN budgets and to augment limited resources. Named for the 1981 Nobel laureate in economic sciences, a proposed tax on international currency transactions—the so-called Tobin tax—is often cited as one possible type of solution to the UN's perennial budgetary shortfalls and agency rivalries. Allowing the UN to manage such independent revenues would alleviate the world organization's reliance on member-state largesse and permit a more rational and less agency-driven agenda regarding priorities and resource availabilities. Critics often forget that the World Bank and its more private-sector-oriented International Finance Corporation raise the vast bulk of their resources on private capital markets. This permits independence, risk-taking, and centralized control in a manner not currently available to the United Nations and other parts of the UN system.

However, the policy authority for tackling global problems remains vested in states, along with the main competence to mobilize the resources to act. The largesse of wealthy individuals, or an international lottery, or proposed taxes on airline tickets or financial transfers, could be helpful on the margins to the United Nations; but they cannot substitute for governments' respecting their commitments and international legal obligations to meet significant cash-flow problems. Dick Thornburg—former UN under-secretary-general for administration, US attorney general, and governor of Pennsylvania— referred to the UN's situation as a "financial bungee jump," even if the amount of money involved appeared almost trivial, or a "bargain" according to a prominent group of bankers.[27]

What sums of money are we talking about? In 2007, the estimated annual cost of UN peace and security missions was approximately $5.3 billion and the UN's regular budget about $2.1 billion; the budget of the entire UN system (not including the international financial institutions) is about $10 billion. The cost of the UN's annual peace operations seems almost laughable compared with the US Defense Department's regular budget of some $500 billion, with another $200–$250 billion currently allocated for Afghanistan, Iraq, and the war on terror. Moreover, the assessed US contribution to UN operations, about 30 percent of the total bill, amounts to only about 0.2 percent of the annual US defense budget, or about one-quarter of conservatively estimated costs for a month of the Iraq occupation.

Independent funds, or more generous financial contributions from governments, if applied in the right way, could help pull together the many moving parts of the UN system, and this would certainly be a strong palliative to feudalism. Donors could apply their financial leverage to assist consolidation and centralization, rather than permit the continued decentralization of UN efforts. But if such structural financing were to be improved and reoriented toward consolidation and centralization, what about the individuals who compose the international civil service? It is to them that we now turn.

CHAPTER EIGHT

Reinvigorating the International Civil Service

The role played by individuals who work at the United Nations is often overlooked, as research by the United Nations Intellectual History Project demonstrates.[1] A way ahead for the world organization would be to rediscover the original idealism and dedication of the international civil service, to make room for creative idea-mongers, and to create more mobile personnel and career development paths for a twenty-first century secretariat.

As in Chapter 4, which diagnosed the ills of the UN's administration, the opening section here focuses on the secretariat's nuts-and-bolts before offering prognoses with illustrations from international peace and security, human rights, and sustainable development. These are small but specific illustrations of what has worked and might be applied more generally to help what ails the world body's personnel and performance. The impetus for change comes from the clouds that still hang over staff as a result of the Volcker Commission and sexual scandals. Also relevant is the absence of action on the sensible recommendations in *Investing in the Future United Nations*, the comprehensive 2006 report about personnel from the by then lame-duck secretary-general, Kofi Annan. This set of suggestions, like many before it, remains in filing cabinets or on office bookshelves rather than in policy.

Reforming the Second UN

The main expenditure of the world organization goes for its employees. These individuals are the UN's main strength and they can be redirected and reinvigorated. The second UN—to reiterate Inis Claude's classic twofold distinction between the world organization as an arena for state decision making and as a secretariat—is in drastic need of repair.[2] What are the main management challenges for the world organization in the administration of the eighth secretary-general, Ban Ki-moon?

The most essential challenge proceeds from the need to change the way that the international civil service and its chief executive actually do business. As such, it is necessary to go substantially beyond the formulaic language of the World Summit's outcome document, which speaks of the need "to enhance the effective management of the United Nations."[3] While Susan Strange and Robert Cox would argue that views from inside can really only be orthodox,[4] I take a different view. The international civil service, properly constituted, can make a difference—not only in field operations but also by engaging in intellectual and policy activities. Indeed, autonomous officials can and should provide essential inputs into UN discussions, activities, advocacy, implementation, and monitoring.

Ignoring standard bureaucratic operating procedures and making waves is an essential part of leadership and is necessary to break down the walls that often separate agencies from one another. For instance, former US Congressman and later UNDP administrator Bradford Morse, together with Canadian businessman Maurice Strong, broke the rules in a feudal system when they headed the temporary Office of Emergency Operations in Africa (OEOA) in the mid-1970s. Thanks to their own experience, reputation, and independence, Morse and Strong were powerful enough to override the UN's institutional rules just as Sir Robert Jackson had broken them on numerous occasions by top-down directives. Jackson applied the military skills and hierarchical command structure that he had used during World War II—defending Malta and working with the Middle East Supply Centre—to United Nations Relief and Rehabilitation Administration (UNRRA) projects in post-war Europe, parts of Africa, and the Far East. And later he did the same for the biggest UN relief operation to that time, the Bangladesh emergency in 1971.[5] These kinds of officials with these kinds of approaches are essential if the second United Nations is to function as it could and should.

International civil servants would not exist without the member states of the first UN, but what would an institution of member states be able to accomplish without a secretariat? The second UN consists of career and long-serving staff members who are paid through assessed and voluntary contributions. In diagnosing the ills, we mentioned that the international civil service is the legacy of the League of Nations, a core of officials charged with tackling international problems as called for in UN Charter Article 101. Old-timers, especially those from the idealist first generation recruited in the 1940s and 1950s, are appalled when nationality baldly trumps competence. They and others were especially upset with the Staff Council's vote of no-confidence in the secretary-general in May 2006.

No other moment offers so much room for consequential change in the secretariat than when a new secretary-general sets out a mandate—Boutros Boutros-Ghali initiated a number of staff changes in 1992, for instance, as did Kofi Annan in 1997 and 2002.

The eighth secretary-general made no such jump-start, despite the low morale that set in after the scandals surrounding the Oil-for-Food-Programme that fed Saddam Hussein's coffers as well as ordinary Iraqis, and sexual exploitation by a few UN officials, as well as troops and civilians on peacekeeping missions. As mentioned earlier, these recent blots on the secretariat's reputation point to serious flaws in the central administration—often inefficient, politicized, and in desperate need of repair.

Both the secretary-general and the High-level Panel on Threats, Challenges and Change proposed, and the summit agreed, to consider a one-time buyout to cut deadwood from the permanent staff. This type of proposal has been around for years and probably would not improve matters—enterprising and competent staff could take a payment and seek alternative employment while the real deadwood would remain because they have no options. The more pertinent challenge, whether any buyout occurs or not, is how to gather *new* wood for the secretariat of the twenty-first century and ensure that the best and brightest are promoted.

Recruitment should return to the idealistic origins of the League of Nations and early UN secretariats: competence should be the highest consideration rather than geographical origin, gender, and age—these being among the various justifications for cronyism that are shamelessly used in filling both senior and junior posts. If certain affirmative action measures continue, the onus must be put on governments to nominate only their most professionally qualified and experienced candidates—not just someone close to the boss who fancies life in New York or Paris. At a minimum, and in contrast to the take-it-or-leave-it approach of the posts "reserved" for particular nationalities, several candidates should be nominated and the choice left to UN administrators. Of course, better yet, there should be no such reservations, and the United Nations should retain its autonomy in making the selections.

It is not impossible to square the circle regarding quality, independence, and representation. Special recruitment efforts can be focused on under-represented nationalities—including the use of quality-enhancing measures such as examinations for new entrants—without compromising the overall quality of the civil service. As with efforts to achieve a better gender balance, priority can be given to nationals of certain countries by casting the net widely enough to draw fully qualified candidates from those backgrounds but eliminate cronyism. It is a fallacy to think that quality must suffer while moving toward a better balance in various types of representation. The real requirement is to limit pressures from outside influence and patronage—pressures exerted by donors, friends, and family members of candidates from developed as well as Third World countries.

Klaus Sahlgren, a former head of the UN's Centre on Transnational Corporations, used another image in considering the need for a stronger secretariat: "Mao Tse Tung used to say, 'It doesn't matter what color the cat has as long as it catches mice.' I can understand that the UN, in its own operations, will have to set an example to backward countries when it comes to gender or race discrimination. But that should not—and need not—happen at the expense of competence and efficiency."[6]

In addition to addressing the issue of staff quality in the bureaucracy, there is also a need for substantial change in the way the secretariat operates and the way its resources are allocated, as indicated in both *A More Secure World* and *In Larger Freedom*.[7] Indeed, observers often overlook the fact that Annan instituted significant managerial and technical improvements shortly after assuming the mantle in 1997, and again at the beginning of his second term in 2002. One change that made a difference was the introduction of a loosely defined "cabinet" system, with regular high-level meetings among senior officials in the secretariat, agencies, funds, and programs.

Unfortunately, the clash between South and North at the end of Annan's term stopped sensible proposals that would have placed more authority in the hands of the secretary-general.

Many Third World countries are reluctant to authorize more flexibility because it moves power away from the General Assembly, where by virtue of their numbers they call the shots. Mark Malloch Brown, who served as Annan's last deputy after having been UNDP's top administrator, noted with some puzzlement upon assuming his UN post: "taking a demotion to come over from UNDP to be Kofi Annan's chief of staff was a much bigger step down than I anticipated . . . I found when it came to management and budgetary matters, he was less influential than I had been."[8]

Ironically, increased discretionary authority for the secretary-general would be in the interests of developing countries whose populations and governments benefit most from the UN's operations and projects. However, a relatively small number of countries in the global South block agreement on management reform, which they view as a subterfuge. If more discretionary authority and power of the purse were to be given to the UN administration, so the argument goes, it would be more subject to Western (and especially American) influence.

If, however, the institution is to meet new and old challenges and be more accountable, allowing greater authority and responsibility at the top is a minimum requirement. The Volcker team's recommendation to establish an Independent Oversight Board, with a majority of independent members and an independent chair, would also help maintain transparency. The World Summit was far tamer, merely muttering on the "urgent need to substantially improve the United Nations oversight and management processes," which specifically included the "operational independence of the Office of Internal Oversight Services."[9] As the Volcker panel indicated, such a unit should not be "advisory," like the present one, but should actually exercise oversight and blow whistles when necessary.

International Peace and Security: Disciplining Peacekeepers, Resolution 1325

Two examples figure in this section to illustrate how the United Nations might be fixed within the field of international peace and security: code and discipline units; and better representation of women in peace operations.

Discipline for Peacekeepers

In response to allegations that emerged in 2004 of sexual misconduct by peacekeepers in the Democratic Republic of the Congo, the secretary-general invited Prince Zeid Ra'ad Zeid al-Hussein, the permanent representative of Jordan, to the United Nations to act as his Advisor on Sexual Exploitation and Abuse by UN Peacekeeping Personnel. In 2005, he presented *A Comprehensive Strategy to Eliminate Future Sexual Exploitation and Abuse in United Nations Peacekeeping Operations*. The so-called Zeid report recommended a number of reforms, including standard rules regarding sexual exploitation and abuse to apply to all peacekeeping personnel, the establishment of a professional investigative process to examine alleged abuses, and the institution of relevant "organizational, managerial and command measures."[10] He further argued that those guilty of sexual abuse should be subject to disciplinary action and should be held financially and, where appropriate, criminally accountable for their actions.

After being debated in the General Assembly, the report led to the adoption of a "comprehensive strategy" to be implemented by the Department of Peacekeeping Operations (DPKO) over two years. As part of the reform package, conduct and discipline units have been established in nearly 20 peacekeeping operations in order to prevent, track, and punish gender-based crimes. The units "act as principal advisers to heads of mission on all conduct and discipline issues involving all categories of peacekeeping personnel in the missions." They are overseen by a conduct and discipline unit established in DPKO, which in 2006 joined with OCHA, UNICEF, and UNDP to host a high-level conference. The "Statement of Commitment on Eliminating Sexual Exploitation and Abuse by UN and non-UN Personnel" contains 10 commitments to "facilitate rapid implementation of existing UN and non-UN standards relating to sexual exploitation and abuse."[11]

Given the symbolic and actual importance of UN peace operations—in 2007, approximately 80,000 wore blue helmets, the signature headgear for UN soldiers, in addition to 20,000 civilians—these measures are essential steps toward professionalism and enhancing the UN's performance. Zero-tolerance toward such actions—rather than the "boys will be boys" attitude of the recent past—is certainly in order.

Security Council Resolution 1325 on Women, Peace, and Security

While the UN continues to struggle with under-representation of women at senior levels of the organization, some progress has been registered. In 2000, building on the momentum of the Millennium Declaration, the Fourth World Conference on Women held in Beijing in 1995, and the 1997 creation of the Office of the Special Advisor on Gender Issues and Advancement of Women, the Security Council approved resolution 1325. This marked a turning point in the UN's commitment to gender mainstreaming and addressing the impact of war on women.

Recognizing that women have a vital role in conflict resolution and peace-building, and that peace is directly linked to equality between men and women, the resolution urged member states and the secretary-general to mainstream a gender perspective and to appoint more women to decision-making positions at all levels, but particularly senior levels, of institutions. A 2006 assessment of the resolution's implementation noted, however, that women remained under-represented in senior level positions at the UN, with only one female special representative and one envoy.[12] Certain member countries, such as Canada and Liberia, have heeded the call to implement gender mainstreaming and have made conscious and public gestures to appoint women to decision-making positions in government. Liberia, led by Ellen Johnson-Sirleaf—a former international civil servant and the first democratically elected female head of state in Africa—has appointed women to the ministerial posts of defense, finance, sports and youth, justice, and commerce, as well as chief of police and president of the Liberian Truth and Reconciliation Commission. These notable efforts to ensure women are well-represented in decision making should serve as an example for the United Nations.

Human Rights: "Outside-Insiders," Rotation, Contracts

For the human rights field, three examples will be examined here: the use of outsiders; field rotation; and fewer permanent contracts. They demonstrate the need for, and real possibility of, essential changes that also have a wider relevance and applicability.

"Outside-Insiders"
One considerable constraint on UN officials is their status as full-time employees of the international civil service—a status that invites close scrutiny by member states that might be offended by human rights advocacy. With their jobs and family security on the line, officials often avoid not only robust public

confrontation, but even more gentle confrontations away from the limelight.

One possible solution is suggested by the work in relation to internally displaced persons, which has essentially been accomplished by a special representative with a UN title and privileges but who remains outside the UN and without a salary.[13] I outlined earlier the history of conceptualizing internal displacement and the consequences of framing the idea of sovereignty as responsibility. In this discussion, I draw attention to the structural relationship with the UN.

Francis Deng's mandate (1992–2004) as the special representative of the secretary-general (SRSG) was intertwined with the Project on Internal Displacement (PID). His back-up secretariat was directed by Deng himself and Roberta Cohen at the Brookings Institution—and a similar arrangement has continued with Walter Kälin since 2004. The conceptualization of internal displacement made a notable contribution to contemporary thinking about international relations, in particular by reframing the central component of theory and practice—state sovereignty. In addition, *Guidelines on Internal Displacement*, an important piece of soft law, was agreed; and UN institutions and NGOs established special programs for this ignored category of war victim.

A crucial variable was that Deng always had a foot in two camps—taking advantage of being both within the intergovernmental system of the United Nations and outside it. He made good use of having both official *and* private platforms. As someone who has thought about how to get research applied, Richard Haass—now president of the Council on Foreign Relations but formerly director of policy planning at the State Department and vice-president of the Brookings Institution—summed up the intriguing advantages of such an arrangement: "Many of us spend a lot of time figuring out how to get ideas into policy-makers' hands, but Francis had a ready-made solution."[14] The impact of "outside-insiders" on advancing previously unacceptable frameworks, policies, or legal standards is worth pondering for other parts of the UN system where controversy is omni-present and rule-breaking initiatives are in short supply.

The mandate and the PID are intertwined to such an extent that it is difficult to say definitively whether Deng and Cohen conducted themselves as outside-insiders or inside-outsiders. Indeed, they collectively wore whichever hat was most convenient and effective in advancing a particular issue. In the words of the former deputy high commissioner for human rights, Bertrand Ramcharan, the success of this effort represents "the power of the voice of the UN system mixed with independence."[15] In adapting to changed political and institutional landscapes, the role of inside-outsiders and outside-insiders is one that could be emulated by others, perhaps with a comparable impact on research, policy, law, and norms.

Without an official and assessed UN budget, Deng and Cohen were able to move a controversial idea that clashed directly with the high politics of state sovereignty quickly and effectively into the intergovernmental arena. "Model" is perhaps too grandiose a description, but we are looking through a special window into the world of normative and policy change in the international arena. Of special relevance is the financial autonomy to develop a strategy and accompanying tactics. On the one hand, the phenomenon of internal displacement requires governments to take seriously their responsibilities toward human rights; and thus Deng's work was associated intimately with the United Nations. On the other hand, since there is a genuine necessity to defend what he has described as a "quasi-independent" status when engaging and confronting the thuggish policies and behavior of many states, such confrontation requires distance from the world organization.

The PID's base at a public policy think-tank working in tandem with universities allows it a respectable distance from governments and from predictable multilateral diplomatic pressure, processes, and procedures. Rather than maintaining the status quo, the expectation is that the project's activities will extend the outer limits of what passes for conventional wisdom in mainstream diplomatic circles. At the same time, the SRSG can also make use of the UN's official platforms, including in the corridors of the Security Council.

Such an approach requires "soft" resources, because policy institutes and universities rarely devote "hard" tuition income or endowments to subsidize researchers and non-instructional personnel. For its very existence, the PID required support from a wide range of private and public donors. The 2004 and 2005 budgets were approximately $2 million, but earlier operating budgets typically varied from $500,000 to $800,000— by any standard trivial sums in relation to what the PID accomplished. This is not the only topic on the international agenda for which resources do not match the long list of responsibilities enshrined in UN resolutions. But IDPs lie at the far end of a spectrum, representing an extremely ambitious mandate virtually without any guaranteed regular funds.

While being on the "outside" has its disadvantages— among others, no guaranteed budget or access—the blend of outsider-insider offers advantages that could and should be replicated for other controversial issues where independent research is required, institutional protective barriers are high, normative gaps exist, and political hostility is widespread. For instance, we saw earlier that the successful negotiation of the landmine ban took up a hot issue and nurtured a political constituency around an emerging norm. In his behind-the-scenes analysis of that process, Don Hubert specifically compares the Ottawa process leading to the ban of antipersonnel landmines with the process leading to the *Guiding Principles*.[16] More part-time, senior officials pushing from their independent bases outside the United Nations would strengthen many policy formulation processes.

Rotation to the Field

Many readers will have encountered the world organization through a tour at, or pictures of, UN headquarters in New York or Geneva, or of specialized agencies like UNESCO in Paris or FAO in Rome. But the bulk of the UN's operations are in the field in developing countries. A problem for staff morale and competence over the years has been that promotions are mainly the result of work and contacts in pleasant headquarters settings, whereas the real challenges lie with delivery of services in the field. Furthermore, the organization is increasingly called upon to react to major crises by sending staff to emergencies at very short notice. How can the United Nations recruit and train the people whom it needs?

Perhaps the most challenging requirement is to have a flexible personnel policy to meet the unforeseen (although predictable) demands of new crises. UNHCR, UNICEF, and UNDP all have mandatory mobility and staff rotation policies, and similar policies should be a requirement across the UN system. In 1982, UNHCR implemented the first formal rotation policy in order to promote burden-sharing among staff members and to ensure that all take part in postings to more difficult duty stations where families are not usually permitted. All international professional staff recruited on indefinite appointments are subject to rotation; and the Joint Inspection Unit, for one, has cited the policy as a model for replication, which is why it is reviewed here.[17]

UNHCR ranks duty stations on factors such as safety and security, access to healthcare, education and basic services, degree of isolation, and climate. Duty stations are placed in one of six categories according to degree of hardship; field stations are ranked from A to E, with E being the most difficult, and there is a special designation, H, for headquarters. Staff serving in stations B through E are entitled to special monetary hardship allowances in addition to their salaries; and there is an accelerated home leave travel scheme (staff are entitled to paid trips to their home countries once a year as opposed to once every two years) for those in categories C through E. Those serving in war zones or particularly dangerous locations are also entitled to special hazard pay, and for those in non-family duty stations (those deemed unsafe for family members, normally D and E duty stations) there are special leave schemes such as VARS (voluntary absence for the relief of stress) and MARS (mandatory absence for the relief of stress).

Depending on the degree of hardship, staff are assigned to stations for varying periods. Postings to H and A duty stations normally last four to five years, while staff placed in D or E duty stations are normally permitted to rotate to other more desirable duty stations after only one or two years. The rotation policy ensures that staff are not condemned only to difficult duty stations or, conversely, are not allowed to remain indefinitely in the more desirable H or A duty stations.

The mandatory rotation policy creates a sense of equity among staff members and ensures that the vast majority of them are exposed to the field and have some training in the kinds of management skills that might be called upon with little advance warning in future emergencies. The secretary-general's 2006 *Investing in the United Nations* identified promotion and mobility among staff as one of the key strategies for investing in people. He also proposed that the majority of international professional posts be designated as rotational and that staff mobility between headquarters and the field be implemented as a matter of priority. There is much in the experience of UNHCR that could usefully inform personnel policy more generally across the system. Kofi Annan described this wrenching effort as "a radical overhaul of the United Nations Secretariat—its rules, its structure, and its systems and culture."[18] This is not an exaggeration; and unlike other recommendations, it has already been demonstrated to work in practice as well as theory.

Fewer Permanent Contracts

The League of Nations instituted permanent contracts—a practice continued by the United Nations—in order to protect staff who deal with contentious political issues from government pressure and to protect anyone from arbitrary dismissal. Permanent contracts thus have the same justification as university tenure. And both have critics for the same reasons, namely that removing the possibility of being fired can also lead to employees coasting along rather than maintaining or increasing productivity. There remains a widespread perception that such contractual arrangements do not stimulate but rather retard productivity because they do not favor contracting or retaining risk-takers. The result, too often, is an excess of "deadwood." On balance, permanent contracts in the UN system do more harm than good.

During Kofi Annan's 10 years in office, permanent contracts were increasingly phased out. Three types of contracts replaced them: short term—up to a maximum of six months to meet work loads and specific short-term requirements; fixed term—renewable up to a maximum of five years; and continuing—to be granted to staff who have served on fixed term for five years and met the highest standards of efficiency, competence, and integrity.[19]

While institutional memory may be well served by veteran officials, the number of persons with "continuing" contracts (basically the equivalent of "permanent") should be kept to a minimum across the system. Currently standing at about 13 percent of the total,[20] they should be reserved for a very limited number of administrators and be avoided for substantive jobs, especially within highly controversial areas. Within the human rights field in particular, an argument could be made that virtually no one should have a long-term contract. If a staff member, especially a senior one, were doing his or her job, many member states should be irritated and be asking for his or her head. Indeed, the fact that human rights officials would have only fixed assignments would put pressure on them to make a mark before exiting and to use the bully-pulpit to maximum effect. There are more than enough qualified persons worldwide to fill such UN posts for fixed periods of time. While there are problems that may be created by adopting this approach—for instance, possible loss of continuity and institutional memory—they are outweighed by the benefits.

By placing the emphasis on fixed-term contracts, the world organization would have a guaranteed influx of younger and hungry staff. They would be anxious to make a mark and a contribution within a short period of time as a first step in a career in international affairs, rather than seeking the guaranteed benefits of a lifelong UN position regardless of subsequent performance.

Sustainable Development: Ideas, the Next Generation

As the reader should by now be aware, the bulk of the UN's staff and resources are devoted to activities designed to foster sustainable development. Despite substantial efforts over the last six decades, the litany of failures is clear. We live in a world with widening extremes in wealth and income and with almost half the global population surviving on incomes equivalent to less than $2 a day.[21] As a result of substantial progress in Asia (mainly in China and India), the number of people living on $1 a day, worldwide, fell slightly from about 1.3 billion in 1990 to

1.2 billion in 2001, although in sub-Saharan Africa it rose from about 230 to 315 million. While the global poverty rate fell, the absolute number of people living on less than $2 a day actually rose from 2.7 to 2.8 billion. The gaps between the richest and the poorest countries have widened over the past two centuries.[22] The poorest and least developed countries have gained least, and in the last two decades a score or more have even slipped back from levels achieved in the 1970s.

At the same time, UN development efforts have also contributed to genuine advances in human welfare. Average life expectancy has increased to double the estimated level of the late 1930s. Child mortality has been lowered by more than three-quarters. Adult literacy has been raised to nearly three-quarters, with basic education extended to over 85 percent of the world's children. Malnutrition has been reduced in all regions of the world except Africa. As we saw earlier, smallpox was eradicated by 1977; and the scourges of yaws, guinea worm, and polio have been virtually eliminated.

In this section, two possible solutions suggest themselves for what ails the United Nations in its development efforts. Better ideas and younger staff are crucial to help ensure that the United Nations comes close to the aspirations set out in the Charter. From the earliest days, the world body very much sought to remain in the forefront of the contemporary human struggle to fill the development glass a bit fuller. There are ways to ensure that the level rises.

Ideas Matter: the Human Development Report

The relevance of John Maynard Keynes's famous statement about the power of ideas is hard to deny. Even so-called practical men and women who think they have no time to read are often acting on the basis of the theories of dead "scribblers." As Keynes wrote: "the ideas of economists and political philosophers, both when they are right and when they are wrong, are more powerful than is commonly understood."[23] If such ideas are essential to human progress, how can the UN improve its production of them?

Powerful minds—those who have the courage to break rules and are encouraged to do so—are essential. Such staff members as Hans Singer, Raúl Prebisch, and W. Arthur Lewis are paragons. The launch by UNDP of the *Human Development Report* in 1990 provides us with a more recent example of an underappreciated variable: intellectual output. This report continues to put forth an annual view of people-centered development. "Human development" is defined as the process of strengthening human capabilities and broadening choices so as to enable people to live the lives that they have reason to value. The market is not ignored, but participation, empowerment, equity, and justice are placed on an equal footing with growth.

The annual report has sometimes stressed human rights, sometimes women, sometimes ecology. It ranks countries not just by GDP per capita, but by a more complex formula attempting to measure quality of life. Wealth and prosperity loom large, of course, but so do education and medical care. Various indices seek to measure discrimination against women, not only legally and politically but also in terms of basic health and education.

Mahbub ul Haq, the Pakistani UN economist who had the vision to create the *Human Development Report*, died in 1998, but not before he ensured the continued existence of its controversial approach. A useful step toward more people-centered development was to create indicators for ranking countries for their performance on the Human Development Index (HDI), a composite measure based on three indicators: longevity, as measured by life expectancy at birth; educational attainment, as measured by a combination of adult literacy and the combined gross primary, secondary, and tertiary enrolment ratio; and access to the resources needed for a decent standard of living, measured by real per capita income (or what is called purchasing power parity, PPP$). It ranks countries from 1 to 177. In 2007, Norway was number one, the United States was in eighth place, and Niger and Sierra Leone brought up the rear.

As might be imagined, calling a spade a shovel in numerical terms does not always gain friends and fans among governments that fare less well than they thought they should have. In the *Human Development Report 1999*, Nobel laureate Amartya Sen, who has been associated with the effort from the outset, wrote about his initial skepticism on the merits of the HDI as an alternative indicator to growth. The intrinsic difficulty for Sen was the attempt "to catch in one simple number a complex reality about human development and deprivation."[24] He later spelled out in more detail what he meant: "The *Human Development Reports*, under Mahbub ul Haq's visionary leadership, consolidated the criticisms that had emerged in the literature on heavy reliance on the GNP and such commodity-based indicators, which was standard practice when Mahbub got going."[25]

In a different version of a temperamental outsider becoming a temporary UN insider, ul Haq and others in the office also took the political flack from governments irritated by the publicity their embarrassing positions in the rankings attracted.[26] Many such governments resented the fact that poorer neighbors actually got higher ratings because they were better at making decisions about priorities, having devoted more of their limited resources to education and health instead of spending them on weapons. Moreover, the methodology used by UNDP to establish its comparative ratings was, in fact, sometimes open to serious criticism.

Certainly, some UNDP staff members were keen on the approach, including UNDP administrator William Draper, but the technical details were the work of outsiders and scholars. Indeed, many governments disputed the appropriateness of Draper's using their financial contributions to commission research that resulted in embarrassing comparative data. Some talked rudely about "biting the hand that feeds."

At all levels of the world organization there should be persons capable of such intellectual leadership, and this is far more likely to come from fixed-term officials, specialized consultants, and academics on leave, than from permanent civil servants whose careers are partially dependent upon reactions from superiors and governments, and who do not have time to stay abreast of the analytical literature and other developments in the worlds of policy and scholarship. This means strengthening the institutional capacity to generate and disseminate original ideas—in short, to fortify mechanisms that ensure creative thinking.[27]

In the myriad official proposals for UN reform, none has emphasized the vital intellectual dimensions of the world organization. Yet many assessments of the UN system, including anecdotal appraisals, have concluded that a lack of knowledge has undermined the ability of the organization to recognize markers of instability and deploy suitable responses—primarily diplomatic, but in some cases also involving economic tools (aid versus sanctions) or military enforcement. Research since 1999 undertaken by the independent United Nations Intellectual History Project has documented the lasting legacy of both principled and operational ideas and norms.

The world organization should invest in analytic capabilities for three reasons. First, hard-hitting evaluations are a prerequisite to better planning, to developing measurements of performance, and to holding personnel accountable. Second, up-to-date and well-grounded analysis is critical to addressing the shortfalls in strategic planning during times of crisis that quickly produce incoherent and undesirable outcomes. Third, investing in analytic capabilities to produce, refine, and disseminate digestible research better prepares the United Nations at both individual and organizational levels for challenges, known and unknown.

Would this be so difficult? Specific measures are required to strengthen this aspect of the UN in the immediate future, but they are not pie-in-the-sky aspirations. The two suggestions that follow are "Track II"-type reforms that do not require constitutional changes (that is, official approval by member states) or even additional resources. They do, however, require a degree of vision and courage on the part of the secretary-general and other heads of agencies.

First, all parts of the UN system should acknowledge straightforwardly that contributions to ideas, thinking, analysis, and monitoring in their areas of international action should be *the* major emphasis of their work. To this end, the UN needs to foster an environment that encourages and rewards creative thinking of the highest caliber. This has implications for recruitment and promotion, it being especially crucial to assemble under one roof professionals from different disciplines and from different national and cultural backgrounds. The quality of staff is essential, and no compromise can be justified in ensuring the highest standards of competence and professional qualifications.

Second, the mobilization of more financial support for research, analysis, and policy exploration should be a top priority. The terms for providing such resources are of special importance—not only are longer-term availability and flexibility necessary, but, more crucially, in order to guarantee autonomy there should be no strings attached. Part of this exercise will consist in strengthening the means to disseminate new ideas. UN outreach with a core of key reports is sometimes impressive, but too many languish on bookshelves and coffee tables or in filing cabinets. Discussion of findings should take place not only in intergovernmental meetings but also in national capitals with governments, and within such diverse constituencies as business, the media, and members of civil society.

Investing in the Next Generation

Launched in the 1960s by UNDP to recruit young and qualified staff to the United Nations, the Junior Professional Officer (JPO) program currently provides nearly 13 percent of UNDP's international staff.[28] JPOs are selected and sponsored (i.e., fully funded) by their governments to work for a fixed period of time (usually two to three years) in the United Nations. The program has become the key entry point for a career—in the UN or elsewhere in the international arena—for a growing number of international professional staff, and has been adopted by numerous other UN agencies, including UNICEF, UNHCR, and WFP. Other agencies have adopted similar programs under different titles—e.g., the IMF's Economist Program and the Asian Development Bank's Young Professional Program.

UN agencies have also implemented new programs for recruiting younger staff. For example, UNHCR has created the International Professional Roster to fill gaps in staffing that arise when suitable internal candidates cannot be identified. Those interested in being added to the roster must fulfill a number of requirements, including passing an entry test, and be willing to work in the harshest duty stations.

There are no silver bullets—indeed, some observers criticize the fact that JPO programs offer a jump-start to the careers of nationals from wealthy countries, a shortcoming that could be, and in some cases already has been, overcome by creative financing for individuals from developing countries. What is essential, however, is to use these or other means to lower the average age at the professional entry level (currently 37) and the average age of the secretariat as a whole (currently 46) over the next five years, when about 15 percent of the total staff will reach retirement age.

Adlai Stevenson once joked that diplomacy at the United Nations involves "protocol, Geritol and alcohol."[29] While little can be done to reduce diplomatic procedures and the consumption of fermented beverages, sclerosis is a guarantee of mediocrity for the secretariat. The world organization should find ways to infuse new blood continually.

The Way Forward

The second UN has been the subject of this chapter's analysis not because therein lies the main illness—the lack of political will and myopia of the first UN of member states clearly wins that award—but because it can and therefore should be changed. Indeed, in spite of the myriad problems laid out in these pages, the UN's residual legitimacy and the mere idea of international cooperation actually keep a surprisingly large number of competent people committed to its work. But the potential is far from realized. James O. C. Jonah, an international civil servant for over three decades, including a stint as head of personnel, tells us:

> It is a common practice of politicians to blame the civil service for their failures and inadequacies. More often than not, their citizens join them in complaining about the evils and sloppiness of bloated bureaucracies. The UN Secretariat is not immune to such criticisms, and over the years all and sundry have decried its waste and ineffectiveness. Despite these complaints about perceived defects, it would be inconceivable for member states to contemplate the dismantling of the Secretariat or parts of it. Surely, they would not abolish their own civil services despite their dissatisfaction?[30]

Renewing and reinvigorating the secretariat is critical as we move toward the second decade of the twenty-first century. In a series of follow-up reports to *Investing in the United Nations*, Kofi Annan lamented the "silos" that characterize staff appointments and promotions and spelled out his "vision of an independent international civil service with the highest standards of performance and accountability. The Secretariat of the future will be an integrated, field-oriented, operational Organization."[31] The so-called Four Nations (Chile, South Africa, Sweden, and Thailand) Initiative (FNI) sought to come up with consensus proposals for improved governance and management of the secretariat. Human resources were not originally a focus, but they "came to the fore" during conversations with other member states. While predictably the FNI expressed concern about "geographical representation," the main thrust of their 2007 recommendations pointed to "merit-based" recruitment and the use of "expert hearings" for the most senior positions that "should not be monopolized by nationals of any state or group of states."[32]

The international civil service can and should be fixed.

Conclusion: What's Next?

The book began with a discussion of John Godfrey Saxe's fable "The Blind Men and the Elephant," in which six visually challenged individuals attempt, and ultimately fail, to describe an elephant to one another's satisfaction. Transforming the current United Nations into an institution capable of addressing the challenges that threaten human survival poses a similar challenge: diagnoses of what ails the UN reflect a wide variety of perceptions—indeed, a variety of realities depending on the viewers' analytical lenses.

These pages reflect the perspective of someone who has both worked in the institution itself for 10 years, and analyzed its behavior and misbehavior for almost four decades. The first four chapters contain my diagnoses of four essential shortcomings in the United Nations: unreconstructed Westphalian state sovereignty; empty North–South confrontation; the feudal nature of the so-called UN system; and the troubled international civil service. The next four chapters extend the medical analogy from identification to prognoses that could mitigate problems and suggest how the UN's institutional ills might be "cured" or at least alleviated: redefining national interests; moving beyond the theater of North–South relations; consolidating and centralizing international efforts; and reinvigorating the secretariat.

At the end of this journey, I permit myself a subjective moment involving less academic inhibition and more reflective passion. Readers should not be put off by what may strike them as such a puffed-up billing. In a self-critical essay, I argue that we have strayed too far from the kind of paradigmatic rethinking of human relations that is absolutely crucial if we are to solve the more intractable problems faced by the United Nations.

Much of the preceding analysis might very well even "depress Dr. Pangloss," the character in Voltaire's *Candide* who believes that all is for the best in this best of all possible worlds. The gaps are enormous between what is on the books— spelled out in the UN Charter, treaties, or public statements by UN officials and national diplomats—and what actually transpires. This final chapter examines the growing familiarity of the concept of global governance before moving on to a discussion of the absence of contemporary thinking about world government.

What is Global Governance?

The notion of world government is decidedly old-fashioned; mainstream thinking about the future of international cooperation has shifted decidedly away from beefing up the United Nations and other intergovernmental organizations and toward "global governance."[1] The coinage of this term in the 1990s reflected an interesting marriage between academic and policy concerns. James Rosenau and Ernst Czempiel's theoretical *Governance without Government* was published in 1992, just about the same time that the policy-oriented Commission on Global Governance under the chairmanship of Sonny Ramphal and Igmar Carlsson began its deliberations. In 1995, the publication of its report, *Our Global Neighbourhood*,[2] coincided with the first issue of the quarterly refereed journal that I helped get off the ground and later edited, *Global Governance: A Review of Multilateralism and International Organization*, whose subscribers are both scholars and practitioners.

As we have seen, the importance of international organization in contemporary world politics is highlighted by many analysts of international relations—especially those identifying themselves as liberal institutionalists and constructivists. Yet we have also observed that the evolution of intergovernmental institutions to facilitate robust international responses lags considerably behind burgeoning collective problems with trans-border dimensions, especially those that are worldwide in scope or potentially so. And the evolution has been especially disappointing in the most representative and universal of such institutions, those of the United Nations system.

While there is much talk of "prevention," anticipating problems before they overwhelm us is not a strength of our species and even less so of the system of states. About the best that we can hope for is playing catch-up in the face of life-menacing threats. So, for example, dramatic climate change and environmental deterioration, weapons proliferation and run-away technology, massive poverty and pandemics, lethal ethnic clashes and destabilizing financial flows have compelled states to react, to cope, and eventually to agree under duress to construct the feeble intergovernmental organizations that we have.

Perhaps there have always been too few such institutions, and perhaps they have always arrived too late on the scene with too little punch. But in the twenty-first century, the nature of many of the collective problems threatening the planet suggests that we must build more robust intergovernmental institutions with greater scope and resources, and very soon indeed. As the US civil rights champion Martin Luther King, Jr., pointed out in a famous 1967 address at Riverside Church: "Over the bleached bones and jumbled residues of numerous civilizations are written the pathetic words: 'Too late.'"[3]

Not to put too fine a point on it, the market will not graciously provide the kinds of global institutions required to ensure human survival with dignity. Adam Smith's "invisible hand" does not operate to solve problems among states; and the supply of global public goods lags far behind the demand. That said, the state remains essential for national, regional, and global problem-solving, and nothing in this book gainsays this stark reality. Yet put simply, states and their creations in the form of the current generation of intergovernmental bureaucracies cannot address the transnational problems confronting the world. As a result, and ironically, we have embraced global governance.

Governance is the sum of laws, procedures, norms, policies, and institutions that define and constitute relations among citizens, the market, and the state. It is the glue of societies, both informal and formal values, norms, practices, and institutions that provide more order than occurs spontaneously. The substance of governance thus is the sum of purposeful systems of rules and norms that ensure order, or at least a better order than would be likely if we relied only upon purely formal regulations and public institutions.

Of course, confusion may arise from the fact that the Latin root of governance, *gubernare*, is the same for the units that we study as political scientists. So, traditionally, "governance" has been closely associated with "governing" and "government"— that is, with political authority, institutions, and control. Governance in that sense encompasses formal political institutions that aim to coordinate and control interdependent social relations and that also possess the capacity to enforce decisions. However, we now routinely use "governance" to denote a mushier notion applied to the planet as a whole. It captures the regulation of interdependent relations in the *absence* of any overarching political authority and with institutions that have virtually no power to compel behavior or exert effective control in the international system.[4]

Quite a difference exists, then, between the national and international versions of governance. At the national level, we have governance *plus* government which, whatever its short-comings in countries like Mexico or the United States, can usually exert authority and control as well as secure wide-spread compliance. At the international level, however, we have governance *minus* government, which means precious little, if any, authority or control to ensure compliance with collective decisions about providing global public goods.

Further confusion may arise because international financial institutions have labeled as "good governance" a host of policies designed to counteract the top-down, anti-market state policies of the 1960s, 1970s, and 1980s. Here, the term "governance" incorporates or implies participation and empowerment with respect to public policies, choices, and offices; the rule of law and an independent judiciary to which the executive and legislative branches of government are subject along with citizens and other actors and entities; and standards of probity and incorruptibility, transparency, accountability, and responsibility. Good governance thus has a normative connotation—as a practice distinct from and opposed to the corrupt centralized state of an earlier era.

And so, what of "global governance"? For me, it refers to collective efforts to identify, understand, or address worldwide problems that go beyond the capacity of individual states to solve. Global governance reflects the capacity of the international system at any moment to provide government-like services in the absence of a world government—the capacity, in short, for collective problem-solving to bring more orderly and reliable responses to international social and political problems than would occur naturally. It can be good, bad, or indifferent, but global governance encompasses an extremely wide variety of cooperative problem-solving arrangements. These may be visible but informal (e.g., practices or guidelines) or result from temporary units (e.g., coalitions of the willing). But the arrangements may also be far more formal, taking the shape of hard rules (laws and treaties) as well as institutions with administrative structures and practices established to manage collective affairs through a variety of actors, including state authorities, intergovernmental organizations, nongovernmental organizations, private sector entities, and other civil society actors.

Thus, global governance consists of the complex of formal *and* informal institutions, mechanisms, relationships, and processes between and among states, markets, citizens, and organizations through which collective international interests are *occasionally* articulated, collective international rights and obligations are *occasionally* established, collective international differences are *occasionally* mediated, and collective international problems are *occasionally* solved.

That is a mouthful. The emphasis is on "occasionally" rather than "routinely"—the adverb I would have used had we been describing national governance. As has been indicated but is worth repeating, at the national level we have governance plus government. And, despite well-known weaknesses, lapses, and inabilities to exert absolute control, the expectation is that existing institutions—in Berlin, New Delhi, Brasilia, or Johannesburg—are routinely expected to exert authority and control. For the globe as a whole, we have only the feeblest imitation: institutions that routinely help ensure certain daily services (e.g., postage rates and airline regulations), but which do almost nothing to help address life-threatening problems (e.g., climate change or ethnic cleansing).

There are two reasons why the term "global governance" emerged in the face of extremely weak intergovernmental institutions with no real authority. First, beginning in the 1970s, growing economic interdependence and rapid technological advances fostered a recognition of problems that defy solutions by a single state. The development of a consciousness about the human environment and especially the 1972

Stockholm conference are usually seen as key developments in this evolution, but there are many other examples ranging from population explosion to nuclear proliferation. The environmental examples, however, are especially apt to illustrate why we are in the same boat: it is simply impossible—in spite of laudable actions like attempted environmental legislation in California—to halt global warming or acid rain through isolated actions.

Second, and equally important, the growing interest in global governance also reflected the sheer growth in numbers and importance of nonstate actors (both civil society and market). Intergovernmental organizations like the UN no longer occupy the center stage for students of international organization. They are not the only act in town. Indeed, this reality was symbolized by the creation of the Global Compact at the Millennium Summit of 2000, when the private sector—both the for-profit and the not-for-profit species—was recognized as a necessary partner for states and the United Nations.

The increased influence of nonstate actors along with technological advances and various forms of interdependence mean that state-centric structures (i.e., either states or their creations in intergovernmental organizations, especially those of the UN system) are no longer seen as having a natural monopoly over collective efforts to improve international society and world order. They share the governance stage with a host of other actors.

For those trying to understand how human beings might better address global problems in the absence of robust UN organizations, global governance became the preferred lens through which to examine contemporary world affairs. Global governance can best be thought of as referring to the various patterns in which actors—public and private, and at the global, regional, national, and local levels—come together to solve problems in the absence of centralized government-like authority. To borrow an image from James Rosenau, there is a "crazy quilt"[5] of authority that is constantly shifting, forming a patchwork of institutional elements that varies by sector and over time. Perhaps a better image, however, might be Gertrude Stein's characterization of Oakland: "there's no there, there." Or perhaps better still would be the Cheshire cat in *Alice in Wonderland*, a head floating with no body, no real substance, basically an ethereal reality in terms of authority. But the UN system with universal state membership and mechanisms for involving nonstate actors is as close as we have got to a central clearing house for information and action.

To state the obvious, contemporary global governance is highly uneven, often giving the impression of coverage but not necessarily with effect. Appearances can be deceiving: a well-populated institutional terrain can mask a lack of coherence, substance, and accomplishment. We may persuade ourselves that we are making progress when we are merely treading water or, worse, drowning by wasting time and energy rather than moving from danger toward safety.

I define global governance in the following way: the totality of institutions, policies, rules, practices, norms, procedures, and initiatives by which states and their citizens try to bring order and predictability to their responses to such universal problems as warfare, poverty, and environmental degradation.

What Happened to World Government?

For many analysts, global governance overlaps with the rise of international organizations, both intergovernmental and nongovernmental. These institutions, according to Craig Murphy's masterful history of global governance beginning in the nineteenth century, are customarily seen as "what world government we actually have."[6] Murphy is right, but the crux of the problem is elsewhere. To repeat, at the national level we have the authoritative structures of government supple-mented by governance. Internationally, however, we simply have governance with some architectural drawings that are over six decades old and not up to present building codes, along with unstable ground and shifting foundations for the institutions that we need to build.

The United Nations is a makeshift expedient, the best orga-nizational structure to date which our feeble imaginations (and certainly those of politicians and diplomats) have been able to imagine for addressing problems that cannot be solved by states within the existing multilateral system. While it was not originally conceived as a world government, neither was it the creation of pie-in-the-sky idealists. As one historian notes, "its wartime architects bequeathed us this system as a realist necessity vital in times of trial, not as a liberal accessory to be discarded when the going gets rough."[7]

But one significant change is noticeable in the contempo-rary landscape of internationalists. Not only is there no world government or likely to be one in my lifetime, but the goal of most contemporary proponents of global governance—unlike many earlier analysts of international organization—is *no longer* the creation of world government.[8] This is a dramatic change in relation to the more idealistic generations of the past, for whom such thinking was not anathema and indeed was not even far from mainstream.

Beginning with Dante's *Monarchia* at the beginning of the fourteenth century, there is a long tradition of criticizing the existing state system (at that time only European) and replac-ing it with a universal government.[9] The idealist tradition also includes Hugo Grotius, the Dutch jurist whose *On the Laws of War and Peace* (1625) usually qualifies him as the "father" of international law; Emeric Cruce, the French monk who died in the same year the Peace of Westphalia was struck, and who had dreamed of a world court, a place for nations to meet and work out disputes, and disarmament; and, of course, Immanuel Kant, whose *Perpetual Peace* (1795) envisioned a confederation of democratic and pacific states.

The late Harold Jacobson, an international organization scholar from the University of Michigan, noted that this view of world government was woven into the tapestries in the *Palais des Nations* in Geneva—the headquarters of the League of Nations and now the UN's European Office. He observed that they "picture the process of humanity combining into ever larger and more stable units for the purpose of governance— first the family, then the tribe, then the city-state, and then the nation—a process which presumably would eventually culminate in the entire world being combined in one political unit."[10]

This now seems quaint. Starry-eyed optimists seem almost extinct, although from time to time a visible contemporary international relations theorist, Alexander Wendt for instance, will suggest that "a world state is inevitable."[11] Or an international lawyer like Richard Falk will call for an irrevocable transfer of sovereignty upwards.[12] For such proponents, current UN institutions constitute the precursors of that world state.

Such perspectives, however, definitely represent a minority view, and nothing covered in the present volume would lead one even to hope for such an outcome. Most analysts of global governance view world government as a distinctly old-fashioned concept, simply indicative of an idealism that is now beyond the pale. To hazard such a view is seen as naive at best, and demented at worst.

Where does that leave us? I see global governance as providing a half-way house between the international anarchy underlying Realist analysis and a world state. The current generation of intergovernmental institutions and procedures help overcome structural obstacles to international cooperation—that this matters is clear to anyone looking at the responses to the

2004 tsunami or to ongoing humanitarian crises. We can observe a wonderful constellation of helping hands—soldiers from a variety of countries, UN organizations, large and small NGOs, and even Wal-Mart.

To that degree, Realists miss many elements of cooperation and possible solutions. At the same time, their emphasis on the absence of central authority and, to use John Mearsheimer's expression, the "false promise of international institutions"—at least the current generation—is on target.[13] Global governance certainly is not the continuation of traditional power politics. But neither is it the expression of an evolutionary process necessarily leading to the formation of an institutional structure able to address contemporary let alone future global threats.

The disappearance of the passion for strengthening intergovernmental institutions appears to be the downside of pursuing enhanced global governance through nonstate actors. Most of us are certainly not complacent about what is at stake, or satisfied that global governance can accomplish what a world government could. Rather, our approach reflects a judgment about how to spend limited analytical energies in the immediate term.

Nonetheless, I continually remind myself that E. H. Carr, the father of the Realists,[14] recommended a mixture of utopia and power in order to avoid stagnation and despair. A vision of where ideally we should be headed is necessary, for without it we risk going nowhere. By abandoning a utopian vision of world government, we should ask ourselves whether we are throwing out the baby with the bath water. At a minimum, without such a vision, we risk accepting and strengthening the contours of the current unacceptable international system, including the feeble United Nations. By not imagining a fundamentally different system, we make the continuation of the current lackluster one all the more inevitable. Even among those considered modestly enlightened on matters of international relations, we are, alas, no longer even imagining what is required beyond tinkering with current institutions. This is ironic, to say the least.

Three important features distinguish global governance from earlier thinking about collective responses to international problems, and they have serious implications for how we act because they restrict our thinking and advocacy. First, many analysts viewed the development of international cooperation and law not only as a step in the right direction, and as more effective than unilateral efforts and the law of the jungle, but also as an unstoppable progression. But it was still typical to recognize—even for a rabid world federalist—that a powerful state could solve certain problems on its own, or at least could insulate itself from most outside menaces.

Earlier efforts to eradicate malaria within a geographic area by preventing those affected from entering a territory are qualitatively different from attempts to halt terrorist money-laundering or acid rain, or numerous other contemporary threats. Today, no state, no matter how powerful, can guarantee success in protecting its population from such threats. Earlier problems could be addressed by a rich state within its own borders, and by erecting effective barriers, but a growing number of today's "problems without passports" respect no such boundaries. Yet, we no longer see the necessity of increased international cooperation as indicative of a continuing march forward. Many even ask whether, in light of what's wrong with the UN, we should dismantle the world organization itself.

Second, earlier conceptual efforts emphasized the state and only grudgingly admitted the presence and capacities of other actors. But starting in the 1980s, and earlier in some cases, both civil society and market-oriented groups were recognized as having a crucial impact and reach. They were more systematically embraced and became an increasingly integral part of comprehensive solutions either promulgated or actually undertaken by the United Nations and many of its member states. But while they remain absolutely essential, we have gone overboard in our enthusiasm for nonstate actors. NGOs and corporations will not eliminate poverty, fix global warming, or halt the slaughter in Darfur. By thinking otherwise, we are grasping firmly some very thin reeds.

Third, we continue to celebrate ad hoc approaches and pragmatism, but to what end? For "one-off" problems, ad hoc solutions are acceptable. But several decades after the recognition of many types of interdependence, and amidst the proliferation of both for-profit and non-profit institutions, the approach of cobbling together solutions and ad hoc coalitions appears increasingly tenuous, even if that is all we seem to be able to do or even imagine. Recurrent problems require predictable and institutionalized responses, but intergovernmental institutions are rarely central to our visioning, to our imagining.

Given the burgeoning numbers of NGOs and corporations, many with impressive resources and problem-solving energies, robust intergovernmental institutions now often seem almost an afterthought, even in "cutting edge" international relations, organization, and law. They should not be. The current generation of such institutions is inadequate, and we have to do more than throw up our hands and hope for the best from norm entrepreneurs, activists crossing borders, members of the Global Compact, and transnational social networks.

Global governance is an intriguing analytical tool—if I were choosing an expensive word, I would say a good "heuristic" device—to understand what *is* happening in today's world. At the same time, I am beginning to feel uncomfortable about its lack of prescriptive power in pointing toward where we *should* be headed and suggest what we *should* be doing. We require more creative thinking about the absolute necessity for more robust intergovernmental institutions, as well as more passionate (or less embarrassed) advocacy of steps leading toward world government—rather than hoping that the decentralized system of states and a pooling of corporate and civil society efforts will somehow be sufficient to ensure human survival and dignity.

What unifies both the most and the least idealistic observers of international politics is an agreement that there is no world government. To repeat again, in the domestic context governance is more than government, implying shared purpose and goal orientation *in addition to* formal authority and police or enforcement powers. For the planet, governance is essentially the whole story. Worse yet, institutions and rules sometimes create the appearance of moving toward effective action, but usually without the desired effects.

So global governance is not a supplement to political authority and legitimate institutions but more what the French would call a "faute de mieux"—a make-do surrogate in the contemporary world because we have nothing else, neither in reality nor even on the drawing boards. But the basic question remains: can global governance without a global government actually address the range of problems faced by humanity?

Proponents of global governance—and it would be difficult to claim that I am not in this category, having edited a journal with that title from 2000 to 2005—make a good-faith effort to emphasize how best to realize a stable, peaceful, and well-ordered international society of the type that Hedley Bull sought in the absence of a unifying global authority. But this pragmatism essentially reflects a judgment that no powerful global institutions will appear in the near future. Because agency is essential, improved problem-solving will not simply materialize without more robust intergovernmental institutions, first and foremost those of the United Nations system. Yet no one is investing intellectual energy or resources pursuing the impossible ideal of world government.

Paradoxically then, intergovernmental organizations seem to be marginal—or at least less central—to our thinking at exactly the moment when enhanced multilateralism is so sorely required. What gets lost as we struggle to understand an indistinct patchwork of authority is that current IGOs are insufficient in number, inadequate in resources, and incoherent in their disparate policies and philosophies.

It is humbling to think how far our vision has shrunk. Returning to John Maynard Keynes's thinking during World War II is unsettling. His vision for what eventually became the International Monetary Fund foresaw an institution whose resources would amount to 50 percent of total world imports. Although the IMF is reputed to be one of the most powerful institutions on earth and comes under much criticism for throwing its weight around, its resources at present represent less than 1.5 percent of world imports. It is true that a denser network of international institutions exists than when Keynes was writing, but the tasks that he sought to accomplish remain. We must ask ourselves why we are satisfied—though indeed, many are uneasy—that the contemporary intergovernmental organization with the sharpest economic teeth in terms of enforcement pales in comparison with what the twentieth century's greatest economist had proposed.

Realizing that the epithet "Pollyannaish" will come my way, it is nonetheless time to reaffirm a seemingly out-of-date belief in the ability of human beings to create powerful intergovernmental institutions and solve problems. Craig Murphy encourages us: "the longer history of industry and international organizations indicates that the task of creating the necessary global institutions may be easier than many of today's liberal commentators believe."[15] We need to be honest and ask ourselves whether the emphasis on global governance postpones a reckoning with the fact that the sum of actions by decentralized NGOs, profit-seeking firms mixing a bottom-line with corporate responsibility, and informal networks of government officials will simply not be enough to address most of the problems that ail the planet.

Are Anomalies No Longer Anomalous?

In his classic work *The Structure of Scientific Revolutions*, Thomas S. Kuhn outlined the process by which a dominant scientific paradigm—or "way of seeing the world"—is replaced by a new one.[16] A paradigm is concerned with solving puzzles within a particular framework. The process starts with a theory—the formal starting point for all research in normal science. The theory directs research by defining the problem, explaining it, and predicting solutions. Normal science is concerned with determining significant facts, matching them with the theory, and with the articulation, refinement, and extension of the theory. The normal procedure for scientific inquiry is not to find anomalies but rather to solve puzzles arising from the paradigm. However, in the course of ongoing research, anomalies often are uncovered. An awareness of unanticipated results creates both an awareness of a deficiency in the theory or existing paradigm and a proliferation of versions of old theory. Anomalies have to be addressed through the generation of auxiliary hypotheses, the main purpose of which is to explain the anomaly within the existing paradigm.

But what if there are too many anomalies and, as a result, too messy a web of auxiliary hypotheses? If so, a new paradigm is required because, in Kuhn's terms, "the anomalous has become the expected."[17] Kuhn's basic example was the shift from Ptolemy's model of planets rotating around a fixed earth to the model introduced by Copernicus. The shift occurred when the old model simply had too many anomalies—in common language, it could not explain what was actually going on, let alone predict what was going to happen and provide prescriptive guidance.

We are not yet at a Copernican moment regarding the inadequacies of state sovereignty because it still works in a number of ways and is useful in predicting much of international relations. At the same time, a growing sense of profound disconnect exists. Global governance is an attempt to make do in the interim, but it certainly does not provide "comprehensive perspectives that organize our understanding,"[18] which is the usual definition of a paradigm change.

What typically happens is that adherents of the old paradigm cling to it desperately for as long as possible. They ignore or downplay the kinds of anomalies that we have routinely encountered in these pages. The malfunctioning of today's international system has not led to a new paradigm but rather to experiments with a useful analytical tool, global governance, which helps us understand what *is* happening but does not push us to prescribe what *should* happen. More and more of us are willing to admit that we are living in a "post-Westphalian" era, but such a label is as unsatisfactory as "post-Cold War"— it captures accurately the fact that we are leaving behind one era (begun in 1648), but it provides neither a catchy nor accurate label for the era to come.

Like the United Nations, global governance is a bridge between the old and the as yet unborn. Global governance also resembles the UN in that we are unable to use either to solve those pesky problems without passports that are staring us in the face—global warming, genocide, money-laundering by terrorists, and worldwide pandemics like AIDS.

Nonetheless, I maintain an unquenchable optimism. As a product of the Enlightenment, I still believe that human beings can organize themselves rationally to solve global problems—the real bottom-line is that we will survive. A Westphalian pessimist[19] should feel free to eat, drink, and be merry, as nuclear apocalypse is inevitable shortly before or after the planet's average temperature increases by several degrees. A post-Westphalian pessimist might as well do the same, since globalization's inequities and technological proliferation will lead to a different kind of chaos and undermine or even doom civilization as we know it.

However, I trust that many readers have not yet resigned themselves to either fate. From the perspective of either a Westphalian or post-Westphalian optimist—I personally vacillate between the two but keep looking for enough data to put me firmly in the latter category—global government rather than global governance is a necessary part of future analytical perspectives. Westphalian optimists are those who believe that the state system can be adapted and modified; they possess a basic Kantian faith in the warming of international relations. For them, the growth of trade and economic progress, combined with the consensual strengthening of existing international organizations, will ultimately result in a world state. David Held is the best example of a Westphalian optimist, more humanistic and less militaristic than most other observers.[20]

Optimists like Peter Singer view globalization as creating a post-Westphalian context of global unity—what he dubs "one world"—in which sovereign states will no longer represent the outer limits of political community and ethical obligations.[21] Over time, there will be voluntary actions by governments and peoples—akin to what is happening in the European Union, with all its ups and downs—and this gradual process will result in a world government. Singer recognizes the danger of creating a lumbering behemoth and the potential for tyranny. Indeed, even the existing UN is anathema to extremist libertarians, some of whom still imagine the world organization as a communist-inspired plot to take over the world and destroy individual freedoms. But he nonetheless sees the growing influence of transnational social forces as making possible a different kind of post-Westphalian global unity.

If solutions without passports are necessary, how soon will we revert to an old-fashioned concept, world government?

Selected Readings

This brief selection highlights a few recent key books that are a starting point for reading about the main topics covered in this book; the endnotes for each chapter contain more detailed recommendations about specialized readings, especially about international peace and security, human rights, and sustainable development. Here, readers will find a handful of more general works that should be readily available in most college and university libraries. I avoid a comprehensive list of "classics"—which would have been too lengthy and in any case many are dated—and instead emphasize up-to-date overviews of the subject matter.

For Chapters 1 and 5 regarding the conceptual building blocks for state sovereignty, readers may wish to consult Stephen Krasner, *Sovereignty: Organized Hypocrisy* (Princeton, NJ: Princeton University Press, 1999) to learn more about the "normal" reasons why Westphalian sovereignty is routinely violated and nonintervention may or may not be a respected in international relations. Kalevi J. Holsti, in *Taming the Sovereigns: Institutional Change in International Politics* (Cambridge: Cambridge University Press, 2004) provides an overview of how to conceptualize continuity and change. Robert Jackson, in *The Global Covenant: Human Conduct in a World of States* (Oxford: Oxford University Press, 2000) revisits the classical international society approach (or "English school") and brings it into the new era, including discussions of war and intervention, human rights, and humanitarian disasters.

For Chapters 2 and 6, views about the South and its relations with the North have received little attention by researchers. One exception is Jacqueline Ann Braveboy-Wagner, in her *Institutions of the Global South* (London: Routledge, 2008) and her edited volume *The Foreign Policies of the Global South: Rethinking Conceptual Frameworks* (Boulder, Colo.: Lynne Rienner, 2003). Global gatherings have been important scenes for North–South encounters, and readers may wish to consult Michael G. Schechter, *United Nations Global Conferences* (London: Routledge, 2005). As UNCTAD was the place within the UN system where much of the South's economic agenda was formulated, readers may wish to consult Ian Taylor and Karen Smith, *United Nations Conference on Trade and Development (UNCTAD)* (London: Routledge, 2007), and John Toye and Richard Toye, *The UN and Global Political Economy: International Trade, Finance, and Development* (Bloomington: Indiana University Press, 2004).

For Chapters 3 and 4 as well as 7 and 8 there is a veritable cottage industry of recent publications about the United Nations and the UN system. Two authoritative compendia on the law and the politics of the UN are: Bruno Simma, ed., *The Charter of the United Nations: A Commentary*, 2nd edn. (Oxford: Oxford University Press, 2002), and Thomas G. Weiss and Sam Daws, eds., *The Oxford Handbook on the United Nations* (Oxford: Oxford University Press, 2007). Two textbooks covering the same topics are: José E. Alvarez, *International Organizations as Law-makers* (Oxford: Oxford University Press, 2005), and Thomas G. Weiss, David P. Forsythe, Roger A. Coate, and Kelly-Kate Pease, *The United Nations and Changing World Politics*, 5th edn. (Boulder, Colo.: Westview, 2007). Three of the UN's principal organs are discussed in some detail in this book, and readers may wish to take a look at more in-depth presentations: for the Security Council, Edward C. Luck, *UN Security Council: Practice and Promise* (London: Routledge, 2006), and David M.

Malone, ed., *The UN Security Council: From the Cold War to the 21st Century* (Boulder, Colo.: Lynne Rienner, 2004); for the General Assembly, M. J. Peterson, *The UN General Assembly* (London: Routledge, 2005); and for the Secretariat, Leon Gordenker, *The Secretary-General and Secretariat* (London: Routledge, 2005), Simon Chesterman, ed., *Secretary or General? The UN Secretary-General in World Politics* (Cambridge: Cambridge University Press, 2007), and Thant Myint-U and Amy Scott, *The UN Secretariat: A Brief History (1945–2006)* (New York: International Peace Academy, 2006).

In relation to the conclusion and looking to the future, readers may wish to begin with Ramesh Thakur, *The United Nations, Peace and Security: From Collective Security to the Responsibility to Protect* (Cambridge: Cambridge University Press, 2006), and Donald J. Puchala, Katie Verlin Laatikainen, and Roger A. Coate, *United Nations Politics: International Organization in a Divided World* (Upper Saddle River, N.J.: Prentice Hall, 2007). In terms of understanding the UN's limitations and strengths after September 11, 2001, a relevant collection of essays is Jane Boulden and Thomas G. Weiss, eds., *Terrorism and the UN: Before and After September 11* (Bloomington: Indiana University Press, 2004). The role of the United States in the multilateral era is discussed in several edited volumes: Rosemary Foot, S. Neil MacFarlane, and Michael Mastanduno, eds., *The United States and Multilateral Organizations* (Oxford: Oxford University Press, 2003); Michael Byers and Georg Nolte, eds., *United States Hegemony and the Foundations of International Law* (Cambridge: Cambridge University Press, 2003); Stewart Patrick and Shepard Forman, eds., *Multilateralism & U.S. Foreign Policy: Ambivalent Engagement* (Boulder, Colo.: Lynne Rienner, 2002); and David M. Malone and Yuen Foong Khong, eds., *Unilateralism & U.S. Foreign Policy: International Perspectives* (Boulder, Colo.: Lynne Rienner, 2003).

Notes

ACKNOWLEDGEMENTS

1 For a discussion, see Dan Plesch, "How the United Nations Beat Hitler and Prepared the Peace," *Global Society* 22, no. 1 (2008): 137–58.
2 Charles Lichenstein quoted in Robert Gregg, *About Face? The United States and the United Nations* (Boulder, Colo.: Lynne Rienner, 1993), p. 68.
3 Thomas G. Weiss, *Humanitarian Intervention: Ideas in Action* (Cambridge: Polity Press, 2007).
4 See, Thomas G. Weiss, David P. Forsythe, Roger A. Coate, and Kelly-Kate Pease, *The United Nations and Changing World Politics*, 5th edn. (Boulder, Colo.: Westview, 2007); and Thomas G. Weiss and Sam Daws, eds., *The Oxford Handbook on the United Nations* (Oxford: Oxford University Press, 2007).
5 Brian Urquhart, *Hammarskjöld* (New York: Knopf, 1972), *Ralph Bunche: An American Life* (New York: W.W. Norton, 1993), and *A Life in Peace and War* (New York: Harper & Row, 1997).

INTRODUCTION

1 Edward C. Luck, *Mixed Messages: American Politics and International Organization 1919–1999* (Washington, DC: Brookings, 1999).
2 Mark Malloch Brown, "Can the UN Be Reformed?," *Global Governance* 13, no. 1 (2008): 1–12.
3 Kalevi J. Holsti, *Taming the Sovereigns: Institutional Change in International Politics* (Cambridge: Cambridge University Press, 2004), p. 8.
4 Theodore C. Sorensen, "JFK's Strategy of Peace," *World Policy Journal* 20, no. 3 (2003): 4.

5 G. John Ikenberry, "Is American Multilateralism in Decline?,"
   Perspectives on Politics 1, no. 3 (2003): 545.

6 Center for Defense Information, Table on "Fiscal Year 2007
   Budget," based on data provided by the US Department of
   Defense and International Institute for Strategic Studies,
   Washington, DC, available at www.cdi.org/budget/2007/
   world-military-spending.cfm

7 Joseph S. Nye, Jr., *The Paradox of American Power: Why the World's
   Only Superpower Can't Go It Alone* (Oxford: Oxford University
   Press, 2002).

8 See Rosemary Foot, S. Neil MacFarlane, and Michael
   Mastanduno, eds., *US Hegemony and International Organizations:
   The United States and Multilateral Institutions* (Oxford: Oxford
   University Press, 2003); Steward Patrick and Shepard Forman,
   eds., *Multilateralism & U.S. Foreign Policy: Ambivalent Engagement*
   (Boulder, Colo.: Lynne Rienner, 2002); David M. Malone and
   Yuen Foong Khong, eds., *Unilateralism & US Foreign Policy:
   International Perspectives* (Boulder, Colo.: Lynne Rienner, 2003);
   and Michael Byers and Georg Nolte, eds., *United States Hegemony
   and the Foundations of International Law* (Cambridge: Cambridge
   University Press, 2003).

9 Charles Krauthammer, "The Unipolar Moment," *Foreign Affairs*
   70, no. 1 (1990/1991): 23–33; and "The Unipolar Moment
   Revisited," *National Interest* 70 (Winter 2002/2003): 5–17.

10 Quoted by James Traub, *The Best Intentions: Kofi Annan and the
   UN in the Era of American World Power* (New York: Farrar, Straus
   and Giroux, 2006), p. 266.

11 Paul Kennedy, *The Parliament of Man: The Past, Present, and
   Future of the United Nations* (New York: Random House, 2006).

12 Thomas G. Weiss, Tatiana Carayannis, and Richard Jolly, "The
   Third UN," *Global Governance* 14, no. 1 (forthcoming, 2009).

13 Inis L. Claude, Jr., *Swords Into Plowshares: The Problems and
   Prospects of International Organization* (New York: Random
   House, 1956) and "Peace and Security: Prospective Roles for the
   Two United Nations," *Global Governance* 2, no. 3 (1996):
   289–98.

14 *Foreign Policy*, no. 132 (September/October 2002): 28–46.

15 Ramesh Thakur and Thomas G. Weiss, *The UN and Global
   Governance: An Unfinished Journey* (Bloomington: Indiana
   University Press, forthcoming).

16 James N. Rosenau and Ernst-Otto Czempiel, eds., *Governance without Government: Order and Change in World Politics* (Cambridge: Cambridge University Press, 1992).

17 Robert W. Cox and Harold K. Jacobson, eds., *The Anatomy of Influence: Decision Making in International Organization* (New Haven, Conn.: Yale University Press, 1973).

18 See Richard Jolly, Louis Emmerij, and Thomas G. Weiss, *UN Ideas Changing History* (Bloomington: Indiana University Press, forthcoming).

CHAPTER I WESTPHALIA, ALIVE BUT NOT WELL

1 Jack Donnelly, "Sovereign Inequality and Hierarchy in Anarchy: American Power and International Society," in *American Foreign Policy in a Globalized World*, ed. David P. Forsythe, Patrice C. McMahon, and Andy Wedeman (New York: Routledge, 2006), pp. 81–104.

2 Stephen Krasner, *Sovereignty: Organized Hypocrisy* (Princeton, NJ: Princeton University Press, 1999).

3 Ramesh Thakur, "Global Norms and International Humanitarian Law: An Asian Perspective," *International Review of the Red Cross* 83, no. 841 (2001): 31.

4 Quoted by Kathleen Newland with Erin Patrick and Monette Zard, *No Refuge: The Challenge of Internal Displacement* (New York and Geneva: United Nations, Office for the Coordination of Humanitarian Assistance, 2003), p. 37.

5 Edward C. Luck, *Mixed Messages: American Politics and International Organization 1919–1999* (Washington, DC: Brookings Institution, 1999).

6 Richard N. Haass, *The Opportunity: America's Moment to Alter History's Course* (New York: Public Affairs, 2005), p. 41.

7 Hedley Bull, *The Anarchical Society: A Study of Order in World Politics*, 3rd edn. (London: Macmillan, 2002). See also Robert Jackson, *The Global Covenant: Human Conduct in a World of States* (Oxford: Oxford University Press, 2000).

8 For more recent arguments, see Jackson, *The Global Covenant*, and Christopher Bickerton, Philip Cunliffe, and Alexander Gourevitch, *Publics Without Sovereignty: A Critique of Contemporary International Relations* (London: Routledge, 2007).

9 Scott Barrett, *Why Cooperate? The Incentives to Supply Global Public Goods* (Oxford: Oxford University Press, 2007).

10 Francis Fukuyama, *The End of History and the Last Man* (New York: Free Press, 1992); and J. Michael Grieg, "The End of Geography," *Journal of Conflict Resolution* 46, no. 2 (2002): 225–43.

11 *National Security Strategy of the United States of America, September 2002*, available at http://usinfo.state.gov/topical/pol/terror/secstrat/htm (March 1, 2004).

12 Adam Roberts, "The United Nations and Humanitarian Intervention," in *Humanitarian Intervention and International Relations*, ed. Jennifer Welsh (Oxford: Oxford University Press, 2004), p. 90.

13 Joseph S. Nye, Jr., "U.S. Power and Strategy After Iraq," *Foreign Affairs* 82, no. 4 (2003): 60–73.

14 The discussion draws on Peter J. Hoffman and Thomas G. Weiss, *Sword & Salve: Confronting New Wars and Humanitarian Crises* (Lanham, Md.: Rowman & Littlefield, 2005), Chapter 3.

15 See Bertrand Badie, *The Imported State: The Westernization of the Political Order* (Stanford, Calif.: Stanford University Press, 2000).

16 John Gerard Ruggie, "Territoriality and Beyond: Problematizing Modernity in International Relations," *International Organization* 47 (Winter 1993): 165.

17 Peter Wallensteen and Margareta Sollenberg, "Armed Conflict, 1989–2000," *Journal of Peace Research* 38, no. 5 (2001): 632.

18 Andrew Mack, *Human Security Brief 2006* (Vancouver: University of British Columbia, 2006).

19 *Relief Web: Complex Emergencies*, available at www.ReliefWeb.int/w/rwb.nsf/WCE?OpenForm.

20 Max Weber, *Politics as Vocation* (Philadelphia: Fortress, 1965); first published 1919.

21 Amin Sakil, "Dimensions of State Disruption and International Responses," *Third World Quarterly* 21, no. 1 (2000): 39–49.

22 William Reno, "Shadow States and the Political Economy of Civil War," in *Greed and Grievance: Economic Agendas in Civil Wars*, ed. Mats Berdal and David Malone (Boulder, Colo.: Lynne Rienner, 2000), pp. 44–5; and *Corruption and State Politics in Sierra Leone* (Cambridge: Cambridge University Press, 1995).

23 Jean-François Bayart, *The State in Africa: Politics of the Belly* (London: Longman, 1993); and Jean-François Bayart, Stephen Ellis, and Beatrice Hibou, eds., *The Criminalization of the State in Africa* (Bloomington: Indiana University Press, 1999).

24 Robert H. Jackson, *Quasi-states: Sovereignty, International Relations, and the Third World* (Cambridge: Cambridge University Press, 1990), p. 21.

25 I. William Zartman, ed., *Collapsed States: The Disintegration and Restoration of Legitimate Authority* (Boulder, Colo.: Lynne Rienner, 1995).

26 Tanisha M. Fazal, "State Death in the International System," *International Organization* 58 (Spring 2004): 311–44.

27 Joel Migdal, *Strong States, Weak Societies: State–Society Relations and State Capabilities in the Third World* (Princeton: Princeton University Press, 1988); and Peter Evans, *Embedded Autonomy: States and Industrial Transformation* (Princeton: Princeton University Press, 1995).

28 Janice E. Thomson, "State Sovereignty in International Relations: Bridging the Gap between Theory and Empirical Research," *International Studies Quarterly* 39 (June 1995): 213–33; and Kalevi J. Holsti, *Taming the Sovereigns: Institutional Change in International Politics* (Cambridge: Cambridge University Press, 2004), pp. 82–98.

29 Samuel Huntington, *Political Order in Changing Societies* (New Haven, Conn.: Yale University Press, 1968), and Migdal, *Strong States, Weak Societies.*

30 William J. Reno, *Warlord Politics and African States* (Boulder, Colo.: Lynne Rienner, 1998), p. 226.

31 Gerald B. Helman and Steven R. Rather, "Saving Failed States," *Foreign Policy* 89 (Winter 1992–93): 3–20.

32 Robert I. Rotberg, "Failed States in a World of Terror," *Foreign Affairs* 81, no. 4 (2002): 127–40. For a fuller discussion of Africa's problems, see Martin Meredith, *The State of Africa: A History of Fifty Years of Independence* (London: Free Press, 2005).

33 Mark Duffield, "Globalization, Transborder Trade, and War Economies," in *Greed and Grievance*, pp. 70–4.

34 Bull, *The Anarchical Society*, p. 245.

35 Jessica Matthews, "Power Shift," *Foreign Affairs* 76 (January–February 1997): 61.

36 Mohammed Ayoob, *The Third World Security Predicament: State Making, Regional Conflict, and the International System* (Boulder, Colo.: Lynne Rienner, 1995).

37 Kalevi J. Holsti, *State, War, and the State of War* (Cambridge: Cambridge University Press, 1996), p. 318.

38 US Department of State, "US Signs 100th Article 98 Agreement," press statement 2005/463 by Richard Boucher, Spokesman, Washington, DC, May 3, 2005; http://www.state.gov/r/pa/prs/ps/2005/45573.htm

39 See Benjamin Ferencz, "Misguided Fears about the International Criminal Court," *Pace International Law Review* 15 (Spring 2003): 223–46.

40 Brian Knowlton, "Rights Chief Talks of U.S. Role in Her Leaving," *International Herald Tribune*, July 31, 2002.

41 This discussion draws on Thomas G. Weiss, David P. Forsythe, Roger A. Coate, and Kelly-Kate Pease, *The United Nations and Changing World Politics*, 5th edn. (Boulder, Colo.: Westview, 2007), pp. 182–4.

42 Bertrand G. Ramcharan, ed., *Human Rights Protection in the Field* (Leiden, Netherlands: Martinus Nijhoff, 2006).

43 *2005 World Summit Outcome*, UN document A/60/L.1, September 15, 2005, para. 160.

44 Yvonne Terlinghen, "The Human Rights Council: A New Era in UN Human Rights Work?," *Ethics & International Affairs* 21, no. 2 (2007): 167–78.

45 Nico Schrijver, "The UN Human Rights Council: A New 'Society of the Committed' or Just Old Wine in New Bottles?" *Leiden Journal of International Law* 20, no. 4 (2007): 809.

46 Human Rights Watch, "UN: Rights Council Ends First Year With Much To Do," Geneva, June 19, 2007; http://hrw.org/english/docs/2007/06/18/global16208.htm

47 Quoted by James Traub, *The Best Intentions: Kofi Annan and the UN in the Era of American World Power* (New York: Farrar, Straus and Giroux, 2006), p. 227.

48 Article 25 (1) of the Kyoto Protocol to the United Nations Framework Convention on Climate Change states that the protocol "shall enter into force on the ninetieth day after the date on which not less than 55 Parties to the Convention, incorporating Parties included in Annex I which accounted in total for at least 55 per cent of the total carbon dioxide emissions

for 1990 of the Parties included in Annex I, have deposited
their instruments of ratification, acceptance, approval or
accession."

49 "China Now No. 1 in CO_2 Emissions; US in Second Position,"
Netherlands Environmental Assessment Agency, retrieved
September 26, 2007; http://www.mnp.nl/en/dossiers/
Climatechange/moreinfo/Chinanowno1inCO2emissionsUSA
insecondposition.html

50 Juliette Jowit, Caroline Davies, and David Adam, "Late-Night
Drama Pushes US into Climate Deal," *Observer*, December 16,
2007.

51 George Monbiot, *Guardian Unlimited*, December 17, 2007.

52 Ben Cubby, *The Sydney Morning Herald*, December 18, 2007.

53 John Vidal, "US Pours Cold Water on Bali Optimism," *Guardian
Unlimited*, December 17, 2007.

54 Ibid.

55 Jowit et al., "Late-Night Drama."

CHAPTER 2 NORTH–SOUTH THEATER

1 Conor Cruise O'Brien, *United Nations: Sacred Drama* (London:
Hutchinson & Company, 1968).

2 Jacqueline Ann Braveboy-Wagner, *Institutions of the Global South*
(London: Routledge, forthcoming 2008).

3 Maggie Black, *The No-Nonsense Guide to International Development*,
2nd edn. (Oxford: New Internationalist, 2007), p. 16.

4 Richard Wright, *The Color Curtain* (Jackson, Miss.: Banner Books,
1956), pp. 13–14.

5 Mark T. Berger, "After the Third World? History, Destiny and the
Fate of Third Worldism," *Third World Quarterly* 25, no. 1 (2004):
13. Berger was the guest editor of this special issue whose articles
review the problems and prospects of the so-called Third World.
Interested readers may also wish to consult such recent works as:
Robert Malley, *The Call From Algeria: Third Worldism, Revolution
and the Turn to Islam* (Berkeley: University of California Press,
1996); and Geir Lundestad, *East, West, North, South: Major
Developments in International Politics Since 1945* (New York: Oxford
University Press, 1999). Older references include: Roeslan
Abdulgani, *Bandung Spirit: Moving on the Tide of History* (Djakarta:

Prapantja, 1964); Carlos P. Romulo, *The Meaning of Bandung*
(Chapel Hill: University of North Carolina Press, 1956); and, Peter
Worsley, *The Third World* (London: Weidenfeld and Nicolson,
1964).

6 Georges Balandier and Alfred Sauvy, *Le "Tiers-Monde," Sous
Développement et Développement* (Paris: Presses Universitaires de
France, 1961).

7 See www.g77.org

8 Joseph S. Nye, "UNCTAD: Poor Nations' Pressure Group," in
*The Anatomy of Influence: Decision Making in International
Organization*, ed. Robert W. Cox and Harold K. Jacobson (New
Haven, Conn.: Yale University Press, 1973), pp. 334–70.

9 See Ian Taylor and Karen Smith, *United Nations Conference on
Trade and Development (UNCTAD)* (London: Routledge, 2007);
John Toye and Richard Toye, *The UN and Global Political
Economy: International Trade, Finance, and Development*
(Bloomington: Indiana University Press, 2004); Thomas G.
Weiss, *Multilateral Development Diplomacy in UNCTAD: The
Lessons of Group Negotiations, 1964–84* (London: Macmillan,
1986); Michael Zammit Cutajar, ed., *UNCTAD and the South-
North Dialogue: The First Twenty Years* (London: Pergamon,
1985); Robert L. Rothstein, *Global Bargaining: UNCTAD and the
Quest for a New International Economic Order* (Princeton:
Princeton University Press, 1979); Branislav Gosovic, *UNCTAD:
Compromise and Conflict* (Leiden, Netherlands: Sijthoff, 1972);
Diego Cordovez, *UNCTAD and Development Diplomacy: From
Conference to Strategy* (London: Journal of World Trade Law,
1970); and Kamal Hagras, *United Nations Conference on Trade
and Development: A Case Study in UN Diplomacy* (New York:
Praeger, 1965).

10 Stephen Lewis, *Race against Time* (Toronto: Anansi Press, 2005),
p. 145.

11 This discussion is based on Thomas G. Weiss and Barbara
Crossette, "The United Nations: The Post-Summit Outlook," in
Great Decisions 2006 (New York: Foreign Policy Association,
2006), pp. 9–20.

12 M. J. Peterson, "Using the General Assembly," in *Terrorism and
the UN: Before and After September 11*, ed. Jane Boulden and
Thomas G. Weiss (Bloomington: Indiana University Press,
2004), pp. 173–97.

13 High-level Panel on Threats, Challenges and Change, *A More Secure World: Our Shared Responsibility* (New York: UN, 2004), para. 161.

14 Kofi Annan, *In Larger Freedom: Towards Development, Security and Human Rights for All*, UN document A/59/2005, March 21, 2005, para. 91.

15 *2005 World Summit Outcome*, UN document A/60/L.1, September 15, 2005, para. 81.

16 The Stanley Foundation, *Implementation of the UN Global Counterterrorism Strategy* (Muscatine, Iowa: Stanley Foundation, 2007), p. 2.

17 In a letter to Russian ambassador Sergey Lavrov, dated October 23, 1997.

18 Morris B. Abram, "Human Rights and the United Nations: Past as Prologue," *Harvard Human Rights Law Journal* 4 (Spring 1991): 69–83.

19 Economic Commission for Africa, *Economic Report on Africa 2007* (Addis Ababa: ECA, 2007), p. 32.

20 Permanent Mission of the Republic of Zimbabwe to the United Nations, "Statement by the Honorable Minister of Justice, Legal and Parliamentary Affairs of Zimbabwe, Mr Patrick A. Chinamasa (MP) at the Inaugural Session of the Human Rights Council, Geneva, 19–22 June 2006," available at www.ohchr.org/english/bodies/hrcouncil/docs/statements/zimbabwe.pdf

21 For a snapshot, see UNDP, *Human Development Report 2000* (New York: Oxford University Press, 2000). For historical developments, see Jack Donnelly, *International Human Rights* (Boulder, Colo.: Westview, 1993); Tim Dunne and Nicholas J. Wheeler, eds., *Human Rights in Global Politics* (Cambridge: Cambridge University Press, 1999); and David P. Forsythe, *The Internationalization of Human Rights* (Lexington, Mass.: D. C. Heath, 1991).

22 See Thomas G. Weiss, David P. Forsythe, Roger A. Coate, and Kelly-Kate Pease, *The United Nations and Changing World Politics*, 5th edn. (Boulder, Colo.: Westview, 2007), Chapters 5–7.

23 UN Environment Programme, "Development and Environment: The Founex Report: In Defense of the Earth," *The Basic Texts on Environment*, UNEP Executive Series 1 (Nairobi: UNEP, 1981).

24 Quoted by Maurice Strong, "Policy Lessons Learned in a Thirty Years' Perspective," Ministry of the Environment, *Stockholm Thirty Years On* (Stockholm: Ministry of the Environment, 2002), p. 18.

25 Branislav Gosovic, *The Quest for World Environmental Cooperation: The Case of the UN Global Environment Monitoring System* (London: Routledge, 1992).

26 World Commission on Environment and Development, *Our Common Future* (Oxford: Oxford University Press, 1987).

27 Shanna Halpern, *The United Nations Conference on Environment and Development: Process and Documentation* (Providence, RI: Academic Council on the United Nations System, 1992).

28 Michael McCoy and Patrick McCully, *The Road from Rio: An NGO Guide to Environment and Development* (Amsterdam: International Books, 1993). For a more general discussion, see Kerstin Mertens, *NGOs and the United Nations* (New York: Palgrave, 2006), and three reports by Helmut Anheier, Marlies Glasius, and Mary Kaldor, eds., *Global Civil Society* (Oxford: Oxford University Press, 2001, 2002 and 2003).

29 Maurice Strong, *Where on Earth Are We Going?* (New York: Norton, 2001).

30 Soo Yeon Kim and Bruce Russett, "The New Politics of Voting Alignments in the United Nations General Assembly," *International Organization* 50, no. 4 (1996): 629–52. See also Evan Luard, *A History of the United Nations: The Years of Western Domination* (London: Macmillan, 1982).

CHAPTER 3 THE FEUDAL SYSTEM, OR
DYSFUNCTIONAL FAMILY

1 Louis Emmerij, Richard Jolly, and Thomas G. Weiss, *Ahead of the Curve? UN Ideas and Global Challenges* (Bloomington: Indiana University Press, 2001), pp. 26–42.

2 Harold K. Jacobson, *Networks of Interdependence: International Organizations and the Global Political System*, 2nd edn. (New York: Knopf, 1984); and Christer Jönsson, "Interorganization Theory and International Organization," *International Studies Quarterly* 30, no. 1 (1986): 39–57.

3 Erskine Childers with Brian Urquhart, *Renewing the United Nations System* (Uppsala: Dag Hammarskjöld Foundation, 1994), p. 32.

4 United Nations, *A Capacity Study of the United Nations Development System* (Geneva: United Nations, 1969), volume I, document DP/5, p. iii.

5 This discussion draws on Thomas G. Weiss and David A. Korn, *Internal Displacement: Conceptualization and its Consequences* (London: Routledge, 2005), Chapters 5 and 7.
6 David A. Korn, *Exodus within Borders* (Washington, DC: Brookings Institution, 1999).
7 Norwegian Refugee Council, *Internal Displacement: Global Overview of Trends and Developments in 2007* (Geneva: Global IDP Project, 2007), pp. 9–10. See also USCR, *World Refugee Survey 2007* (Washington, DC: USCR, 2005). These statistics reflect the usual practice of referring only to persons uprooted by conflict, but some observers press for much broader notions to encompass millions more uprooted by natural disasters and development. Moreover, there is also no consensus about when displacement ends, thereby inflating figures in some cases. See Erin D. Mooney, "The Concept of Internal Displacement and the Case for IDPs as a Category of Concern," *Refugee Survey Quarterly* 24, no. 3 (2005): 9–26. This entire issue is devoted to "Internally Displaced Persons: The Challenges of International Protection"— Articles, Documents, Literature Survey.
8 Roberta Cohen and Francis M. Deng, *Masses in Flight: The Global Crisis of Internal Displacement* (Washington, DC: Brookings Institution, 1998), p. 3. See also Roberta Cohen and Francis M. Deng, eds., *The Forsaken People: Case Studies of the Internally Displaced* (Washington, DC: Brookings Institution, 1998); and Francis M. Deng, *Protecting the Dispossessed: A Challenge for the International Community* (Washington, DC: Brookings Institution, 1993).
9 Donald Steinberg, *Orphans of Conflict: Caring for the Internally Displaced* (Washington, DC: U.S. Institute of Peace, 2005), Special Report #148.
10 Centers for Disease Control, "Famine-Affected, Refugee, and Displaced Populations: Recommendations for Public Health Issues," *Morbidity and Mortality Weekly Report* 41, RR-13 (1992). More recent estimates are essentially unchanged. See Peter Salama, Paul Spiegel, and Richard Brennan, "Refugees-No Less Vulnerable: The Internally Displaced in Humanitarian Emergencies," *The Lancet* 357, no. 9266 (5 May 2001): 1430–1.
11 Cohen and Deng, *Masses in Flight*, pp. 128–9.
12 See Cécile Dubernet, *The International Containment of Displaced Persons: Humanitarian Spaces without Exit* (Aldershot, UK:

Ashgate, 2001). For a rebuttal, see Erin D. Mooney, "In-country Protection: Out of Bounds for UNHCR?," in *Refugee Rights and Realities: Evolving International Concepts and Regimes*, ed. Frances Nicholson and Patrick Twomey (Cambridge: Cambridge University Press, 1999), pp. 200–19. For a balanced treatment of the agency, see Gil Loescher, *The UNHCR and World Politics: A Perilous Path* (Oxford: Oxford University Press, 2001), and Gil Loescher, Alexander Betts, and James Milner, *UNHCR: The Politics and Practice of Refugee Protection into the Twenty First Century* (London: Routledge, 2008).

13 Sadako Ogata, *The Turbulent Decade: Confronting the Refugee Crises of the 1990s* (New York: Norton, 2005), pp. 29–49.

14 Interview with author, October 11, 2005.

15 International Organization on Migration, *Internally Displaced Persons: IOM Policy and Activities* (Geneva: IOM, 2002), IOM document MC/INF/258, p. 3.

16 InterAction's position has changed: "UNHCR should be vested with the authority and resources to be able to coordinate response for internally displaced persons." See "Statement by Dr. Mohammad N. Akhter, President & CEO, InterAction," September 16, 2005; http://www.interaction.org/newswire/detail.php?id=4358

17 Kofi Annan, *Renewing the United Nations: A Programme for Reform* (New York: UN, 1997). See Thomas G. Weiss, "Humanitarian Shell Games: Whither UN Reform?," *Security Dialogue* 29, no. 1 (1998): 9–23.

18 Interview with the author, October 11, 2005.

19 See Catherine Phuong, *The International Protection of Internally Displaced Persons* (Cambridge: Cambridge University Press, 2004).

20 Interview, October 11, 2005.

21 "Statement by Ambassador Richard C. Holbrooke to the Security Council," January 13, 2000, USUN Press Release #6(00).

22 "Ambassador Richard C. Holbrooke, Statement at Benjamin N. Cardozo School of Law," March 28, 2000, USUN Press Release #44(00).

23 See Thomas G. Weiss and Amir Pasic, "Dealing with Displacement and Suffering from Yugoslavia's Wars: Conceptual and Operational Issues," in Cohen and Deng, eds., *The Forsaken*

People, pp. 175–231. A more recent study of the institution calls some of this thinking into doubt. See Barb Wigley, *The State of UNHCR's Organization Culture* (Geneva: UNHCR Policy and Evaluation Unit, 2005), document EPAU/2005/08.

24 Elizabeth Stites and Victor Tanner, *External Evaluation of OCHA's Internal Displacement Unit: Final Report* (New York: OCHA, 2004), p. 12.

25 This discussion is based on Peter J. Hoffman and Thomas G. Weiss, *Sword & Salve: Confronting New Wars and Humanitarian Crises* (Lanham, Md.: Rowman & Littlefield, 2005), Chapter 5; and Michael Barnett and Thomas G. Weiss, "Humanitarianism: A Brief History of the Present," in *Humanitarianism in Question: Politics, Power, Ethics*, ed. Michael Barnett and Thomas G. Weiss (Ithaca, NY: Cornell University Press, 2008), pp. 1–48.

26 James Fearon, "The Rise of Emergency Relief Aid," in *Humanitarianism in Question*, pp. 49–72.

27 Randolph Kent, "International Humanitarian crises: Two Decades Before and Two Decades Beyond," *International Affairs* 80, no. 5 (2004): 851–69.

28 Development Initiatives, *Global Humanitarian Assistance 2003* (London: Overseas Development Institute, 2003), p. 56.

29 Rachel McCleary and Robert Barro, "U.S.-Based Private Voluntary Organizations: Religious and Secular PVOs Engaged in International Relief and Development, 1939–2004," paper presented at the American Political Science Association annual meetings, Philadelphia, Pennsylvania, August 29–31, 2006.

30 Abby Stoddard, Adele Harmer, and Katherine Haver, *Providing Aid in Insecure Environments: Trends in Policy and Operations*, HPG Report 23 (London: Overseas Development Institute, 2006), p. 16.

31 Abdel-Rahman Ghandour, *Jihad Humanitaire* (Paris: Flammarion, 2002).

32 Adele Harmer and Lin Cotterrell, *Diversity in Donorship: The Changing Landscape of Official Humanitarian Aid* (London: ODI, 2005), quotations from pp. 3 and 6, statistics from pp. 7 and 5.

33 Hugo Slim, "Global Welfare," *ALNAP Review of Humanitarian Action in 2005* (London: ODI, 2005), p. 21. See also his *Killing Civilians: Method, Madness, and Morality in War* (New York: Columbia University Press, 2008).

34 Ian Smillie and Larry Minear, *The Charity of Nations: Humanitarian Action in A Calculating World* (Bloomfield, Conn.: Kumarian, 2004), pp. 8–10, p. 195.

35 Joanna MacRae et al., *Uncertain Power: The Changing Role of Official Donors in Humanitarian Action*, Humanitarian Policy Group Report 12 (London: Overseas Development Institute, 2002), p. 15. See also Judith Randel and Tony German, "Trends in Financing of Humanitarian Assistance," in *The New Humanitarianisms: A Review of Trends in Global Humanitarian Action*, ed. Joanna Macrae (London: Overseas Development Institute, 2002), pp. 19–28.

36 Development Initiatives, *Global Humanitarian Assistance 2003* (London: Overseas Development Institute, 2003), pp. 14–15.

37 Ibid.

38 Inter-Agency Standing Committee, "Working Paper on the Definition of Complex Emergency" (December 1994), in *Humanitarian Report 1997*, by the Department of Humanitarian Affairs, United Nations (New York: United Nations, 1997), p. 9. See also David Keen, *Complex Emergencies* (London: Blackwell Publishers, 2008).

39 John Mackinlay, *Globalisation and Insurgency*, Adelphi Paper 352 (Oxford: Oxford University Press, 2002), p. 100.

40 Sue Graves, Victoria Wheeler, and Ellen Martin, *Lost in Translation: Managing Coordination and Leadership Reform in the Humanitarian System*, HPG Policy Brief 27 (London: Overseas Development Institute, July 2007), p. 3.

41 Antonio Donini, "The Evolving Nature of Coordination," in *The Humanitarian Decade: Challenges for Humanitarian Assistance in the Last Decade*, vol. 2, (New York: OCHA, 2004), ed. OCHA p. 131, which updates *The Policies of Mercy: UN Coordination in Afghanistan, Mozambique, and Rwanda*, Occasional Paper 22 (Providence, RI: Watson Institute, 1996), p. 14.

42 High-level Panel on UN System-wide Coherence in the Fields of Development, Humanitarian Assistance and Environment, *Delivering as One* (New York: UN, 2006).

43 See Division for the Advancement of Women, *Women Go Global: The United Nations and the International Women's Movement, 1945–2000*, CD-ROM developed with the National Council for Research on Women (New York: United Nations, 2002); and Hilkka Pietilä, *Engendering the Global Agenda: The Story of Women*

and the United Nations, 2nd edn. (New York: United Nations Non-Governmental Organization Liaison Service, 2007); and Devaki Jain, *Women, Development, and the UN: A Sixty Year Quest for Equality and Justice* (Bloomington: Indiana University Press, 2005).

44 Quoted in Jain, *Women, Development, and the UN*, p. 8.

45 Charlotte Bunch, "Women and Gender," in *The Oxford Handbook on the United Nations*, ed. Thomas G. Weiss and Sam Daws (Oxford: Oxford University Press, 2007), p. 497.

46 UNIFEM, www.unifem.org

47 High-Level Panel on UN System-Wide Coherence, *Delivering as One*, p. 15.

48 Bunch, "Women and Gender," p. 506.

49 Based on Thomas G. Weiss, David P. Forsythe, Roger A. Coate, and Kelly-Kate Pease, *The United Nations and Changing World Politics*, 5th edn. (Boulder, Colo.: Westview, 2007), Chapter 9.

50 Michael G. Schechter, *United Nations Global Conferences* (London: Routledge, 2005).

51 *UNEP 2006 Annual Report* (UNEP, 2007), p. 82; http://www.unep.org/pdf/annualreport/UNEP_AR_2006_English.pdf

52 Katherine Marshall, *The World Bank: From Reconstruction to Development to Equity* (London: Routledge, 2008), Chapter 3.

53 "World Bank Lending by Theme and Sector: Fiscal 2002–2007," *The World Bank Annual Report 2007*, www.worldbank.org

54 Environmental expenditures cover "costs incurred that relate to the prevention, control, abatement, or elimination of environmental pollution. Expenditures are the incremental costs reported by a unit in a facility that would not have been incurred if environmental issues had not been considered." *Environmental Expenditures by the U.S. Oil and Natural Gas Industry* (Washington, DC: API, 2005), p. 11; http://www.api.org/ehs/performance/upload/ENVIRON_EXPENDITURES_REPORT_LO.pdf

55 Ibid., p. 2.

56 Richard Benedick, *Ozone Diplomacy: New Directions in Safeguarding the Planet* (Cambridge, Mass.: Harvard University Press, 1998).

57 This discussion is from Thomas G. Weiss, Tatiana Carayannis, Louis Emmerij, and Richard Jolly, *UN Voices: The Struggle for*

Development and Social Justice (Bloomington: Indiana University Press, 2005), p. 205.

58 Ibid., p. 205.

59 Ibid., p. 206.

CHAPTER 4 OVERWHELMING BUREAUCRACY AND UNDERWHELMING LEADERSHIP

1 Simon Chesterman, ed., *Secretary or General? The UN Secretary-General in World Politics* (Cambridge: Cambridge University Press, 2007). See also Kent J. Kille, *From Manager to Visionary: The Secretary-General of the United* Nations (Houndsmills, Basingstoke, UK: Palgrave, 2006); Edward Newman, *The UN Secretary-General from the Cold War to the New Era: A Global Peace and Security Mandate?* (London: Macmillan, 1998); and Benjamin Rivlin and Leon Gordenker, eds., *The Challenging Role of the UN Secretary-General: Making "The Most Impossible Job in the World" Possible* (Westport, Conn.: Praeger, 1993).

2 This idea was first spelled out in 1921 and is known as the "Nobelmaire Principles," named after the chairman of the committee convened to codify the international character of secretariats.

3 Egon Ranshofen-Wertheimer, *The International Secretariat: A Great Experiment in International Administration* (Washington, DC: Carnegie Endowment for International Peace, 1945).

4 See, for example, Thomas George Weiss, *International Bureaucracy: An Analysis of the Operation of Functional and Global International Secretariats* (Lexington, Mass.: DC Heath, 1975); Leon Gordenker, *The UN Secretary-General and Secretariat* (London: Routledge, 2005); James O. C. Jonah, "Secretariat: Independence and Reform," in *The Oxford Handbook on the United Nations*, ed. Thomas G. Weiss and Sam Daws (Oxford: Oxford University Press, 2007), pp. 160–74; Manuel Frohlich, *Political Ethics and the United Nations: Dag Hammarsköld as Secretary General* (London, Routledge, 2008).

5 Dag Hammarskjöld, "The International Civil Servant in Law and in Fact," lecture delivered to Congregation at Oxford University, May 30, 1961, reprinted by permission of Clarendon Press, Oxford, quotations at p. 329 and p. 349. Available at http://www.un.org/depts/dhl/dag/docs/internationalcivilservant.pdf

6 See Thomas G. Weiss, Tatiana Carayannis, Louis Emmerij, and Richard Jolly, *UN Voices: The Struggle for Development and Social Justice* (Bloomington: Indiana University Press, 2005), pp. 315–43. See also *The Complete Oral History Transcripts from UN Voices* CD-ROM (New York: United Nations Intellectual History Project, 2007).

7 Thant Myint-U and Amy Scott, *The UN Secretariat: A Brief History (1945–2006)* (New York: International Peace Academy, 2007), pp. 126–8.

8 Francesco Mezzalama, *Young Professionals in Selected Organizations of the United Nations System: Recruitment, Management and Retention* (Geneva: United Nations Joint Inspection Unit, 2000); http://www.unjiu.org/data/reports/2000/en2000_7.pdf; quotations at pp. v–vi.

9 Donald J. Puchala, Katie Verlin Laatikainen, and Roger A. Coate, *United Nations Politics: International Organization in a Divided World* (Upper Saddle River, NJ: Prentice Hall, 2007), p. x.

10 This number represents UN civilian staff members killed as a result of malicious acts in the period since reporting began in 1992 through September 2006. *Safety and Security of Humanitarian Personnel and Protection of UN Personnel*, Report of the Secretary-General, UN document A/61/463, September 26, 2006. In fact, 2007 was one of the deadliest years for UN personnel, with 33 civilian staff members killed. UN document ORG/1489, January 2, 2008.

11 Fatalities from 1948 through February 7, 2008 as compiled by the UN Department of Peacekeeping Operations; http://www.un.org/Depts/dpko/fatalities/StatsByYear%201.pdf

12 Paul A. Volcker, Richard J. Goldstone, and Mark Pieth, *The Management of the Oil-for-Food Programme*, Volume I, September 7, 2005, pp. 4–5, available at www.iic-offp.org

13 Paul A. Volcker, "Introduction," in a summary version of the principal findings done by two staff members, Jeffrey A. Meyer and Mark G. Califano, *Good Intentions Corrupted: The Oil-for-Food Scandal and the Threat to the U.N.* (New York: Public Affairs, 2006), p. xii and p. x.

14 Devaki Jain, *Women, Development, and the UN: A Sixty-year Quest for Equality and Justice* (Bloomington: Indiana University Press, 2005), p. 149.

15 Ibid., p. 40.

16 Quoted in Ibid., p. 72.

17 Office of the Special Advisor on Gender Issues and Advancement of Women, "The Status of Women in the United Nations System and Secretariat," September 28, 2006; http://www.un.org/womenwatch/osagi/pdf/Fact%20sheet%2028%20september.pdf

18 "Special and Personal Representatives and Envoys of the Secretary General," Department of Peacekeeping Operations; http://www.un.org/Depts/dpko/SRSG/table.htm

19 Ambassador Swanee Hunt's Remarks to the UN Security Council on UN Resolution 1325 and the Status of Women's Inclusion in Peace Processes Worldwide at The Initiative for Inclusive Security, Arria-style Meeting between Members of the Security Council and NGO's Security Council Resolution 1325—5th Anniversary, October 25, 2005, available at www.huntalternatives.org/download/253_10_25_05_hunt_haf_statement_to_un_security_council_on_resolution_1325.pdf

20 Ibid., pp. 150–1.

21 Ibid., p. 168.

22 Samantha Power, *"A Problem from Hell": America and the Age of Genocide* (New York: Harper Perennial, 2003); and Michael Barnett, *Eyewitness to Genocide: The United Nations and Rwanda* (Ithaca, NY: Cornell University Press, 2003).

23 Roméo Dallaire, *Shake Hands with the Devil: the Failure of Humanity in Rwanda* (New York: Carroll and Graf Publishers, 2004).

24 Alan J. Kuperman, *The Limits of Humanitarian Intervention: Genocide in Rwanda* (Washington, DC: Brookings Institution, 2001).

25 Warren Hoge, "Khartoum Expels U.N. Envoy Who Has Been Outspoken on Darfur Atrocities," *New York Times*, October 23, 2006.

26 Graham Hancock, *Lords of Poverty: the Power, Prestige, and Corruption of the International Aid Business* (New York: The Atlantic Monthly Press, 1989).

CHAPTER 5 REDEFINING NATIONAL INTERESTS

1 See Nicholas J. Wheeler and Tim Dunne, "Good International Citizenship: A Third Way for British Foreign Policy," *International Affairs* 74, no. 4 (1998): 847–70.

2 Lloyd Axworthy, "Human Security and Global Governance: Putting People First," *Global Governance* 7, no. 1 (2001): 19–23.

See also S. Neil MacFarlane and Yuen Foong-Khong, *The UN and Human Security: A Critical History* (Bloomington: Indiana University Press, 2006).

3 See Andrew Linklater, "The Good International Citizen and the Crisis in Kosovo," in *Kosovo and the Challenge of Humanitarian Intervention: Selective Imagination, Collective Action, and International Citizenship*, ed. Ramesh Thakur and Albrecht Schnabel (Tokyo: UN University Press, 2000), p. 493.

4 Stephen G. Brooks and William C. Wohlforth, "International Relations Theory and the Case against Unilateralism," *Perspectives on Politics* 3, no. 3 (2005): 509.

5 Jane Boulden and Thomas G. Weiss, "Tactical Multilateralism: Coaxing America Back to the UN," *Survival* 46, no. 3 (2004): 103–14.

6 "Statement of H.E. George W. Bush, President of the United States of America, 2005 World Summit, High Level Plenary Meeting, September 14, 2005," available at: www.whitehouse.gov/news/releases/2005/09/20050914.html

7 Brian Urquhart, "The New American Century," *New York Review of Books*, August 11, 2005, p. 42.

8 Robert S. McNamara and James Blight, *Wilson's Ghost: Reducing the Risk of Conflict, Killing, and Catastrophe in the 21st Century* (New York: Public Affairs, 2001), p. 3.

9 Andrew Moravcsik argues for a division of labor between American enforcement and European peacekeeping in "Striking a New Transatlantic Bargain," *Foreign Affairs* 82, no. 4 (2003): 74–89.

10 Alan J. Kuperman, *The Limits of Humanitarian Intervention: Genocide in Rwanda* (Washington, DC: Brookings Institution, 2001).

11 *A Secure Europe in a Better World*, available at http://ue.eu.int/pressData/en/reports/78367.pdf

12 See Bastian Giegrich and William Wallace, "Not Such a Soft Power: The External Deployment of European Forces," *Survival* 46, no. 2 (2004): 163–82, quotation: 179.

13 EUFOR website; http://www.euforbih.org/mission/mission.htm

14 See Thomas G. Weiss, ed., *Beyond UN Subcontracting: Task-sharing with Regional Security Arrangements and Service-Providing NGOs* (Houndmills, Basingstoke, UK: Macmillan 1998), pp. 3–138, 227–58.

15 Alhaji M. S. Bah and Ian Johnstone, "Sudan: Faltering Protection and Fragile Peace," in Center on International Cooperation,

Global Peace Operations 2007 (Boulder, Colo.: Lynne Rienner, 2007), pp. 29–43.

16 "Scandinavian 'no' to Darfur role," January 9, 2008, available online at: http://english.aljazeera.net/NR/exeres/C7D3DFB0-F7E0-4461-BDC9-AF91178E81D2.htm (February 8, 2008).

17 Tom J. Farer and Felice Gaer, "The UN and Human Rights: At the End of the Beginning," in *United Nations—Divided World*, ed. Adam Roberts and Benedict Kingsbury (Oxford: Oxford University Press, 1993), pp. 240–96.

18 "Displacement Studies and the Role of Universities," lecture by Francis Deng to a Conference of the German Academic Exchange Service, University of Kassel, Germany, June 2002.

19 International Commission on Intervention and State Sovereignty, *The Responsibility to Protect* (Ottawa: ICISS, 2001); and Thomas G. Weiss and Don Hubert, *The Responsibility to Protect: Research, Bibliography, and Background* (Ottawa: International Development Research Centre, 2001). See also J. L. Holzgrefe and Robert O. Keohane, eds., *Humanitarian Intervention: Ethical, Legal, and Political Dilemmas* (Cambridge: Cambridge University Press, 2003).

20 For a discussion, see Thomas G. Weiss, *Military–Civilian Interactions: Humanitarian Crises and the Responsibility to Protect*, 2nd edn. (Lanham, Md.: Rowman & Littlefield, 2005).

21 Kofi A. Annan, *The Question of Intervention: Statements by the Secretary-General* (New York: UN, 1999), p. 7.

22 Frances M. Deng et al., *Sovereignty as Responsibility: Conflict Management in Africa* (Washington, DC: Brookings, 1996); Kofi Annan, *The Question of Intervention* and *"We the Peoples": The United Nations in the 21st Century* (New York: UN, 2000).

23 S. Neil MacFarlane, Carolin Thielking, and Thomas G. Weiss, "The Responsibility to Protect: Is Anyone Interested in Humanitarian Intervention?," *Third World Quarterly* 25, no. 5 (2004): 979–94.

24 Anthony Lewis, "The Challenge of Global Justice Now," *Dædalus* 132, no. 1 (2003): 8.

25 Mohammed Ayoob, "Humanitarian Intervention and International Society," *The International Journal of Human Rights* 6, no. 1 (2002): 84. For the context that drives Ayoob's skepticism, see Simon Chesterman, Michael Ignatieff, and Ramesh Thakur, eds., *State Failure and the Crisis of*

Governance: Making States Work (Tokyo: UN University Press, 2005).

26 Gareth Evans, "When is it Right to Fight?," *Survival* 46, no. 3 (2004): 59–81.

27 Richard N. Haass, *The Opportunity: America's Moment to Alter History's Course* (New York: Public Affairs, 2005), p. 41.

28 See Thomas G. Weiss and Barbara Crossette, "The United Nations: Post-Summit Outlook," in *Great Decisions 2006* (New York: Foreign Policy Association, 2006), pp. 9–20.

29 General Assembly, *2005 World Summit Outcome*, paras. 138–9.

30 José E. Alvarez, *International Organizations as Law-makers* (Oxford: Oxford University Press, 2005), p. 591.

31 Alexander J. Bellamy, "What Will Become of the Responsibility to Protect?," *Ethics and International Affairs* 20, no. 2 (2006): 143–69.

32 This discussion is based on Thomas G. Weiss, David P. Forsythe, Roger A. Coate, and Kelly-Kate Pease, *The United Nations and Changing World Politics*, 5th edn. (Boulder, Colo.: Westview, 2007), Chapter 5.

33 Joe W. Pitts III and David Weissbrodt, "Major Developments at the UN Commission on Human Rights in 1992," *Human Rights Quarterly* 15, no. 1 (1993): 122–96.

34 Nico Schrijver, "The UN Human Rights Council: 'A Society of the Committed' or Just Old Wine in New Bottles?," *Leiden Journal of International Law* 20, no. 4 (2007): 809–24.

35 In total, 64 countries ran for the 47 seats on the Human Rights Council in its first year.

36 Schrijver, "The UN Human Rights Council": 818–19.

37 *2005 World Summit Outcome*, para. 124.

38 OHCHR, Funding and Budget; http://www.ohchr.org/EN/ AboutUs/Pages/FundingBudget.aspx (accessed February 8, 2008).

39 This discussion draws on Louis Emmerij, Richard Jolly, and Thomas G. Weiss, *Ahead of the Curve? UN Ideas and Global Challenges* (Bloomington: Indiana University Press, 2001), Chapters 2 and 7.

40 Frank Fenner et al., *Smallpox and its Eradication* (Geneva: WHO, 1988), History of International Public Health No. 6; and Maggie Black, *The Children and the Nations: The Story of UNICEF* (New York: UNICEF, 1986).

41 Quoted in *The Washington Post*, July 5, 2000.

42 See Leon Gordenker, Roger A. Coate, Christer Jönsson, and Peter Söderholm, *International Cooperation in Response to AIDS* (London: Pinter, 1995).

43 World Health Organization, *World Health Report 1998* (Geneva: WHO, 1998) and *World Health Report 1999* (Geneva: WHO, 1999).

44 Quoted in *The Washington Post*, July 5, 2000.

CHAPTER 6 MOVING BEYOND THE NORTH–SOUTH DIVIDE

1 Benedict Anderson, *Imagined Communities: Reflections on the Origin and Spread of Nationalism* (London: Verso, 1983).

2 Don Hubert, *The Landmine Ban: A Case Study in Humanitarian Advocacy*, Occasional Paper #42 (Providence, RI: Watson Institute, 2000), p. xviii.

3 Richard Price, "Reversing the Gun Sights: Transnational Civil Society Targets Landmines," *International Organization* 52, no. 3 (1998): 613–44.

4 Eveline Herfkens, "Foreword," in Juan Somavía, *People's Security: Globalizing Social Progress* (Geneva: ILO, 1999), p. viii.

5 Richard H. Ullman, "Redefining Security," reprinted in Sean M. Lynn-Jones and Steven E. Miller, *Global Dangers: Changing Dimension of International Security* (Cambridge, Mass.: MIT Press, 1995), pp. 15–39, quotation at p. 39.

6 "What Is 'Human Security'?," special section of *Security Dialogue* 35, no. 3 (2004): 347–71, quotations at 347 and 351.

7 Roland Paris, "Human Security: Paradigm Shift or Hot Air?," *International Security* 26, no. 2 (2001): 87–102.

8 *Copenhagen Declaration and Programme of Action* (New York: UN, 1995).

9 UN Office of the Special Advisor on Gender Issues and Advancement of Women website; http://www.un.org/womenwatch/osagi/gendermainstreaming.htm

10 S. Neil MacFarlane and Yuen Foong Khong, *The UN and Human Security: A Critical History* (Bloomington: Indiana University Press, 2006), p. 270.

11 Ibid., p. 264.

12　See Michael G. Schechter, *United Nations and Global Conferences* (London: Routledge, 2005), pp. 128–34.

13　Vienna Declaration and Programme of Action, General Assembly A/CONF.157/23, July 12, 1993.

14　Julie Mertus, *The United Nations and Human Rights: A Guide for a New Era* (London: Routledge, 2005).

15　Germain Katanga, the former chief of staff of the Patriotic Force of Resistance in Ituri (FRPI), the military wing of the Front for National Integration (FNI) militia, was transferred from the DRC to The Hague on October 18, 2007. Thomas Lubanga, former leader of the Union of Congolese Patriots, was transferred to the court on March 17, 2006.

16　See Program in Law and Public Affairs, *The Princeton Principles on Universal Jurisdiction* (Princeton, NJ: Princeton University, 2001); Council on Foreign Relations, *Toward an International Criminal Court?* (New York, Council on Foreign Relations, 1999); and Steven R. Ratner and James L. Bischoff, eds., *International War Crimes Trials: Making a Difference?* (Austin: University of Texas Law School, 2004).

17　Richard Goldstone, "International Criminal Court and Ad Hoc Tribunals," in *The Oxford Handbook on the United Nations*, ed. Thomas G. Weiss and Sam Daws (Oxford: Oxford University Press, 2007), pp. 463–78. See also Richard Goldstone and Adam Smith, *International Judicial Institutions: The Architecture of International Justice at Home and Abroad* (London: Routledge, 2008).

18　Fanny Benedetti and John L. Washburn, "Drafting the International Criminal Court Treaty," *Global Governance* 5, no. 1 (1999): 1–38.

19　Teresa Whitfield, *Friends Indeed? The United Nations, Groups of Friends, and the Resolution of Conflict* (Washington, DC: US Institute of Peace, 2007), p. 9 and p. 2.

20　Stanley Foundation, *Implementation of the UN Global Counterterrorism Strategy* (Muscatine, Iowa: Stanley Foundation, 2007), p. 7.

21　David M. Malone and Lotta Hagman, "The North–South Divide at the United Nations: Fading at Last?" *Security Dialogue* 33, no. 4 (2002): 410–11.

22　Thomas G. Weiss, *Multilateral Development Diplomacy in UNCTAD: The Lessons of Group Negotiations, 1964–84* (London: Macmillan, 1986).

23 Mahfuzur Rahman, *World Economic Issues at the United Nations: Half a Century of Debate* (Dordrecht: Kluwer, 2002), p. 145.

24 For a more in-depth discussion see Louis Emmerij, Richard Jolly, and Thomas G. Weiss, *Ahead of the Curve? UN Ideas and Global Challenges* (Bloomington: Indiana University Press, 2001).

25 For a discussion of the distance, see Mahbub ul Haq, Richard Jolly, and Paul Streeten eds., *The UN and the Bretton Woods Institutions: New Challenges for the Twenty-First Century* (Houndsmills, Basingstoke, UK: Macmillan, 1995).

26 United Nations, *2005 World Summit Outcome* (UN document A/60/L.1), September 15, 2005. See also Millennium Project, *Investing in Development: A Practical Plan to Achieve the Millennium Development Goals*, ed., Jeffrey D. Sachs (New York: United Nations Development Programme, 2005); and Jeffrey Sachs, *The End of Poverty: Economic Possibilities for Our Time* (New York: Penguin Books, 2005).

27 Thomas G. Weiss, Tatiana Carayannis, Louis Emmerij, and Richard Jolly, *UN Voices: The Struggle for Development and Social Justice* (Bloomington: Indiana University Press, 2005), p. 308.

28 See Devaki Jain, *Women, Development, and the UN: A Sixty-Year Quest for Equality and Justice* (Bloomington: Indiana University Press, 2005); Lourdes Benería, *Gender, Development, and Globalization: Economics As If All People Mattered* (New York: Routledge, 2003); Suzanne Bergeron, *Fragments of Development: Nation, Gender, and the Space of Modernity* (Ann Arbor: University of Michigan Press, 2006); and Jael Silliman and Ynestra King *Dangerous Intersections: Feminist Perspectives on Population, Environment, and Development* (Cambridge, Mass.: South End Press, 1999).

29 Quoted in Center for Global Solutions, Analysis of International Affairs Budget Proposal for FY 2007, Millennium Challenge Account: *U.S. Development Assistance*; http://www.globalsolutions.org/hill/in_the_beltway/2006a/in_the_beltway FY07_broadanalysis.html#Millennium_Challenge_Account.

30 According to the US Department of State website (http://usinfo.state.gov/ei/economic_issues/mca.html), the Millennium Challenge Corporation has approved over $5.5 billion in aid for 16 countries—Madagascar, Cape Verde, Honduras, Nicaragua, Georgia, Armenia, Vanuatu, Benin, Ghana, Mali, El Salvador,

Mozambique, Lesotho, Morocco, Mongolia, and Tanzania—since its inception in 2004.

31　See John Gerard Ruggie, "global_governance.net: The Global Compact as Learning Network," *Global Governance* 7, no. 4 (2001): 371–8; and Jean-Philippe Thérien and Vincent Pouliot, "The Global Compact: Shifting the Politics of International Development?," *Global Governance* 12, no. 1 (2006): 55–75. For an enthusiastic endorsement from the head of the Davos annual gathering, see Klaus Schwab, "Global Corporate Citizenship: Working with Governments and Civil Society," *Foreign Affairs* 87, no. 1 (2008): 107–18.

32　Weiss et al., *UN Voices*, p. 310.

CHAPTER 7 TRULY DELIVERING AS ONE

1　See "Part VIII: Prospects for Reform," including Edward C. Luck, "Principal Organs," Jeffrey Laurenti, "Financing," and Chadwick G. Alger, "Widening Participation," in *The Oxford Handbook on the United Nations*, ed. Thomas G. Weiss and Sam Daws (Oxford: Oxford University Press, 2007), pp. 653–715.

2　*Delivering as One: The Report of the Secretary-General's High-level Panel* (New York: UN, 2006).

3　*Statement by Representative Jim Leach to the House of Representatives Committee on International Relations*, January 26, 2005; http://commdocs.house.gov/committees/intlrel/hfa98206.000/hfa98206_0.HTM

4　Andrew Cooley and James Ron, "The NGO Scramble: Organizational Insecurity and the Political Economy of Transnational Action," *International Security* 27, no. 1 (2002): 5–39.

5　"Delivering the Promise: Aid Problems," *BBC News*, January 11, 2005; http://news.bbc.co.uk/go/pr/fr/-/2/hi/asia-pacific/4152285.stm

6　Annelies Z. Kamran, "Structure of a Transnational Human Security Network: The Response to the Indian Ocean Tsunami of 26 December 2004," Proceedings of The Institute of Mathematics and its Applications and ONCE-CS Conference on Mathematics in the Science of Complex Systems, University of Warwick, UK, September 18–21, 2006, available at http://phoenixweb.open.ac.uk/complexity/MITSOCS%2706b.pdf

7 David J. Scheffer, "Challenges Confronting Collective Security: Humanitarian Intervention," in *Three Views on the Issue of Humanitarian Intervention*, ed. US Institute of Peace (Washington, DC: US Institute of Peace, 1992), p. 5.

8 Thomas G. Weiss, "Humanitarian Shell Games: Whither UN Reform?" *Security Dialogue* 29, no. 1 (1998): 9–23.

9 Center for International Cooperation, *Global Peace Operations 2007* (Boulder, Colo.: Lynne Rienner, 2007).

10 Stephanie Nebehay, "UN Plans Rapid Reaction Aid Force," *Reuters*, March 18, 2005; http://www.globalpolicy.org/security/peacekpg/reform/2005/0318announce.htm

11 Robert C. Johansen, ed., *A United Nations Emergency Peace Service to Prevent Genocide and Crimes against Humanity* (New York: World Federalist Movement, 2006).

12 Commission on Global Governance, *Our Global Neighborhood* (Oxford: Oxford University Press, 1995), pp. 110–11.

13 International Consultative Group chaired by Brian Urquhart and John C. Polanyi, *Towards a Rapid Reaction Capability for the UN* (The Government of Canada, 1992).

14 Central Emergency Response Fund; http://ochaonline2.un.org/Default.aspx?tabid=8770.

15 Quoted in William Korey, *NGOs and the Universal Declaration of Human Rights: "A Curious Grapevine"* (New York: St. Martin's Press, 1998), p. 9.

16 Julie Mertus, *The United Nations and Human Rights: A Guide for a New Era* (London: Routledge, 2005), p. 9 and p. 16.

17 Office of the High Commissioner for Human Rights website; http://www.unhchr.ch/development/approaches-04.html

18 Craig G. Mokhiber, "Toward a Measure of Dignity: Indicators for Rights-Based Development," *Statistical Journal of the United Nations Economic Commission for Europe* 18, no. 2–3 (2001): 155–62, quoted in Mertus, *The United Nations and Human Rights*, p. 25.

19 Mertus, *The United Nations and Human Rights*, p. 34.

20 *OHCHR Annual Report 2003* (Geneva: Office of the High Commissioner for Human Rights, 2003), pp. 9–10.

21 *Delivering as One*, p. 1 of transmittal letter and p. 1 of report.

22 Robert Wade, "Greening the Bank: The Struggle over the Environment," in *The World Bank: Its First Half Century*, vol. 2, "Perspectives" (Washington, DC: Brookings Institute, 1997), pp. 611–734.

23 This discussion draws on Richard Jolly, Louis Emmerij, and Thomas G. Weiss, *The Power of UN Ideas: Lessons from the First 60 Years* (New York: United Nations Intellectual History Project, 2005), p. 63.

24 Robert Jenkins, *Peacebuilding: From Concept to Commission* (London: Routledge, forthcoming).

25 HLP, *A More Secure World: Our Shared Responsibility* (New York: UN, 2004), p. 72.

26 Alberto Cutillo, *International Assistance to Countries Emerging from Conflict: A Review of Fifteen Years of Interventions and the Future of Peacebuilding* (New York: International Peace Academy, The Security-Development Nexus Program, 2006), p. 60.

27 See *Financing an Effective United Nations* (New York: Ford Foundation, 1993), a report of an expert group chaired by Paul Volcker and Shijuro Ogata.

CHAPTER 8 REINVIGORATING THE INTERNATIONAL CIVIL SERVICE

1 For details of the book series and of the oral history, see www.unhistory.org.

2 Inis L. Claude, Jr., *Swords Into Plowshares: The Problems and Prospects of International Organization* (New York: Random House, 1956) and "Peace and Security: Prospective Roles for the Two United Nations," *Global Governance* 2, no. 3 (1996): 289–98.

3 *2005 World Summit Outcome*, UN document A/60/L.1, September 15, 2005, paras. 161–7, quotation in 163.

4 Susan Strange, *The Retreat of the State: The Diffusion of Power in the World Economy* (Cambridge: Cambridge University Press, 1996); and Robert C. Cox, *The New Realism: Perspectives on Multilateralism and World Order* (New York: St. Martin's Press, 1997).

5 James Gibson, *Jacko, Where Are You Now?* (Richmond, UK: Parsons Publishing, 2006), pp. 247–80.

6 Thomas G. Weiss, Tatiana Carayannis, Louis Emmerij, and Richard Jolly, *UN Voices: The Struggle for Development and Social Justice* (Bloomington: Indiana University Press, 2005), p. 327.

7 High-level Panel on Threats, Challenges and Change, *A More Secure World: Our Shared Responsibility* (New York: United

Nations, 2004); and Kofi A. Annan, *In Larger Freedom: Towards Development, Security and Human Rights for All*, UN document A/59/2005, March 21, 2005.

8 Mark Malloch Brown, "Can the UN be Reformed?," *Global Governance* 14, no. 1 (2008): 1–12.

9 *2005 World Summit Outcome*, para. 164.

10 Zeid Ra'ad Zeid al-Hussein, *A Comprehensive Strategy to Eliminate Future Sexual Exploitation and Abuse in United Nations Peacekeeping Operations*, UN document A/59/710, March 24, 2005.

11 See www.un.org/Depts/dpko/CDT/whats_new.html

12 "Peace and Security: Implementing UN Security Council Resolution 1325," Global Conflict Prevention Pool, UK Commonwealth Secretariat, Canadian International Development Agency, Gender Action for Peace and Security, May 30–June 2, 2006, p. 4, available at www.peacewomen.org/resources/1325/Wilton%20Park%20Report.pdf

13 This discussion draws on Thomas G. Weiss and David A. Korn, *Internal Displacement: Conceptualization and its Consequences* (London: Routledge, 2006), Chapter 8.

14 Interview with the author, November 30, 2005.

15 Interview with the author, June 18, 2005.

16 Don Hubert, *The Landmine Ban: A Case Study in Humanitarian Advocacy* (Providence, R.I.: Watson Institute, 2000), Occasional Paper # 42, pp. 57–71.

17 *Staff Mobility in the United Nations*, prepared by Even Fontaine Ortiz and Guangting Tang, Joint Inspection Unit (UN document JIU/REP/2006/7) Geneva, 2006.

18 Kofi Annan, *Investing in the UN: for a Stronger Organization Worldwide*, UN document A/60/692, March 7, 2006, p. 10.

19 *Human Resources Management Reform: Report of the Secretary General – Addendum: Contractual Arrangements*, UN document A/59/263/Add.1, September 9, 2004.

20 Thant Myint-U and Amy Scott, *The UN Secretariat: A Brief History* (New York: International Peace Academy, 2007), p. 127.

21 Figures here are based on World Bank, *Global Poverty Monitoring*, available at www.worldbank.org/research/povmonitor/index.htm

22 UNDP, *Human Development Report 1999* (New York: Oxford University Press, 1999), p. 3.

23 John Maynard Keynes, *The General Theory of Employment, Interest and Money* (London: Macmillan, 1936), p. 383.

24 Amartya Sen, "Assessing Human Development," in UNDP, *Human Development Report 1999*, p. 23.

25 Weiss et al., *UN Voices*, p. 291.

26 Craig N. Murphy, *The United Nations Development Programme: A Better Way?* (Cambridge: Cambridge University Press, 2006), pp. 232–62.

27 See Richard Jolly, Louis Emmerij, and Thomas G. Weiss, *The Power of UN Ideas: Lessons from the First 60 Years* (New York: UNIHP, 2005), Chapter 6; and *UN Ideas Changing History* (Bloomington: Indiana University Press, forthcoming).

28 See www.jposc.org

29 Quoted in "Thoughts on the Business of Life," *Forbes*, January 20, 2003, p. 120.

30 James O. C. Jonah, "Secretariat: Independence and Reform," in *The Oxford Handbook on the United Nations*, ed. Thomas G. Weiss and Sam Daws (Oxford: Oxford University Press, 2007), p. 171.

31 Kofi Annan, *Investing in People: Report of the Secretary-General*, UN document A/61/255, August 9, 2006, p. 3.

32 Four Nations Initiative Secretariat, *Towards a Compact: Proposals for Improved Governance and Management of the United Nations Secretariat* (Stockholm: 4NI, 2007), pp. 32–3.

CONCLUSION

1 See Ramesh Thakur and Thomas G. Weiss, *The UN and Global Governance: An Unfinished Journey* (Bloomington: Indiana University Press, forthcoming).

2 Commission on Global Governance, *Our Global Neighbourhood* (Oxford: Oxford University Press, 1995).

3 Martin Luther King, Jr., "Beyond Vietnam," Address delivered to the Clergy and Laymen Concerned about Vietnam, Riverside Church, April 4, 1967, available at: www.ratical.org/ratville/JFK/MLKapr67.html

4 Ernst-Otto Czempiel, "Governance and Democratization," in *Governance without Government: Order and Change in World Politics*, ed. James N. Rosenau and Ernst-Otto Czempiel

(Cambridge: Cambridge University Press, 1992), pp. 250–71. See also Leon Gordenker and Thomas G. Weiss, "Pluralizing Global Governance: Analytical Approaches and Dimensions," in *NGOs, the UN, and Global Governance*, ed. Leon Gordenker and Thomas G. Weiss (London: Lynne Rienner, 1996), pp. 17–47.

5 James N. Rosenau, "Toward an Ontology for Global Governance," in *Approaches to Global Governance Theory*, ed. Martin Hewson and Timothy J. Sinclair (Albany: State University of New York, 1999), p. 293.

6 Craig N. Murphy, "Global Governance: Poorly Done and Poorly Understood," *International Affairs* 76, no. 4 (2000): 789.

7 Dan Plesch, "How the United Nations Beat Hitler and Prepared the Peace," *Global Society* 22, no. 1 (2008): 137.

8 For an alternative view, see James A. Yunker, *Rethinking World Government: A New Approach* (Lanham, Md.: University Press of America, 2005). See also Robert Latham, "Politics in a Floating World: Toward a Critique of Global Governance," in *Approaches to Global Governance Theory*, pp. 23–53.

9 Craig N. Murphy, *International Organization and Industrial Change: Global Governance Since 1850* (Cambridge: Polity Press, 1994), p. 1.

10 Harold K. Jacobson, *Networks of Interdependence: International Organizations and the Global Political System*, 2nd edn. (New York: Knopf, 1984), p. 84.

11 Quoted by J. Martin Rochester, *Between Peril and Promise: The Politics of International Law* (Washington, DC: CQ Press, 2006), p. 27.

12 Richard Falk, "International Law and the Future," *Third World Quarterly* 27, no. 5 (2006): 727–37.

13 John J. Mearsheimer, "The False Promise of International Institutions," *International Security* 19, no. 3 (1994–95): 5–49.

14 Edward Hallett Carr, *The Twenty Years' Crisis, 1919–1939* (New York: Harper Torchbooks, 1964), p. 108.

15 Murphy, *International Organization and Industrial Change*, p. 9.

16 Thomas S. Kuhn, *The Structure of Scientific Revolutions*, 2nd edn. (Chicago: University of Chicago Press, 1970), p. 4.

17 Ibid., p. 53.

18 James N. Rosenau and Mary Durfee, *Thinking Theory Thoroughly* (Boulder, Colo.: Westeview, 1995), p. 6.

19 These terms are Richard Falk's in "International Law and the Future."

20 See David Held, *Global Covenant: The Social Democratic Alternative to the Washington Consensus* (Cambridge: Polity, 2004).
21 Peter Singer, *One World: The Ethics of Globalization*, 2nd edn. (New Haven, Conn.: Yale University Press, 2004).

Index